Managerial Skills and Practices for Global Leadership

Bahaudin G. Mujtaba

☆ **International** ☆

ILEAD ACADEMY
Leadership Education and Associate Development Academy

© Bahaudin G. Mujtaba (2014). Managerial Skills and Practices for Global Leadership

Cover Design: Cagri Tanyar

Subject Code & Description
    BUS503010 - Business & Economics: Business Life - Health/Stress
    SEL024000 - Self-Help: Stress Management
    FAM013000 - Family & Relationships: Conflict Resolution

Print: ISBN-13: 978-1-936237-06-7
e-Book: ISBN-13: 978-1-936237-07-4

ILEAD Academy, LLC

Fort Lauderdale (USA), Ho Chi Minh City (Vietnam),
Bangkok (Thailand), Islamabad (Pakistan)

* * * Dedication * * *

Effective managers are those who think with their heads, act with their hearts, and demonstrate through their habits!

*

*

*

*

*

*

*

TABLE OF CONTENTS

Preface

Managerial Skills and Practices for Global Leadership book is about leading people through effective management practices across cultures and borders. The book is about building one's management skills and organizational practices according to principles of leadership and professionalism. A manager has to understand each individual employee and empower them to freely voice their opinion in order to maximize their efficiency and productivity toward the complex solutions we all face in today's cross-cultural work environments. Likewise, professionals need to have great management skills while working toward the objectives of maximizing shareholder benefits in the organization.

Some of the topics and discussions presented in this book are in a summary format, as they come from previous books where the original contributors are credited, and those interested in more details can look at the following books for the comprehensive coverage:

1. Mujtaba, B. G. (2010). *Workforce Diversity Management: Challenges, Competencies and Strategies (2nd edition)*. ILEAD Academy Publications: Florida, USA.
2. ___ (2008). *Coaching and Performance Management: Developing and Inspiring Leaders*. ILEAD Academy Publications: Florida, USA.
3. ___ (2007). *Cross Cultural Management and Negotiation Practices*. ILEAD Academy Publications: Florida, USA.
4. ___ (2006). *Cross Cultural Change Management*. Llumina Press, Tamarac, Florida.
5. ___ (2006). *Privatization and Market-Based Leadership in Developing Economies: Capacity Building in Afghanistan*. Llumina Press and Publications, Tamarac, Florida.

The author and contributors have used the concepts discussed in this book both nationally and internationally with academic and practitioner audiences to help increase their awareness of management, international management, negotiations, communication, and different cultures. The concepts, cases and skills have been gleaned from a variety of sources and professionals around the globe. As such, these are very relevant to today's work environment, and thus can easily fit most management, international management, or cultural competency courses, seminars, and employee development workshops. Management trainers, corporate universities, colleges or professors wishing to adopt this book or any of its chapters may contact the publisher or the author to request the available supplementary facilitator's materials such as the electronic Power Point files for presentation, chapter summaries for usage with lectures and online postings, test questions for discussions or exams, and/or other supplementary material for exercises. The Instructor's CD (resources) come electronically using Microsoft Power Point, Word, and Excel files; as such, they can be adjusted by each educator and facilitator for his or her lectures, training and presentations.

I wish you harmony in your head (thoughts), heart (feelings), and habits (behaviors).

Bahaudin

Acknowledgements

Special thanks to my family members, colleagues and friends for their guidance and valuable input in the review of this material. In particular, I thank and acknowledge the following individuals for generously sharing their thoughts, suggestions, writings, and other contributions in this book.

- Ayesha Zahid
- Belay Seyoum
- Belal Kaifi
- Bina Patel
- Cindy Nguyen
- Cuneyt Oskal
- Donovan McFarlane
- Edward F. Murphy, Jr.
- Elizabeth Danon-Leva
- Frank Cavico
- Frank Wolf
- Han Ping
- Helen Turnbul
- Jane W. Gibson

- Jatuporn Sungkhawan
- Joseph Heinzman
- Joseph W. Kennedy
- Lam D. Nguyen
- Mahmoud Bodla
- Matthew Kenney
- Michela de Gennaro
- Mohammed Ahmed
- Naveed A. Malik
- Paul Knapp
- Phuong Ngo Thai
- Nisarat Aimkij
- Pedro Pellet
- Phong Nguyen Nguyen

- Piboon Puriveth
- Preston Jones
- Quan Tran
- Randolph Pohlman
- Razia Begum
- Regina A. Greenwood
- Ricky Hieu Nguyen
- Rhonda Polak
- Satin Soonthornpan
- Somsak Kaveetriphop
- Talat Afza
- Tanin Kaweevisultrakul
- Timothy O. McCartney
- Tracie Cooper

Thank you for helping with this material which can assist many professionals better "serve" humanity in the dream of creating a more peaceful world through effective management, communication and negotiation practices.

Bahaudin

CHAPTER 1

Management and Culture

Leaders and managers of a diverse work environment require cross-cultural awareness, communication, negotiation, and international management skills. Cultures tend to strongly influence how one should manage the company's resources to achieve organizational goals. A starting place is the awareness of cultural challenges, complexities and influences in today's workplace. This book discusses the fundamental elements of management, cultural diversity, and international management skills in a global context.

Modern managers can best increase their organization's competitiveness and productivity by understanding effective management and cross-cultural leadership skills. One cannot always "go with the flow" as per the practices of one's mentors or previous managers.

There is a story about a Japanese company and an American company from the United States that decided to have a canoe race on a major river. Both teams practiced long and hard to reach their peak performance before the race. On the big day, the Japanese won by a mile. The Americans, very discouraged and depressed, decided to investigate the reason for the crushing defeat. A management team made up of senior managers was formed to investigate and recommend appropriate actions. Their conclusion was the Japanese had eight people rowing and one person steering, while the American team had eight people steering and one person rowing. So American management hired a consulting company and paid them a large amount of money for a second opinion. The consultant advised that too many people were steering the boat, while not enough people were rowing. To prevent another loss to the Japanese, the rowing team's management structure was totally reorganized to four steering supervisors, three area steering superintendents and one assistant superintendent steering manager. They also implemented a new performance system that would give the one person rowing the boat greater incentive to work harder. It was called the *"Rowing Team Quality Performance Program."* It involved meetings, dinners and free pens for the rower. There was discussion of getting new paddles, canoes and other equipment, extra vacation days for practices and bonuses. The next year the Japanese won by two miles. Feeling disappointed and angry, the American management laid off the rower for poor performance, halted development of a new canoe, sold the paddles, and canceled all capital investment on new equipment. The money saved was distributed to the senior executives as bonuses. Next year's racing team has been outsourced to India.

This fictional story exaggerating real-world decisions in some modern firms demonstrates that instead of automatically restructuring, outsourcing, or trying the latest "fad" of the year, managers must be cognizant of proper long-term decision-making and relevant management skills if they are to compete effectively with today's global organizations.

Introduction

There is an old adage which says, "If you don't know where you are going, any road will take you there." This is the essence of why proper strategic planning must be an essential part of today's organization and a manager's duties. Strategic planning determines where the organization is now, where it wants to be, and how it is going to get there. The three stages of the strategic planning process are: (1) determining or understanding the company's mission statement and general goals, (2) strategy formulation, and (3) strategy implementation.

For a modern firm, there are at least three levels of planning which are corporate, business and functional. For example, at the corporate level, the executives, founders, and other senior managers with assistance from their employees create the corporation's mission. The business level consists of determining divisional goals; and at the functional level, managers determine functional goals. All the levels of planning need to be integrated, and effective communication, therefore, becomes a key element to planning effectiveness. Another way to look at planning is the time horizon considered. *Short-range plans* typically are called operational or tactical plans and consist of one year or less.

Intermediate-range plans cover a 1-2 year time horizon, and *long-range* or *strategic plans* cover 3 years and further into the horizon. These plans do not have to roll over if they are no longer relevant and strategic plans should be constantly revised if the organization is to remain responsive to the changing environment. The characteristics of successful plans are that they are relevant, realistic, flexible, measurable, time-bounded, aligned with predicted results, and that they provide accountability and responsibility for results. Strategic plans, once put into implementation, should be controlled through an effective follow-up process. Control is the process where managers monitor and regulate how an organization and its employees are performing the activities necessary to achieve the stated goals. Managers should be able to compare and contrast various methods of control to see how useful they are for one's industry and department. Managers should also be familiar with the common types of organizational control systems such as output controls, behavioral controls, and culture or clan control. The application of such concepts can help managers create an effective organizational culture that matches their core values.

So, what exactly is management? Simply stated, *management* is the process of achieving organizational goals with and through people using available resources in the most efficient manner possible. The functions of management include planning, organizing, leading, and controlling (POLC). The main functions of management are likely to stay the same regardless of where one is managing. *International management* can be defined as the process of planning, organizing, leading, controlling, and performing relevant management tasks and techniques within an international environment to efficiently achieve organizational goals through the available resources. Therefore, as implied through these definitions, managers can practice standard management roles within cross-cultural work environments. The management functions can be used to classify the manager's job and responsibilities at different levels in the hierarchy.

Management Functions

Planning means defining an organization's goals, establishing an overall strategy for achieving these goals, and developing comprehensive plans to integrate and coordinate activities. *Organizing* includes determining what tasks must be done, who will do them, how the tasks will be grouped, who will report to whom, and where decisions will be made. *Leading* includes motivating and directing employees, and communicating and resolving conflicts. *Controlling*, on the other hand, means monitoring performance, comparing results and goals, and making corrections and adjustments as needed in a timely manner.

Effectiveness and Efficiency

Besides performing the regular management functions, managers must also be concerned with doing the rights things (effectiveness) in the right manner (efficiency) in order to increase the organization's performance. *Organizational performance* measures how efficiently and effectively managers use resources to satisfy customers and achieve their goals. *Efficiency*, or doing things right, is a measure of how well resources are used to achieve a goal. The key about efficiency is to be doing the right things right. *Effectiveness*, doing the right things, is a measure of the appropriateness of the goals chosen to get the firm to its destination, and the degree to which the stated goals are achieved. Effectiveness is concerned with selecting the right goals and making sure they are achieved. As a manager and leader, one must consider what might be the results of not being both efficient and effective in the department and/or organization.

Managers must take responsibility for the morale of their people in the department. Morale is the nature of a relationship between employees and the organization. Morale reflects the nature of the department and reveals the heart of an organization at its best or worst depending on the outcome of the assessment. Management should keep their finger on the pulse of the organization and measure morale on a regular basis. Managers and leaders must have the ability to create a sense of pride among employees about the organization and its objectives. Managers and leaders must also recruit, retain, develop, and motivate a high-performance workforce if they are to be productive and efficient in their individual positions, tasks and departments. The number of years employees stay in an organization is directly linked to the type of relationship they maintain with their superiors. Managers and leaders can motivate and increase organizational morale by engaging all employees in the mission and vision of the firm. Engaging everyone in the organization requires ongoing and effective strategic planning, appreciation, communication, and employee recognition programs. Managers can "LEAD" by:

- *Learning* about the needs and wants of their people on a continuous basis.
- *Educating* and *"empowering"* their people about the mission, vision and objectives of the organization and department. Empowering, at its best, comes with proper education, training, development, responsibility, and the authority to get the job done. Through effective and timely education, true empowerment and enthusiasm will be the natural results in a given department or organization.
- *Acknowledging* and *"appreciating"* the contributions of all employees on an individual basis.
- *Demanding* high performance and total integrity from everyone in the organization.

Management History

Management is "an activity that performs certain functions to obtain the effective acquisition, allocation, and utilization of human efforts and physical resources to accomplish some goals" (Wren, 2005, p. 3). Similarly, *management thought* is seen as the existing body of relevant knowledge about the activities of management, the various functions involved in getting things done and its overall purpose and scope. While management functions and activities have been around for hundreds of years, as a profession management is only less than about one hundred years old.

Management and Leadership Dependency

Management functions include planning, organizing, leading, and controlling. Management is also divided into three general levels: first-level supervisors (managers), middle managers, and senior managers or executives. The changing story in management today, of course, is that the many layers of middle managers which most large organizations used to have in developed economies are giving way to self-empowered teams and "flatter" organizations. The three basic skills that managers use, to different extents at all levels, are technical, human relations, and conceptual. Technical skill is naturally very important for doing a job successfully and for working with one's employees and customers. Human relations skills tend to be important at all levels of the profession. As a person rises in the hierarchy of management, the need for conceptual skills becomes greater. To determine your inventory of skills in each of the three areas, complete the Management Skills Inventory survey at the end of this chapter.

The proportion of one's time spent in each of these areas may change depending on the organizational structure, one's span of control, level of experiences, and the manager's position in the hierarchy. For example, senior managers may not spend as much time in technical functions as those who are in front-line management. Top managers tend to spend more time using their conceptual skills. Finally, it is a good idea for management scholars to reflect upon Henry Mintzberg's important study about what managers really do, and the three categories of roles he identified: interpersonal, informational, and decisional.

As can be seen in Figure 1, management is about efficiency (how things get done), and leadership is about effectiveness (what gets done); yet, they closely relate to one another and a manager must practice both in order to be successful. Since leaders usually provide the vision (what to do or effectiveness) and managers focus on getting it done with the least amount of resources (doing things right or efficiency), one can see that leadership and management skills are interdependent and must be done jointly in harmony with one another.

Figure 1 – Leadership and Management Interdependency

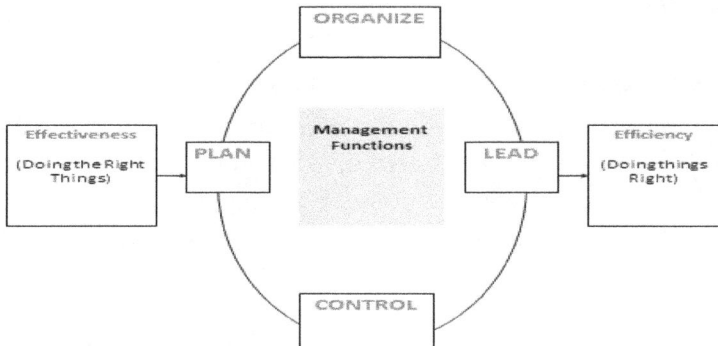

F. W. Taylor and Scientific Management

The Father of Scientific Management is Frederick Taylor, an engineer at the Stevens Institute of Technology, who was one of the initial contributors in management history. Taylor, while focusing on efficiency, believed that the best way to increase output was to streamline procedures used by workers in completing their tasks. He initiated time and motion studies to determine the best way to do each segment of a task, and then imposed upon workers the requirement that they do their work exactly as instructed.

The needs of the organization were separated from the needs of the individual. The result of Taylor's scientific management research was that he suggested four principles to increase efficiency:

1. *Study the way the job is performed* now and determine new ways to do it. Gather detailed, time and motion information. Try different methods to see which is best.
2. *Codify the new method into rules.* Teach to all workers.
3. *Select workers whose skills match* the rules set in step two.
4. *Establish a fair level of performance* and pay for higher performance. Workers should benefit from higher output.

According to Taylor, *"natural soldiering"* was part of organizational life and it is defined as the natural instinct and tendency of workers to take it easy rather aiming to performing at the optimal level. Taylor blamed management for not designing jobs properly and offering proper incentives to motivate employees toward great performance. Taylor thought that a supervisor may be able to inspire or force workers to stop natural soldiering. Regardless of the efforts of supervisors and managers, researchers observed what is known as *"systematic soldiering,"* which resulted from group pressures for individuals to conform to output norms set by the work group. Taylor felt managers can overcome soldiering and improve the situation if workers knew that the production standards were established by a study of the job, rather than by historical data, and if incentives could be provided.

Taylor also believed that everyone was best or *"first class"* at some type of work. There should be a match between a person's abilities and the person's job placement. Of course, today this concept is known as having a "job-fit" between a worker and his/her responsibilities. If a worker enjoys the job, then he or she will likely be more productive doing it.

Frank and Lillian Gilbreth

Frank Gilbreth is known as the Father of "Time and Motion Studies," and it was his filming of individual movements in physical labor that allowed the scientific managers to break a job down into its component parts and streamline the process. Scientific managers, as demonstrated by the concept's founder Frederick Taylor, were efficiency experts. They believed in finding the one best way to do things. Then, managers had the responsibility of training workers in this one "best" way. Efficiency would be improved and productivity would go up.

Lillian Gilbreth was one of the first female psychologists with a doctorate degree and she wrote a famous book entitled, "*The Psychology of Work*." Together, Frank and Lillian had 12 children, a story made famous by one of their daughters who wrote the play, "*Cheaper by the Dozen*." The original movie version of the play demonstrates how scientific management techniques were used to organize and run the Gilbreth household. The "Cheaper by the Dozen" movie which came out in late 2003, and its second part which was out in 2005 and 2006, starring Steve Martin and Bonnie Hunt, however, is not based on the life of Frank and Lillian Gilbreth.

Henri Fayol

An important historical aspect of management is that its functions were originally described by Henri Fayol in the early 1900's. Henri Fayol was born in 1841 in Istanbul, Turkey, and his parents moved to France in 1847. Eventually, Fayol became an engineer and worked in the mining industry where he observed and experimented with management tasks. At about the same time as the studies being conducted on scientific management, Henri Fayol, an industrialist, was working to develop a framework for studying management. Known as the Father of Modern Management, Fayol identified the original "five functions of management." Fayol's original management functions were planning, organizing, directing, coordinating, and controlling.

Studying these five activities is the way to study management. This work was significant given the fact that there were no management majors and no business schools at that time. "Management" was a newly developing field.

Mary Parker Follett

Mary Parker Follett was one of the few women who were making a mark with predominantly male businesspeople at the time. Follett generally is more studied by public administration majors than business administration majors because she worked for social service agencies. Nonetheless, she was a popular speaker of the day in Western countries during the mid-1950's and made presentations to many business (men's) groups on her views of how individual behavior influenced work. This was a very unorthodox viewpoint at the time but initiated the next school of management thought.

Three of Follett's most noteworthy concepts were the "Universal Goal," the "Universal Principle," and her "Law of the Situation." According to Follett, the "universal goal" of organizations was "integration" of individual effort into a synergistic whole. The "universal principle" was "circular or reciprocal response," which stated that no communication transactions should be seen as one way from supervisor to employer, but that every message had a result which served as "feedback" to the sender; that is the concept of two-way communications. Follett's "law of the situation" was even more prophetic in that she taught that there is no one best way to do anything since it all depends on the situation. Today, of course, the dominant way of thinking, as demonstrated by situational leadership concepts, is that Follett was right and thus "it all depends" on the situation. This thinking is now called "contingency theory" or "situational theory," and it is in the mainstream of today's management thinking. Follett's writing of the interrelationships of the behavioral and holistic school was to capture the essence of integration within business, to replace inadequate or damaging hierarchical controls which de-humanized employee value and allowed corruption within organizations to emerge. Such realities are of concern today as people see the widespread popularity of unethical practices by organizational leaders.

Mary Parker Follett identified three compelling steps of giving orders, which internalizes ethical decision-making on the part of the business leader. Follett stated that experiential learning is "the conscious" affect toward people's behavior, turned inward, to learn from what they do as business leaders. The three steps to giving orders are:

1. *Conscious attitude.* The realization that people can imply context and act appropriately.
2. *Responsible attitude.* Ethical behavioral constraints, which determine the moral judgments of different people's perceptions. This is based on the manner in which the person giving the order will act on, based on individual preferences.
3. *Experimental attitude.* Follett identified this third aspect as the test phase, to experiment and review findings to determine the best set of circumstances in issuing orders.

According to Follett's writing, giving the correct orders should be ascertained by the greatest opportunity, which culminates in the best set of factors for the organizational members. This is a very important aspect of ethical behavior for business leaders. Organizational leaders should not base their orders and decisions on what they perceive are right for them. Rather, they should base their decisions, orders and actions on the creation of overall value to the entire organization.

According to Follett, as stated earlier, the "universal goal" of organizations was "integration" of individual effort into a synergistic whole, the group or team philosophy, which culminates the entire behavioral aspects of all organizational members for the integration effort. This is basically the focus of systems thinking mentality today. According to Follett, the business leaders' work is to provide a basis of understanding for all organizational members, by allowing them to make cognitive choices, thus all information is shared openly, seeking to solve organizational problems for the betterment of the entire organization. Follett stated that true powers in small and large organizations are based on the co-mingling of various organizational teams through "effective relations." The leader of the organization divulges his/her will to create synergy within the organization, through organizational integration. Follett stated that in order to discern this process, the object (environment) is either an independent variable or an interdependent variable, and each scenario precipitates different factors based on each observed or implied response. This process is instantaneous, however, if a leader of an organization fails to consider the ramifications of his or her communications, directives, or orders, people in business may respond to it in the wrong way, which can result in unethical practices by an organization.

Another factor discussed by Follett, is the level of job satisfaction an employee may have towards his/her employer.

Employees respond to intrinsic and extrinsic motivational factors, such as:

- Wages, profit sharing, employee benefits.
- Leadership and management proficiency from the organization.
- Working conditions.
- Immediate employee needs and desires.
- Future employee aspirations.

According to Follett, employees respond to various sets of intrinsic and extrinsic factors differently, based on each employee's own desires, internally or externally. However the employee discerns value based on external factors, such as what other employees receive, increased pay, increased benefits, advanced training and development, increased opportunities by others, etc. Thus, employee needs are espoused based on changing external factors in the organizational environment. Follett stated that intrinsic and extrinsic behavioral processes are linked, and must be analyzed together to determine the best set of stimuli for organizational behaviors.

One of the key elements of Mary Parker Follett's contribution to the management discipline is her belief that organizational leadership is "situational;" leadership is in place throughout an organization, at different levels and in different situations. When leadership transforms an organization to higher levels; achieving greater market share, or when an organization becomes the dominant business within their market, leadership has achieved the genius level (Follett, 1933, p. 51). Follett taught that there is no one best way to do anything, it depends on the situation. The business leader must appropriately diagnose the situation, and visualize the situation entirely, in order to correlate its indigenous parts. The business leader's most notable asset is his/her ability to recognize changing situations and to respond effectively. This was in direct contrast to the scientific management approach of her time. In today's business environment, Follett's philosophy is correct; the situation depends on the correct course of action to be taken by the organizational leaders; however, unethical practices by an organization can be caused by the deficiency of effective leadership.

The Hawthorne Studies

During the 1920's, the dominant management philosophy changed drastically to what management experts call the Human Relations School of thought. This school was based on psychological concepts of man, e.g., man needs to be needed and that the work group is very important psychologically. Instead of the philosophy of "economic man," the concept of "social man" emerged. Managers became more concerned about employees as people and company social events and communication devices such as suggestion boxes became popular to hear employees' thoughts. One reason that human relations became the new school of thought was because of the very famous Hawthorne Studies. As the literature points out, the Hawthorne Studies took place from 1924 to 1933 at the Hawthorne Plant of the Western Electric Company in Cicero, Illinois. Studies show that there were four major components of the Hawthorne Studies.

The first phase was the Illumination Studies sponsored by the General Electric (GE) Company. GE wanted to prove scientifically that better lighting would lead to increased productivity. The experimental group at Hawthorne, however, produced more regardless of whether the lights were turned up (increased) or down (decreased), perhaps as a result of the increased attention the employees were getting. Everyone was amazed and GE withdrew from the study. In 1927, Harvard professors, Elton Mayo (later known as the Father of the Hawthorne Studies) and Fritz Roethlisberger came in to consult at Hawthorne. It was Mayo who identified the "*Hawthorne Effect*," the bias that occurs when people know they are being observed, noticed and studied.

The Relay Assembly Test Room came second. Here, employees who put together small telephone relays were put in a special room and given breaks, the freedom to talk, and a change in supervisor. The female employees involved liked the changes and productivity soared, which was more proof that group norms were at work.

Third, the Bank Wiring Experiments consisted of men, and there was no change of supervision. Again, group dynamics were noted, especially as they related to productivity standards.

Finally, an extensive employee interviewing program ensued. First, direct interviews, then indirect interviews, were used to collect piles of data on how employees felt about the company, what they liked and disliked about their jobs, etc. It was only because of the deepening depression that the interviews were cut short.

So, what was the overall significance of the Hawthorne Studies? According to the literature, the Hawthorne Studies are important for at least several reasons. First, they are the single most significant study in the field of human behavior. Second, they put researchers on the road to shifting to a human relations focus in management. Third, they provided insights into the roles of group dynamics and the importance of leadership style. Fourth, they provided the concept of the "Hawthorne Effect," a bias which can occur in human research.

HR School of Thought

Beginning in the early 1950's, the Human Resources School began to dominate in the American workforce. This school of thought represented a substantial progression from human relations. While the latter believed that "A happy worker is a productive worker," the human resources advocates knew that sometimes happy workers are just happy. It takes more to motivate the increasingly educated and professional workforce.

Overall, in 1950's, most of the workforce in the western world was enjoying unprecedented prosperity. The workforce was becoming more well-to-do and job opportunities were plentiful. It was not by chance that employers began to worry about how to keep their most productive employees. As such, employee satisfaction and motivation became topics of great concern, as managers try to deal with the complexities of the general, task, and global environments while attempting to create sustainable learning organizations in order to stay competitive. Human resources management should be considered a strategic partner in the success of any successful and sustainable organization.

Benjamin Franklin once said: *"Well done is better than well said."* By that, he was implying that words alone cannot achieve much. Rather, they should be supported by well thought actions. In the language of business this means that strategic planning allows companies to put down on paper where they are, where they want to go, and how they plan to get there. But the best planning in the world does nothing for a company if it does not act on those plans in an appropriate manner. In this aspect, strategic human resources management has been defined as the linking of human resources with strategic goals and objectives in order to improve a company's performance and develop an organizational culture that fosters creativity, inclusion, innovation, and flexibility. Strategic HR means accepting the HR function as a strategic partner in the formulation of the company's strategies as well as in the implementation of those strategies through HR activities such as recruiting, selecting, training and rewarding personnel. In addition, among the other roles that a company's strategic HR management should be responsible for include environmental scanning, i.e. identifying and analyzing external opportunities and threats that may be crucial to the company's success. HR is also responsible for supplying of competitive intelligence that may be useful in the long-term planning process. It is well established that supplying timely and useful information regarding the company's strengths and weaknesses can have a determining effect on the long-term viability of the firm's strategic options.

In the modern business world, rather than being supportive, HRM plays a strategic role by aiming at facilitating the accomplishment of a company's mission and ensuring a company's competitive advantage. The goal is to move a company's strategy to action and to design practices that align with the business strategy. By fulfilling this role, HR professionals increase the capacity of a business to execute its strategies and to execute it well.

The role of strategic planning is to provide organizations and agencies with a clear sense of direction by clarifying their mission, priorities, and goals and objectives. The goal of managers should be to link the strategic objectives to efficiently position the firm's human resources to accomplish the stated mission. The goal should be effective performance management in order to ensure accountability and progress. An example of this is the daily tracking of statistics that each employee turns in at the end of the month at some organizations or departments. The firm can use this information to follow the production of its employees and to see if they are actually working toward achieving the desired results. Therefore, regularly monitoring performance to make sure the activities of employees and their results are linked to the strategies is a good initiative for management.

Environmental Forces Impacting Business

By reading about the general, task, and global environments of business, a manager will understand why the organizational environment is so important and why systems theory has been applied to organizations in recent years. An effective manager knows that any system has inputs, a transformation process (where the goods or services are produced), and outputs (such as products or services that are used by end-users or consumers). Around that system circulate various environments.

The *task environment* (or intermediate environment) consists of direct suppliers, competitors, customers, and distributors; in other words, the people and organizations with whom managers are in direct contact on a regular basis.

The *general environment* (or macro environment) extends further out from the organization, and includes all the social, economic, and political forces that have a general impact on business.

The *global environment* consists of national and international forces that operate in both the task and general environments of business. Regardless of the environment, managers and leaders can always use values-driven and values-based management practices to make effective decisions that maximize the long-term value of their stakeholders.

Culture and Management

Twenty-first century managers work with different employees, suppliers and customers. As such, modern managers must be aware of cross-cultural management practices. International management is about the application of traditional management concepts and techniques in a global setting or diverse cultural environments to achieve organizational goals using available resources in the most efficient manner.

Culture is the accumulated acquired knowledge and "know-how" that individuals use to make sense of each experience and produce desired actions and behaviors. Of course, this acquired knowledge forms people's values, creates their attitudes, and influences their behavior in a predictable pattern. In 1980, Geert Hofstede defined culture as "the collective programming of the mind," which distinguishes one group of people from another. For the purposes of this book, *culture* is defined as the collective programming of the mind which drives human behavior in each department, organization, city, or nation in a consistent and predictable manner. Today's managers, with diverse value systems, are global managers as they mostly manage people of diverse beliefs in an international or global environment. Consequently, understanding culture plays a critical role in international management. For an organization to operate in several countries with different cultures, it is important for the management team to understand the culture of the countries in order to efficiently and effectively operate interdependently among them. The norms and practices of one culture may not be the norms and practices of another. A starting place is to understand cultures as a way of improving management practices in the international work environment.

In their 1987 book, Hall and Hall stated that each culture operates according to its own internal dynamic, its own principles, and its own written and unwritten laws. However, there are some common threads that run through all cultures. Cultural programs guide the actions and responses of human beings in every walk of life. This process requires attention to everything people do to survive, advance in the world, and gain satisfaction from life. Furthermore, cultural programs will not work if crucial steps are omitted, which happens when people unconsciously apply their own rules to another system. Culture and cultural conditioning of people can affect technology transfer, managerial attitudes, managerial ideology, and even business-government relations. Furthermore, and perhaps most important, culture affects a person's priorities as well as how people feel, think and behave in society.

Harris, Moran, and Moran provided ten basic categories that are important for understanding culture and these categories can be useful when studying another culture. The ten categories offered by Harris, Moran, and Moran include (2004, p. 5):
1. Sense of Self and Space
2. Communication and Language
3. Dress and Appearance
4. Food and Feeding Habits
5. Time and Time Consciousness
6. Relationships
7. Values and Norms
8. Beliefs and Attitudes
9. Mental Process and Learning
10. Work Habits and Practices.

Culture, in its simplest form, is a way of life. While cultures cannot be changed easily, peoples' thoughts, words, actions, and behaviors can be changed and this change takes place best when it is intrinsically initiated through knowledge, education, awareness, critical thinking, and self-reflection. Regardless of one's culture, each person is likely to achieve success in bringing about changes as per his or her own management skills, initiatives, persistency, efforts, education, self-reflections, behaviors, and ability to effectively work with others.

Understanding cultural differences and work practices are a necessity for the growth and success of doing business with others throughout the world and serving each market in an effective and efficient manner. International expansions have been on the rise in the past few decades, and they present managers with new challenges on how to deal with the differences in culture. One of the benefits that such expansions offer is the access to new markets for economies of scale. With globalization of markets, competition and organizations, individuals increasingly interact, manage, negotiate, and compromise with people from a variety of cultures. Over a quarter of century ago, Geert Hofstede identified five dimensions of cultural values: power distance, uncertainty avoidance, masculinity / femininity (achievement versus nurturing), collectivism / individuality, as well as long-term / short-term orientation that characterize cultural differences among diverse countries or cultures.

According to Hofstede, a country's position, on these five dimensions, allows predictions on the way societies operate, including the management principles that are applied. Other researchers developed theories to explain the extent to which one culture can affect others as people migrate and interact in the global marketplace, and some of them include: convergence, divergence and crossvergence. *Convergence* describes the merging of different cultures due to the influence of globalization and other factors that bring them into close contact with one another. *Divergence* is the extent to which distinctiveness is exhibited by a specific culture despite interaction with other cultures. Finally, *crossvergence* is the development of a new culture with its own characteristics that result from cultures interacting with each other over time.

Culture can impact people physically, mentally and psychologically. Over time though, people and their cultures have been able to integrate new customs and values into their way of life. Cultures and nationalistic trends can condition people to behave toward others based on stereotypes and misinformation. Managers and professional workers need to understand that each culture has its own pace and paradigm with regard to how fast or how slow things should get done.

While some cultures are urgency-driven, others have a more balanced approach to tasks since they put relationships first. In the context of the manufacturing work environment, the balanced approach means spending more time on the planning stage so there is less rework, and spending time to get things done right the first time instead of experimenting until one gets it right. Understanding such differences about cultures and time orientations can help managers avoid stereotyping while leading people toward change according to their local norms and customs.

Cultural Values and Decision Making

Personal, organizational, and cultural values can be subconscious and impact a person's decisions. Values have an impact on one's everyday life and they shape as well as define one's character. Living by a personal universal code of ethics helps managers and leaders remain consistent when defining themselves and shaping the perception of others. The result of a decision oftentimes characterizes the process in which people follow when making decisions. Understanding the reasons behind decisions requires thoughtful consideration of the action one takes. Personal, organizational, or cultural values are the foundation on which decisions are made in the day-to-day operations. If personal values are a definition of who you are and what you do, then ensuring your actions are ethical is crucial to effective management and social development. Personal values are not always perceptible, so you can judge the effect you have on a situation by examining your actions.

Individual values are the products of shared cultures and unique personal experiences. For most individuals, family is the first institution in which values are instilled in children through their parents. Family is where the first and foremost fundamental training on ethics is acquired. Religious institutions are another avenue where values and beliefs are taught. Children are raised not to lie, not to cheat, to be responsible for their actions, and to treat people as they want to be treated. As such, most individuals seem to know the difference between right and wrong. Studies have shown that people who commit unethical acts often know they are doing something wrong.

The most basic moral values are learned as children; and as children enter adulthood, more values are acquired at different institutions. When adults enter the workforce, there are rules of conduct imposed by companies and organizations that employees must follow. Organizational values must be communicated through written codes of ethics, as well as formal and informal training. While there are no "right" or "wrong" values, there are values that are better aligned with the organization's culture and codes of ethics. Corporate values must be explicit, and they should be applied to everyone in the organization including top management. Everyone must see that top managers are responsible for their ethical behavior, and employees need to be rewarded for ethical behavior and face consequences for unethical decisions.

In recent years, many corporate scandals have come to light. As such, ethics has become so important and often emphasized in society that it has become a major academic topic. The cultural values, the workforce and personal standards are interrelated; individuals exposed to these values will need to form their own rules of conduct. Life presents people with many choices, and decisions will be made based on personal rules of conduct. Of course, it is best not to choose the most convenient way to conduct business or personal affairs, but to instead choose the way that is aligned with one's overall life goals.

Summary

Valuing cultural differences and international laws is not just an idea that sounds good and promotes positive publicity for the firm. Valuing cultural and managerial differences and each person's genuine commitment to the thorough implementation of effective management practices are critical to one's success as an individual and to the company's survival. In order to be successful, diverse international workers and managers need to become culturally competent. *Cultural competency* refers to the continuous learning process that enables individuals to function effectively in the context of cultural differences. This chapter discussed management, international / global practices, as well as the history of management and the impact of culture on people and modern organizations.

Reflecting on various topics regarding management, culture and cross-cultural management practices can be fruitful for learning and effective leadership. Perhaps one can use such reflections and experience as a learning tool, while appreciating the alternative courses and attempting to avoid the negative "routes" in the future. Author Anne Bradstreet is quoted has having said that "If we had no winter, the spring would not be so pleasant; if we did not sometimes taste of adversity, prosperity would not be so welcome." Such experiences and thoughts can reshape philosophies and form a person's realistic paradigm of the future. The Dalai Lama states that "This is my simple religion. There is no need for temples; no need for complicated philosophy. Our own brain, our own heart is our temple; the philosophy is kindness." Accordingly, while people can write anything they want, each person should use his or her own brain and analyze the current facts prior to taking an appropriate action.

At the meantime, one must remain patient and persistent toward a better future. A Chinese Proverb, with regard to patience, states that "One moment of patience may ward off great disaster. One moment of impatience may ruin a whole life." While being patient, managers should also think of ways to improve the situation or status quo for themselves and their colleagues. Rollo May has been quoted as saying that "Creativity arises out of the tension between spontaneity and limitations, the latter (like the river banks) forcing the spontaneity into the various forms which are essential to the work of art or poem."

Discussion Questions

1. What is management? Define the typical functions of management.
2. Effective managers are expected to have technical, human and conceptual skills. Which of these skills are the most important for a middle manager? Discuss.
3. Should managers be effective or efficient? Discuss.
4. What is international management and how does it vary from national management? Discuss.
5. Who are some of the pioneers of management history? Briefly discuss what they did and do not limit your answers to those who are discussed in this chapter or book.
6. Are scientific management principles universal? Can they be applied across different cultures and industries?
7. What is culture? How does culture influence a person's behavior? What are some of the functions of culture?
8. What are some important dimensions of culture that relate to teamwork?
9. How does culture impact a person's decision-making process?

Management Skills Inventory (MSI)

Management is the process of achieving organizational goals with and through people using available resources in the most efficient manner possible. There are three basic skills that managers use, and they are technical, human relations, and conceptual. Peter G. Northouse (2007, p. 65) provides a quick and useful instrument, known as Skills Inventory (p. 65), which can be used to understand a person's management and leadership skills and how such skills are measured. The final scores provide a sense of various leadership and management competencies related to technical, human and conceptual skills. The skills inventory survey can be completed by oneself to determine one's strengths and weaknesses regarding the three management and leadership skills.

To determine your leadership competencies, circle one of the following options that best describe how you see yourself regarding each statement. For each statement, indicate the degree to which it describes you. A rating of 1 means the statement is Not True for you and a rating of 5 means the statement is Very True of you. Or, you can complete the survey online at: http://www.huizenga.nova.edu/survey/SIS.

Table 1.2 – Management Skills Inventory

Questions	Not true.................True
1. I enjoy getting into the details of how things work.	1 2 3 4 5
2. As a rule, adapting ideas to people's needs is easy for me.	1 2 3 4 5
3. I enjoy working with abstract ideas.	1 2 3 4 5
4. Technical things fascinate me.	1 2 3 4 5
5. Being able to understand others is the most important part of my work.	1 2 3 4 5
6. Seeing the big picture comes easy for me.	1 2 3 4 5
7. One of my skills is being good at making things work.	1 2 3 4 5
8. My main concern is to have a supportive communication climate.	1 2 3 4 5
9. I am intrigued by complex organizational problems.	1 2 3 4 5
10. Following directions and filling out forms comes easily for me.	1 2 3 4 5
11. Understanding the social fabric of the organization is important to me.	1 2 3 4 5
12. I would enjoy working out strategies for my organization's growth.	1 2 3 4 5
13. I am good at completing the things I've been assigned to do.	1 2 3 4 5
14. Getting all parties to work together is a challenge I enjoy.	1 2 3 4 5
15. Creating a mission statement is rewarding work.	
16. I understand how to do the basic things required of me.	1 2 3 4 5
17. I am concerned with how my decisions affect the lives of others.	1 2 3 4 5
18. Thinking about organizational values and philosophy appeals to me.	1 2 3 4 5

Scoring Guidelines for Management Skills Inventory.

To determine your scores for the management and leadership competencies of technical, human and conceptual skills, do the following:

1. Add the responses on items 1, 4, 7, 10, 13, and 16 to determine your score for technical skills.
2. Add the responses on items 2, 5, 8, 11, 14, and 17 to determine your score for human skills.
3. Add the responses on items 3, 6, 9, 12, 15, and 18 to determine your score for conceptual skills.

Total Management Skills Inventory Scores

Technical Skills: _____   Human Skills: _____   Conceptual Skills: _____

Your management skills inventory scores provide information regarding your leadership skills in the areas of technical, human and conceptual skills. The highest scoring areas are your strengths and the lowest scores might indicate areas for usage of skill-relevant management and leadership behaviors to further develop them. The scores for each area might also indicate various levels of management that you may enjoy.

What is Your Personal Decision-Making Style?

People of all cultures make decisions and cultures tend influence a person's decision-making process. As a result of one's socialization in society as well as observations of parents, elders, teachers, managers, and community leaders, one is likely to develop a specific personal decision-making style. It is very possible that a specific individual or group, such as parents or a person's first or most effective or domineering boss, might have had more of an influence on the development of one's personal decision-making style. What tends to hold true for most individuals, over time, is that they are likely to have one or two dominant personal decision-making styles. The personal decision-making style questionnaire below is one short version of a survey that has been presented by academicians (S. Robbins, 2005; A. J. Rowe and J. D. Boulgarides, 1992) and used by practitioners to determine one's decision-making preference or orientation.

To determine your personal decision making style, circle one of the following options that best describe how you see yourself in a normal or a typical work environment.

1. When performing a specific job or task, I usually look for
   a. The best solutions to the problem.
   b. Pleasant working conditions.
   c. New ideas and approaches to get it done.
   d. Practical results.
2. When faced with a problem, I usually
   a. Analyze it carefully.
   b. Rely on my feelings.
   c. Try to find a creative approach.
   d. Use approaches that have worked in the past.
3. When making plans, I usually emphasize
   a. Attaining objectives.
   b. Developing my career.
   c. Future goals.
   d. The problems I currently face.
4. The kind of information I usually prefer to use is
   a. Complete and accurate data.
   b. Data that is limited and simple to understand.
   c. Broad information covering many options.
   d. Specific facts.
5. Whenever I am uncertain about what to do, I
   a. Look for facts.
   b. Wait, and decide later.
   c. Try to find a compromise.
   d. Rely on my intuition.
6. The people with whom I work best are usually
   a. Self-confident.
   b. Trusting and polite.
   c. Open-minded.
   d. Ambitious and full of energy.
7. The decisions I make are usually
   a. Abstract or systematic.
   b. Sensitive to others' needs.
   c. Broad and flexible.
   d. Direct and realistic.

Scoring Guidelines for Personal Decision-Making Styles:

Each answer equals one point. Total the number of points you have selected for a, b, c, and d answers and write the totals below at the front of each letter.

a_____ = **A**nalytical. b_____ = **B**ehavioral. c_____ = **C**onceptual. d_____ = **D**irective.

The "total points" at the front of each letter is the relative strength of your preference or dominant orientation toward each decision-making style. While some people might rely solely on their dominant style(s) to make decisions, others who are more flexible and conscious of various approaches can use different styles depending on the situational variables impacting the dilemma.

According to organizational behavior experts, a person's decision-making style can range from low tolerance for ambiguity to high tolerance for ambiguity. Similarly, a person's decision-making style or way of thinking can range from using a rational (directive or analytical) style to an intuitive (behavioral or conceptual) style. In other words, a person's way of thinking or processing information can be done serially (logical and rational); or they can see situations holistically by processing information through intuitive and creative approaches. The following are the typical characteristics of each style as presented in the field of organizational behavior (for more information, see Robbins, 2005; Rowe & Boulgarides, 1992).

Analytical style. The analytical style individuals tend to be more willing to consider complex solutions based on ambiguous information. People with this style tend to analyze their decisions carefully using as much data as possible. Such individuals tend to enjoy solving problems. They want the best possible solutions and are willing to use innovative methods to achieve them.

Behavioral style. Behavioral individuals are characterized by having a deep concern for the organization in which they work and the personal development of their co-workers. They are highly supportive of others and very concerned about others' achievements, frequently helping them meet their goals. These individuals tend to be open to suggestions from others and, they tend to rely on group meetings for making important decisions.

Conceptual style. Conceptual style individuals tend to be more socially-oriented in their approach to problems. Their approach is humanistic and artistic. They tend to consider many broad alternatives when dealing with problems and to solve them creatively. They have a strong future orientation and enjoy initiating new ideas.

Directive style. The directive style is characterized by people who prefer simple, clear solutions to problem. Individuals with this style tend to make decisions rapidly because they use little information and do not always consider many alternatives. They tend to rely on existing rules to make their decisions, and aggressively use their status to achieve results.

Whatever one's preference or dominant decision-making style(s), it is usually best to consider the various elements and factors that impact the specific situation and people involved before making a final decision. Furthermore, when a decision impacts individuals that can be involved in the problem's final solution, it is best for the manager or leader to show flexibility and use other styles to reach a consensus with his/her colleagues. For example, let us say that "Dean's" scores for the personal decision-making styles are as follows: **A**nalytical = 1; **B**ehavioral = 3; **C**onceptual = 1; and **D**irective = 2. Data shows that Dean's normal preference for making decisions is to use a behavioral approach or the directive style. While he might be comfortable with these two styles, he also should consciously attempt to use the analytical and conceptual styles in order to make good use of his colleagues' and peers' innovative and creative ideas. As such, the development of new skills and flexibility to effectively use any of the styles, depending on the situational factors, would be essential for effective management and leadership.

Through various decisions, you determine the direction of your leadership style and where you are headed in life, both personally and professionally. With regard to direction, author W. Clement Stone states that "The choice is yours. You hold the tiller. You can steer the course; you choose in the direction of where you want to be - today, tomorrow, or in a distant time to come."

CHAPTER 2

Cultural Research

Cultural influences and practices have been impacting individuals, teams, organizations, and businesses every day since the beginning of time and it will continue to be a major influence in everyone's lives. This chapter discusses culture, cultural research, cultural dimensions, diversity, and other such issues which cross-cultural researchers and global employees should be aware of as they conduct research as well as when they recruit, attract, hire, develop, promote, and develop a strong cross-culturally strong workforce.

The Global Environment of Management

Professional managers in the twenty-first century will get the opportunity to work with diverse individuals or in a decidedly different culture. This poses rigorous and numerous challenges, not the least of which is culture shock. Culture shock occurs when expatriates realize that their old ways of doing things, which have always made them successful, may not work as well as they used to in the new culture and work environment. Hopefully, in a successful scenario, they adapt over time and become successful. Effective adaptation and integration depend on many things, including the manager's personality, his or her flexibility and attitude towards new things and change, his or her ability to rely on local mentors to provide accurate and timely assistance, family support, and willingness to experience a new culture.

There are many cross-cultural researchers who have developed various concepts and theories to explain the extent to which one culture can affect others when people migrate (for example Afghan immigrants moving to Thailand, Vietnam, the United States, Europe, Russia, Pakistan, and Iran) and interact in the global marketplace as is the case with many non-governmental organizations (NGOs) impacting business and entrepreneurship around the globe today. Such global interactions can result in convergence, divergence and crossvergence of cultures or sub-cultures. Convergence explains the merging of different cultures by such factors as technology, globalization, economic growth, and industrialization. Divergence, on the other hand, is a state in which there is a marked strength exhibited by individual cultures despite globalization. Crossvergence occurs as cultures are exposed to each other and some new cultural characteristics are formed that are distinct from any of the cultures that are interacting.

To fully understand culture we must be able to stand back and view our own culture as others might. It is very important to get away from the ethnocentric and narrow-minded view that one's own culture is "right," "normal," or "superior" and that other cultures are inconsistent, strange or inferior to one's own. Oftentimes, we think of "primitive" cultures as practicing outdated rituals, but rarely see such elements in our own culture simply because we are used to it. Of course, our own cultures have rituals just as the so called "primitive" cultures do. What is important about cultures, sub-cultures and other such differences is that managers need to respectfully manage such diversity in the workforce effectively.

Diversity management is the process of becoming culturally competent and conscious by understanding the needs, wants, desires, strengths, weaknesses, beliefs, and values of each team member while providing him or her the opportunity to contribute to the collective genius of the whole; thereby, creating synergistic results that are equal to or greater than the sum of the individual parts. "Diversity consciousness" can be seen as the proactive and progressive activation of the mind or senses to create awareness and develop understanding and skills in the area of diversity. It requires life-long soul searching, self-reflection, and learning. It requires diversity education - strategies that enable one to develop diversity management skills. Diversity consciousness requires effective interaction and communication with all individuals. *Communication*, when effective, is a process of sharing information with another person in such a way that s/he understands what you are saying. On the other hand, *intercultural communication* is the process of sharing information or interacting with a person from another culture. So, managers need to be effective intercultural communicators as they deal with so many different ethnicities, cultures, customs, and languages. Diversity conscious individuals understand that as children, they do not necessarily have much control over their programming and may have received negative or stereotypical information about others. However, as adults they have full control over their behavior and, therefore, are totally responsible for changing and/or controlling any negative programming they may have received as children.

All managers should understand that national cultural values are often embedded into one's subconscious mind during childhood. Therefore, some individuals are unaware of their cultural conditioning. On the other hand, organizational value are usually taught and learned later in life either through general education or workplace training. Therefore, these values are often assimilated into one's conscious thoughts and can be changed quicker through socialization into the new culture. *Transculturation* is the process by which a person adjusts to another cultural environment without sacrificing his or her own cultural identity—making necessary adjustments without assimilating or losing one's cultural distinctiveness. Transculturation can be very empowering when one can adjust to any situation without sacrificing or compromising his or her personal beliefs. Transculturation can be very beneficial for a workforce as it leads to individuals who are familiar with many cultures. For example, a person of mixed cultures may know that there are some differences between monochronic and polychronic time orientations in different cultures. In *monochronic* cultures, time is experienced and used in a linear way. Monochronic time means paying attention to and doing only one thing at a time. *Polychronic* time means being involved with many things at once; as such, there is more emphasis on completing human transactions than on holding to schedules. A mixed culture group is more likely to be synergistic when the task is organized so that diversity is an advantage, the task is non-routine and open-ended, top management is supportive, cultural diversity training is provided, and the commitment of group members is rewarded.

Cultures tend to shift and progress in a uniform and consistent way over time. However, some aspects of a culture may not change as fast as others. For example, *cultural lag* is when parts of how things are done in the culture are not keeping up with the rest of the society. For example, a culture can be technologically developed and still hold on to their deeply-held values and perspectives that are very different from the rest of the world. As a matter of fact, one of the functions of culture is to regularize human behavior in a predictable and systematic way.

As such, many individuals who are new to a totally different culture may experience extreme discomfort and at times depression, known as culture shock. *Culture shock*, as alluded to before, is a sense of psychological disorientation that some people suffer when they move into a different culture or work environment. It is the initial adjusting process of an individual when encountering a new culture. It is a natural response to a new cultural experience. The best way to eliminate culture shock is to become a multicultural person. *Multicultural person* refers to a timeless "universal" person who approaches the ideal world of a person whose lifestyle is one of knowledge and wisdom, integrity and direction, principle and fulfillment, balance and proportion. S/he is neither totally a part of nor totally apart from his/her culture; s/he lives, instead, on the boundary. Perhaps, all managers and expatriates need to become "multicultural persons" if they are to be effective leaders with a diverse workforce and produce synergistic results in today's global world of management.

Shifts in Culture

For thinking and reflections, it is critical to mention the importance of understanding the events that cause shifts in a culture. A manager needs to recognize the affects cultural change and shifts will have on people and the organization. If one does not recognize that a change has occurred, s/he may not understand the implications of that shift. Factors to take into consideration once the shift is recognized are industry, organizational culture, cost, and nature. The affiliation between the environment and the culture shift will affect how the manager performs his/her responsibilities. The speed of the shift can be painful when the cultural change is slow.

Setting up a global business is not as simple as constructing a building in the country of choice. It is about understanding the implication of the culture on people and the business. As sourcing shifts continue to change and pressure increase on multinationals to open more facilities in different parts of the globe, taking the time upfront to learn how to lead people and to effectively communicate with each other, how to interpret body language and the importance of the business relationship definitely will help speed up the growth of the business.

Organizational Culture

Organizational culture is comprised of the assumptions, values, norms, and tangible signs of the organization's members. It is a specific collection of the basic values and norms that are shared by people and groups in an organization that control the way people interact with each other and with stakeholders outside of the organization.

There is no one accepted meaning of the term organizational culture. Some writers use the term organizational culture in preference to corporate culture. *Corporate culture* is the basic assumptions and beliefs that employees hold about the company in which they work. Most definitions of organizational culture fall between two extremes: definitions that focus on structures, systems, and regulations, and definitions that focus on the members' sense of 'how we do things here' (Mead, 2005). Definitions that focus on structures, systems, and regulations are referred to as structural definitions, and definitions that focus on the members' sense of "how we do things here" are referred to as experiential definitions.

Richard Mead provides two simple models which are used to compare different organizational cultures. The organizational structure is assessed in terms of how far it is positive or negative. When members trust and support top management, and the workforce and top management share a commitment to the organization, the culture is said to be positive. When these conditions are not met and the workforce and management relations are unproductive, the organizational culture is negative. Furthermore, the culture is strong when it is cohesive, workers can easily communicate between themselves, and members depend upon each other in meeting individual needs. When none of these occur and the relationships between members are not cohesive, the organizational culture is weak.

When the culture is positive and strong, there is a good relationship between management and the workforce. They are able to communicate easily and openly with each other. Productivity is high at this level. When employees are united in their distrust of management and their alienation from official structures, the culture is negative and strong.

It should be noted that management does not always have total control over the organizational culture because it does not have full control over all the factors that influence employees' attitudes toward their jobs. They cannot totally control employees' informal systems, including informal communications, gossip, informal relationships, friendship, and personal relationships, informal rules and norms for surviving and getting along in the workplace. They also cannot control factors in the business environment, such as economic factors, market forces and competition, and industry factors. The national culture, including values associated with working and the workplace is also something that management has no control over. As such, having a well-functioning organizational culture requires the continuous work and engagement of all managers and employees cohesively working based on the established values and norms.

Hall and Hall's Time Orientations

Cultures can be situated and compared in relation to one another through people's communication styles. In some cultures, such as those of Scandinavians, Germans, and the Swiss, communication tends to occur predominantly through explicit statements, and they are thus categorized as low context cultures. In other cultures, such as the Japanese and Chinese, messages include other communicative cues such as body language and the use of silence. Thus, high context communication involves implying a message through that which is not expressed. In order to understand communication one should look at meaning and context together. Context refers to the situation, background, or environment connected to an event, a situation, or an individual.

Hall and Hall, in their 1987 textbook titled *"Understanding Cultural Differences"* stated that each culture operates according to its own internal dynamic, its own principles, and its own explicit or implied laws. Even time and space are unique to each culture. There are, however, some common threads that run through all cultures that managers and change agents should consider when working with people from that environment. According to Hall and Hall, *culture* is similar to a giant, extraordinarily complex, subtle computer. Culture, as a result of socialization and conditioning, guides the actions and responses of human beings in every walk of life in a consistent and predicable manner. This process requires attention to everything people do to survive, advance in the world, and gain satisfaction from life. Furthermore, cultural programs do not work if crucial steps are omitted, which happens when people unconsciously apply their own rules to another system.

According to Hall and Hall, *cultural communications* are deeper and more complex than spoken or written messages. The essence of effective cross-cultural communication has more to do with sending the right responses than with the "right" messages. *Context* is the information that surrounds an event and it is readily available within the person. The elements, such as the events and context that combine to produce a given meaning, are in different proportions depending on the culture. A *high context* (HC) communication or message is one in which most of the information is already in the person, while very little is in the coded, explicit, transmitted part of the message. A *low context* (LC) communication is just the opposite; i.e., the mass of the information is in the explicit code. Twins who have grown up together can and do communicate more economically (HC) than two lawyers in a courtroom during a trial (LC). Most Asians, Arab, and Mediterranean people, who have extensive information networks among family, friends, colleagues, and clients and who are involved in close personal relationships, tend to be high-context. As a result, for most normal transactions in daily life they do not require, nor do they expect, much in-depth, background information (such information already exists or is common knowledge among them).

There are many kinds of time systems in the world, but the two discussed here, according to Hall and Hall, are most important to international employees and managers. *Monochronic time* means paying attention to, doing and / or focusing on, one thing at a time. *Polychronic time orientation* generally means being involved with many things at once. Monochronic time is perceived as being almost *tangible:* people talk about it as though it were money, as something that can be "spent," "saved," "wasted," and "lost." Monochronic time seals people off from one another and as a result intensifies some relationships while shortchanging others. Monochronic time dominates most businesses in the United States, Switzerland, Germany, and Scandinavia. German and Swiss cultures represent classic examples of monochronic time.

Polychronic time is characterized by the simultaneous occurrence of many things and by a great involvement with people. There is more emphasis on completing human transactions than on holding to pre-determined schedules. Proper understanding of the difference between the monochronic and polychronic time systems can be helpful in dealing with the time-flexible Mediterranean workers. While the generalizations, listed in Table 2.1, do not necessarily apply equally to all cultures, they do convey a pattern. In monochronic time cultures, the emphasis is on the compartmentalization of functions and people.

In polychronic Mediterranean cultures, business offices often have large reception areas where people can wait. Polychronic people feel that private space disrupts the flow of information by shutting people off from one another. In polychronic systems, appointments mean very little and may be shifted around even at the last minute to accommodate someone more important in an individual's hierarchy of family, friends, or associates. Some polychronic people (such as Thais, Vietnamese, Latin Americans, Afghans, Iranians, and Arabs) give precedence to their large circle of family members over any business obligation. Polychronic people, according to Hall and Hall, live in a sea of information.

Table 2.1 – Monochronic and Polychronic Time Orientations

MONOCHRONIC PEOPLE	POLYCHRONIC PEOPLE
Do one thing at a time	Do many things at once
Concentrate on the job	Are highly distractible and subject to interruptions
Take time commitments (deadlines, schedules) seriously	Consider time commitments an objective to be achieved, if possible
Are low-context and need information	Are high-context and already have information
Are committed to the job	Are committed to people and human relationships
Adhere religiously to plans	Change plans often and easily
Are concerned about not disturbing others; follow rules of privacy consideration	Are more concerned with those who are closely related (family, friends, close business associates) than with privacy
Show great respect for private property; seldom borrow or lend	Borrow and lend things often and easily
Emphasize promptness	Base promptness on the relationship
Are accustomed to short-term relationships	Have strong tendency to build lifetime relationships

While working with international firms and diverse cultures, it is important to know which segments of the time frame are emphasized. Cultures in countries such as Afghanistan, Pakistan, Iran, India, and some of the Far East for many individuals are past-oriented; still others, such as those of Latin America, are both past-and present-oriented. In Germany, where historical background is very important, every talk, book, or article seems to begin with background information giving a historical perspective. The Japanese and the French are also steeped in history, and because they are high-context cultures, historical facts are often alluded to in a roundabout way.

Each culture has its own language when it comes to *time*. For example, to function effectively in France, Germany, and the United States, it is essential to understand the local language of time. When people take their own time system for granted and project it onto other cultures, they fail to read the hidden messages in the foreign time system and therefore deny themselves vital feedback. For Americans, the use of appointment-schedule time reveals how people feel about each other, how significant their business is, and where they rank in the status system. In France, almost everything is polychronic, whereas in Germany monochronic promptness is even more important than it is in the United States. Oftentimes, due to these differences, some Americans complain that the Germans take forever to reach decisions.

To conduct business in an orderly manner in other countries, it is essential to know how much or how little lead time is required for each activity: how far ahead to request an appointment or schedule meetings and vacations, and how much time to allow for the preparation of a major report. *Lead time* varies from culture to culture and is itself a communication as well as an element in an organization.

Overall, interactions between monochronic and polychronic people can be stressful unless both parties know and can decode the meanings behind each other's message and view of time. According to Hall and Hall (1987), the language of time is much more stable and resistant to change than other cultural systems. In organizations, everything management does communicates; thus when viewed in the cultural context, all acts, all events, all material things have meaning.

Kluckhohn and Strodtbeck

One of the earliest cultural comparative models was designed in 1961 by Kluckhohn and Strodtbeck. As presented in Table 2.2, these authors hypothesized that people of different cultures tend to have different orientations toward the world and people who are different from themselves. As such, they claimed that people of different cultures can be compared and differentiated as per their orientations toward such dimensions as people, nature, relationships, human activity, and conception of space.

1. With regard to the first question, (What is the nature of people?), persons of a specific culture are likely to be seen as good, evil or a mixture of each. These responses have certain implications for managers and expatriates. People who are seen as "good" are likely to be optimistic and may work best with Theory Y style of management where two-way communication is preferred and participation is mandatory as people want to be involved in the decision-making

process. On the other side, people with dominant orientation toward "evil" would probably be more productive with a Theory X style of management, and they may not trust their superiors and colleagues to the same extent as those who are generally optimistic. Furthermore, people who have a dominant "evil" orientation are likely to be secretive and might want to constantly negotiate regarding most aspects of their jobs and day-to-day activities.

Table 2.2 – Kluckhohn and Strodtbeck Cultural Orientation Model

Orientations	Choice / Range of Variations
1. What is the nature of people?	• Good (changeable/unchangeable) • Evil (changeable/unchangeable) • A mixture of good and evil
2. What is the person's relationship to nature?	• Dominant • In harmony with nature • Subjugation
3. What is the person's relationship to other people?	• Lineal (hierarchical) • Collateral (collectivist) • Individualist
4. What is the modality of human activity?	• Doing • Being in becoming • Being
5. What is the temporal focus of human activity?	• Future • Present • Past
6. What is the conception of space?	• Private • Mixed • Public

2. Regarding a person's relationship to nature, people of a culture who have a dominant orientation tend to prefer control and planning over their activities and schedules. Furthermore, these individuals might also be somewhat ethnocentric and impose their will on the business and environment. People who are harmony-oriented tend to better get along with others by avoiding conflict in the workplace as much as possible, and they are likely to show a high level of respect for people who are different from them. A subjugation orientation means fatalism and these individuals are likely to "go with the flow" of external forces without planning to change their fate or destiny.

3. In regard to a person's relationship with other people, those with lineal or hierarchical orientation tend to show respect for their bosses, teachers, parents, and those who are seen to be in the authority positions. Furthermore, they might expect promotions based on seniority of employment, experience and age. Those with a collateral

(collectivist) orientation are likely to prefer team rewards instead of being singled out from the group. They are also likely to brainstorm with the group and obey the rules set forth by their peers or groups. On the other side, an individualistic orientation is likely to condition people to maximize their own status, wealth, and reward opportunities.

Table 2.3 - Kluckhohn and Strodtbeck's Cultural Orientation Model

Concerns / Orientations	Possible Responses
Human Nature: What is the basic nature of people?	*Good.* Most people are basically pretty good at heart; they are born well. *Evil.* Most people can't be trusted. People are basically bad and need to be controlled. *Mixed.* There are both evil people and good people in the world, and you have to check people out to find out which they are. People can be changed with the right guidance.
Man-Nature Relationship: What is the appropriate relationship to nature	*Subordinate to Nature.* People really can't change nature. Life is largely determined by external forces, such as fate and genetics. What happens was meant to happen. *Harmony with Nature.* Man should, in every way, live in harmony with nature. *Dominant over Nature.* It is the great human challenge to conquer and control nature. Everything from air conditioning to the "green revolution" has resulted from having met this challenge.
Time Sense: How should we best think about time?	*Past.* People should learn from history, draw the values they live by from history, and strive to continue past traditions into the future. *Present.* The present moment is everything. Let's make the most of it. Don't worry about tomorrow: enjoy today. *Future.* Planning and goal setting make it possible for people to accomplish miracles, to change and grow. A little sacrifice today will bring a better tomorrow.
Activity: What is the best mode of activity?	*Being.* It's enough to just "be." It's not necessary to accomplish great things to feel your life has been worthwhile. *Becoming.* The main purpose for being placed on this earth is for one's own inner development. *Doing.* If people work hard and apply themselves fully, their efforts will be rewarded. What a person accomplishes is a measure of his or her worth.
Social Relations: What is the best form of social organization?	*Hierarchical.* There is a natural order to relations, some people are born to lead, and others are followers. Decisions should be made by those in charge. *Collateral.* The best way to be organized is as a group, where everyone shares in the decision process. It is important not to make important decisions alone. *Individual.* All people should have equal rights, and each should have complete control over one's own destiny. When we have to make a decision as a group it should be "one person one vote"

4. Those with a doing modality of human activity orientation are likely to value performance, achievement, results, and getting things done. Without achievement and goal-oriented activities, they are likely to become frustrated and anxious. Those with a being orientation tend to prefer seeing their identity derived from birth, age, sex, culture, family, and place of growth. Furthermore, they prefer living in the moment rather than too much planning for the future. They are likely to

"smell the roses" more often in their lives and be concerned with people's feelings toward their jobs, the firm, and other people. Those with a containing orientation tend to focus on self-restraint, self-control, and more likely to effectively strike a good balance between doing and being.

5. With regard to the temporal focus on human activity, those with a future orientation are more concerned with goal orientation and priorities for the future. They are likely to welcome and value change. They want to know where they are going as an individual and as a professional in the firm; therefore, they value career development and succession planning. Those with a present orientation are naturally going to put more emphasis on the moment rather than future planning. People with a past orientation tend to value the law, precedence, rules, age, seniority, and structure based on previous outcomes. They are likely to solve current problems using past experience and performance.

6. Those who are private in their orientation about the conception of space will show more respect for privacy, ownership, and friendships. As such, they will keep outsiders outside and will feel comfortable working with them from a distance. On the other side, those with a public orientation will want more openness in the organization's decision making, will view secret meeting with suspicion, and will get more involved in public forums and meetings.

While much of the above interpretations tend to be subjective, they are likely to have certain implications for managers, leaders and expatriates when they are working with individuals that have diverse personal, professional, or cultural orientations. For example, people with a private orientation will require more time for building trust and negotiations. As such managers must be prepared not to rush a negotiation or force his/her methods on them without getting their agreement.

The Kluckhohn and Strodtbeck's model presents a cross group analysis of specific value orientations about human nature, concept of time, concept of human activity, and social relations of human beings. The dimensions of difference listed was human nature, the relation between nature and human beings, concept of time, concept of human activity, nature of relations of human beings, relationship to things, self-concept, attitude towards the body, and morality. It is proposed that it is possible to distinguish cultures based on how they each address five common human concerns. Kluckhohn and Strodtbeck did not propose that these were the only concerns but that they were useful in understanding cultural differences.

Andre` Laurent's Study on Power and Relationship

Andre` Laurent who examined people's attitude toward power and relationship in his 1983 publication. He examined and analyzed the values of managers in Switzerland, Germany, Denmark, Sweden, United Kingdom, Netherlands, Belgium, Italy, France, and the United States. Later in the decade, Laurent and his colleagues got more data from such countries as China, Indonesia, and Japan. Laurent claims that managers express their values through the process of management by carrying their management status with them outside of the workplace, capacity to bypass various hierarchies in the organization, and by serving as experts and facilitators.

With regard to managerial status in the wider context, Laurent would ask respondents the following question to see what percentage of them would agree: *"Through their professional activity, managers play an important role in society."* The results presented in Table 2.4 were reported in Laurent's 1983 study.

Table 2.4 – Managerial Status and Role in Society

Countries	% Agree
1. Denmark	1. 32%
2. United Kingdom	2. 40%
3. Netherlands	3. 45%
4. Germany	4. 46%
5. United States	5. 52%
6. Sweden	6. 54%
7. Switzerland	7. 65%
8. Italy	8. 74%
9. France	9. 76%

Data shows that 76% of French managers agree that managers tend to carry their titles and status into the wider society and, therefore, are perceived to play an important role in the community. Similarly, 74% of the Italians agreed that managers carry their status into activities outside of the workplace. On the opposite end, only 32% of managers in Denmark (or Danish respondents) tend to agree that managers play an important role in the society due to their professional activities.

Managers in the United States tend to fall around the middle with 52% of the respondents agreeing that managers play an important role in society.

Table 2.5 – Bypassing the Hierarchy

Countries	% Disagree
1. Sweden	1. 22%
2. United Kingdom	2. 31%
3. United States	3. 32%
4. Denmark	4. 37%
5. Netherlands	5. 39%
6. Switzerland	6. 41%
7. Belgium	7. 42%
8. France	8. 42%
9. Germany	9. 46%
10. Italy	10. 75%
11. People's Republic of China	11. 66%

In regard to bypassing the hierarchy, Laurent would ask respondents the following question to see how many of them would disagree with it: "*In order to have efficient work relationships, it is often necessary to bypass the hierarchical line.*" The percentages of responses, from the studies in the 1980's, in disagreement are presented in Table 2.5. Through data analysis, one can conclude that Swedish employees are likely to bypass hierarchical levels when searching for new knowledge, efficiency and productivity. On the opposite extreme, bypassing the hierarchy in the Italian and Chinese firms would show lack of respect for authority and insubordination since most respondents disagreed with the statement posed to them. This means that Chinese and Italians might prefer to work in a single structure format rather than a matrix organization where employees report to two bosses (i.e. divisional managers as well as functional managers).

With regard to the manager as an expert versus as a facilitator, Laurent's study would require researchers to ask respondents the following question: "*It is important for a manager to have at hand precise answers to most of the questions that his/her subordinates may raise about their work.*" The percentages of respondents in agreement in some of the studies from the 1980's are presented in Table 2.6.

The data with regard to managers as experts or facilitators show that managers in Sweden, Netherlands and the United States are not expected to have all the answers to their employees' questions as they are seen to serve as facilitators (and not experts). On the other side, managers in the Asian countries, Italy and France are expected to have the answers to their employees' questions since they are expected to serve as experts. In other words, Asians want managers that are knowledgeable in technical aspects of their jobs. As such, seniority and promotion from within or, at least, from within the industry are going to be important when working in Asian, Italian and French cultures. While the Asian, Italian and French managers see their positions and titles in terms of who has decision-making authority, the Swedish, Dutch and American managers are likely to use their titles to facilitate problem solving and decision-making processes with and/or through people.

Table 2.6 – Managers as Experts v. Facilitators

Countries	% Agree
1. Sweden	1. 10%
2. Netherlands	2. 17%
3. United States	3. 18%
4. Denmark	4. 23%
5. United Kingdom	5. 27%
6. Switzerland	6. 38%
7. Belgium	7. 44%
8. Germany	8. 46%
9. France	9. 53%
10. Italy	10. 66%
11. People's Republic of China	11. 74%

Overall, to summarize, one can say that Andre` Laurent studied attitudes to power and relationships. He analyzed the values of managers in different countries. The three main points develop based on the parameters identified by Laurent are: a) How far the manager carries his/her status into the wider context outside the workplace; b) The manager's capacity to bypass levels in the hierarchy; and c) The manager as an expert in contrast to the manager as a facilitator.

Geert Hofstede's Cultural Dimensions

Global managers need to pay attention to the work of Geert Hofstede, who studied values in many countries through his work with the IBM organization in the early 1980's. He found that countries could be profiled on at least four variables (his original profile): individualism, power distance, masculinity, and uncertainty avoidance. The masculinity-femininity dimension has been renamed the achievement versus nurturing orientation to be more politically correct. Hofstede (1993) also later added a fifth dimension, long-term versus short-term orientation.

For the purpose of research and further study, the following are the commonly applied definitions for the various dimensions as mentioned by Hofstede:

- *Individualism.* A dimension of culture that stands for a society in which the ties between individuals are loose: Everyone is expected to look after himself or herself and immediate family.
- *Collectivism.* A dimension of culture that stands for a society in which people from birth onwards are integrated into strong, cohesive in-groups, which throughout people's lifetime continue to protect them in exchange for unquestioning loyalty.
- *Power Distance.* The extent to which the less powerful members of institutions and organizations within a country expect and accept that power is distributed unequally.
- *Uncertainty Avoidance.* The extent to which members of a society feel threatened by situations of uncertainty.
- *Masculinity (achievement).* This dimension describes a society in which the social gender roles are clearly distinct: men are supposed to be assertive, tough and focused on material success; women are supposed to be more modest, tender and concerned with the quality of life.
- *Femininity (nurturing).* This stands for a society in which social gender roles overlap: Both men and women are supposed to be modest, and concerned with the quality of life.
- *Long-Term Orientation.* This dimension stands for the fostering of virtues oriented towards future rewards in particular perseverance and thrift.
- *Short-Term Orientation.* This dimension stands for the fostering of virtues related to the past and present, in particular, respect for tradition, preservation of "face," and fulfilling social obligation.

The "typical" western worker is very independent and individualistic; generally speaking, Americans are not group-oriented like the

Japanese, Chinese, Thais, Vietnamese or most other Asians. Americans, again generally speaking, do not have high reverence for status differences in their organizations, thus the low power distance. Americans are high in their desire for material goods and achievement, stereotypically achievement-oriented traits; they are comfortable with ambiguity; and they tend to live for the short-term profit. When you compare their profiles with other countries, you can see the types of cultural challenges that await expatriates as well as both national and international managers.

Fons Trompanaar's Cultural Dimensions

Culture, according to Fons Trompanaar (1993), can be examined on different levels: individual, organizational and national. On an individual level, culture is viewed as the way that people share and express their values. On an organizational level, it can be looked at as the way in which people within an organization express attitudes. On a national level, it can be viewed as the way in which attitudes are expressed in a particular country or geographical region.

Cultures differ greatly and some practices of a specific culture might be very different from others. While cultural practices can be similar, they may still have subtle nuances that might not be apparent to a foreigner. In a Japanese study conducted by the Ministry of Labor it was disclosed that 38% of young men and 36% of young women are not particularly interested in promotion as long as they can work in a job where they can apply their skills and abilities (Women in Japan, 2006). Studies show that only about 11% of the respondents indicated they wanted to get ahead by exerting effort. These results come as a big surprise to many researchers and writers. Young Japanese workers are certainly quite a different breed from their supposedly "workaholic fathers." One guess is that young people have probably found meaningful ways to spend time outside of work, something that the older generation was perhaps unable to do to the same extent. Many companies in Japan still hire only men or only women for certain jobs. There are many justifications for these practices, but one can certainly say that culture is one of them. As to why companies will allow only men to perform certain jobs, the most popular reason cited was that the positions in question had late night shifts for which women were prohibited. As to why only women were allowed to apply for certain jobs, 47% of the respondents said "the job is supportive or seasonal," therefore only women would be appropriate; and 39% said "women can respond more gently to customers," or "the job better utilizes a women's abilities and/or feelings."

Japan is a fine example of a culture where the emphasis is on relationships; the principal criterion for evaluating people is on their loyalty, contribution to group harmony and team spirit, and social "fit." The work group gives an employee his or her social and personal identity; it is amazingly like a family. People change jobs infrequently, sometimes never. So at the time people are selected for hiring, promotion, or special trust, their ascribed characteristics are carefully taken into account. Their on-the-job performance is less important; everyone performs reasonably well on the job, so performance is not a particularly effective way of making choices among them. A Japanese executive provides a fine example of someone who is quite comfortable assuming that people's birth-given or ascribed traits (in this case, male or female) are an appropriate basis for assigning them to an economic role and social status. The Western culture managers often prefer to sort people out on the basis of their demonstrated achievements. A difference among cultures that can undermine mutual understanding concerns the extent to which one's feelings and emotions are openly revealed in the course of professional and managerial work.

Every culture distinguishes itself from others by the specific solutions it chooses to certain problems which reveal themselves as dilemmas. It is convenient to look at such problems under three areas: those which arise from our relationships with other people; those which come from the passage of time; and those which relate to the environment. From the solutions different cultures have chosen to these universal problems, researchers can further identify fundamental dimensions of culture that are emphasized by Fons Trompanaar (1993; Cultural Dimensions, 2006):

A) *Universalism vs. Particularism*: People in universalistic cultures share the belief that general rules, codes, values and standards take precedence over particular needs and claims of friends and relations. In a universalistic society, the rules apply equally to the whole "universe" of members. Any exception weakens the rule. For example: the rule that you should give your honest judgment to the insurance company concerning a payment it is about to make to you, is more important here than particular ties of friendship or family. It is not that in universalistic cultures particular ties are completely unimportant; but the universal truth, the law, is considered logically more significant than these relationships. Particularistic cultures see the ideal culture in terms of human friendship, extraordinary achievement and situations and in intimate relationships. The "spirit of the law" is deemed more important than the "letter of the law."

B) *Individualism vs. Communitarians*: In a predominantly individualistic culture people place the individual before the community. Individual happiness, fulfillment, and welfare set the pace. People are expected to decide matters largely on their own and to take care primarily of themselves and their immediate family. In a particularistic culture, the quality of life for all members of society is seen as directly dependent on opportunities for individual freedom and development. The community is judged by the extent to which it serves the interest of individual members. Communitarian cultures place the community before the individual. It is the responsibility of the individual to act in ways which serve society. By doing so, individual needs will be taken care of naturally.

C) *Specific vs. Diffuse*: People from specific cultures start with the elements, the specifics. First they analyze them separately, and then they put them back together again. In specific cultures, the whole is the sum of its parts. Each person's life is divided into many components: you can only enter one at a time. Interactions between people are highly purposeful and well-defined. The public sphere of specific individuals is much larger than their private sphere. People are easily accepted into the public sphere, but it is very difficult to get into the private sphere, since each area in which two people encounter each other is considered separate from the other, a specific case. Specific individuals concentrate on hard facts, standards, and contracts. People from diffusely oriented cultures start with the whole and see each element in perspective of the total. All elements are related to each other. These relationships are more important than each separate element; so the whole is more than just the sum of its elements. Diffuse individuals have a large private sphere and a small public one. Newcomers are not easily accepted into either. But once they have been accepted, they are admitted into all layers of the individual's life. A friend is a friend in all respects: tennis, cooking, work, etc. The various roles someone might play in your life are not separated.

D) *Affective vs. Neutral*: In an affective culture people do not object to a display of emotions. It isn't considered necessary to hide feelings and to keep them inside. Affective cultures may interpret the less explicit signals of a neutral culture as less important. They may be ignored or even go unnoticed. In a neutral culture people are taught that it is incorrect to show one's feelings overtly. This doesn't mean they do not have feelings, it just means that the degree to which feelings may become manifest is limited. They accept and are aware of feelings, but are in control of them. Neutral cultures may think the louder signals of an affective culture are too excited, and over-emotional. In neutral cultures, showing too much emotion may erode your power to interest people.

E) *Achievement vs. Ascription*: Achieved status refers to what an individual does and has accomplished. In achievement-oriented cultures, individuals derive their status from what they have accomplished. A person with achieved status has to prove what he / she is worth over and over again: status is accorded on the basis of action. Ascribed status refers to what a person is and how others relate to his or her position in the community, in society or in an organization. In a scripture society, individuals derive their status from birth, age, gender or wealth. A person with ascribed status does not have to achieve to retain his/her status: it is accorded to him/her on the basis of his/her being.

F) *Internal vs. External*: In regards to relations with nature, every culture has developed an attitude towards the natural environment. Survival has meant acting with or against nature. The way we relate to our environment is linked to the way we seek to have control over our own lives and over our destiny or fate. Internal people have a mechanistic view of nature. They see nature as a complex machine and machines can be controlled if you have the right expertise. Internal people do not believe in luck or predestination. They are 'inner-directed' - one's personal resolution is the starting point for every action. You can live the life you want to live if you take advantage of the opportunities. Human beings can dominate nature - if they make the effort. External people have a more organic view of nature. Mankind is one of nature's forces, so should operate in harmony with the environment. Man should subjugate to nature and go along with its forces. External people do not believe that they can shape their own destiny. 'Nature moves in mysterious ways', and therefore you never know what will happen to you. The actions of externalist people are 'outer-directed' - adapted to external circumstances.

The work of most management and international management researchers on cultural dimensions can also apply to predict people's behavior, at a general level, based on their culture and cultural orientations. For example, Fons Trompanaar differentiated between *Universalism* and *Particularism* and used dilemmas to see if respondents lean more toward universalism or particularism based on their cultures. *Universalists* believe what is good and right applies everywhere regardless of the situation or extenuating circumstances. *Particularists* emphasize obligations and relationships. The following are two typical scenarios asked of respondents, by Trompanaar, to see if they say "yes or no" or "agreed or disagreed":

Scenario One: "You are working for a large organization with over 10,000 associates. Your boss asks you to help paint his or her house this weekend." *Would you help your boss?* The following results of over 15,000 respondents from different countries represent "*the percentage of people who would NOT paint the house.*" Some of the initial responses were as follows:

–	Australia	96%
–	USA	89%
–	Japan	83%
–	China	28%
–	Hispanics	17%

The 83% response rate of people who would not paint the house in Japan seems surprising to most people as the Japanese live in a collective or team-oriented culture. During a discussion of the results at the 2005 SHRM conference in Orlando, Florida, Trompanaar said that the responses from the Japanese group turned out as such because many of the respondents in Japan did not paint houses; thus, the Japanese respondents could not relate to the question of painting home.

Scenario Two: "You are riding with your friend who is driving 75 MPH in a 45 MPH zone. He accidentally hits a pedestrian and you end up going to court with him. His lawyer tells you "don't worry, you are the only witness." Would you agree or disagree with the following statement: "*My friend has NO right or some right and I will NOT help?*" The following are results of 15,000 respondents from different countries who said: "*My friend has NO right or some right and I will NOT help.*" Some of the initial responses were as follows:

–	USA	95%
–	Germany	91%

–	France	68%
–	South Korea	26%

The answers from respondents from different countries and continents are often driven by cultural influences; as such, facilitators of change and trainers should take such diverse views into consideration when initiating change. Yes it is difficult, even impossible, for firms, expatriates, trainers, managers, and facilitators of change to fully understand every aspect of other cultures in a short period of time, but the differences can be managed if they are predicted, acknowledged, respected, and proactively integrated into an effective training and development program.

Summary

Stereotypes and cultural misunderstandings are likely to exist in various parts of the society for many decades and centuries to come. Professionals should create a work environment that respects human beings and supports them in capitalizing on their unique qualities. This chapter has presented some of the major studies regarding cultural dimensions that have been studied in the past three decades. Studying cultures through actual research and primary data can point to the facts and specific differences and commonalties exist among people in different nations and regions.

Discussion Questions

1. What is culture? What is culture shock and how can one successfully overcome its negative impact? Discuss and provide examples.
2. In what manners can cultures be studied? What are some of the common studies that have been conducted regarding cultures?
3. How are cultures changing today? Are they converging or diverging? Discuss.
4. Discuss the various time orientations across cultures and their impact in the workplace.
5. Discuss the five dimensions of culture as defined by Hofstede.
6. Discuss dimensions of culture as defined by Fons Trompanaar.
7. Is there a relationship between high context cultures and collective cultures? Discuss.
8. Discuss the work of Andre` Laurent and its implications for managers.

9. Discuss the work of Kluckhohn and Strodtbeck and its implications for researchers and managers.
10. Is there a relationship between individualism and ethics? Can there be negative relationships and positive? Discuss.

CHAPTER 3

Motivational Concepts and Practices

People of different cultures, generations and times have different values and, thus, are motivated by different factors. It is assumed that treating others the way we want to be treated is sufficient for healthy interpersonal relationships and, perhaps this is true to some extent. The "Golden Rule" (doing unto others as one would want done to oneself) may not always apply in each case since the population is now more heterogeneous and, thus, some have resorted to adopting the "Platinum Rule" in their workplace. The Platinum Rule states that one should treat others the way they want to be treated. Today's diverse generations and cultural values require flexibility in using management and leadership approaches that are relevant for the culture, time and generations of people. This chapter provides an overview of motivational theories and concepts so managers can create a workplace where employee satisfaction and productivity can be high.

Job Satisfaction and Motivation

Values and attitudes are a basic part of human behavior. *Values* are beliefs about what is right or wrong, good or bad, normal or abnormal. We learn basic values at a very young age from everyone and everything around us. By the time we are in our late teens and early adulthood, we have pretty well developed our value system which we will use in relating to the world from then on. During the first few years, children are value programmed mostly by their parents and immediate family members that come into contact with them. Media, especially television, are important value programmers as well. As the child enters school, the latter becomes a major source of values. In the teenage years, parents and family become secondary to peers as the primary source of values. Also, there is a genetic component to values.

Regardless of cultural backgrounds, values once established tend to stay relatively stable over time. After the value system has been established, only a truly significant emotional event is likely to cause these values to change.

While people hold only a limited number of core values, they may have thousands of attitudes. *Attitudes* are how we feel about something or somebody, either positive or negative. Attitudes, according to experts, have three components: *Cognitive component* - What you believe to be true; for example, "I believe higher education is very important." *Affective component* - what you feel about the belief; example, "I disapprove of parents who discourage their children from going to college." *Behavioral component* - what that feeling leads you to do; example, "I argue with Mrs. Ngo because she is trying to lead her son to go into the army instead of going to college." Much of the management literature deals with the attitudes we have about work, especially job satisfaction, job involvement, and organizational commitment.

An important thing to realize about attitudes is that all humans struggle for consistency between their attitudes and behavior. When you are in a situation which demands that you behave against your beliefs and attitudes you suffer from what experts have identified as "cognitive dissonance." *Cognitive dissonance* refers to an uneasy feeling when beliefs and behavior are in conflict. Individuals will struggle to reorient either their attitudes or behavior in order to bring them back into harmony. As such, dissatisfaction with the job might be the outcome.

Job satisfaction is one of the four outcome variables that are often studied by management researchers and scholars (the other three variables are employee turnover, absenteeism, and productivity). Job satisfaction is an elusive variable and researchers often measure it using attitude surveys. Some research suggests that productivity leads to job satisfaction. Other research says just the opposite that job satisfaction leads to productivity.

Studies that measure overall job satisfaction in the workforce show widely varied results. One guess would be that even as the workforce is getting increasingly professional (an item often associated with increased job satisfaction), the overall workforce is less satisfied now than they were in the 1980's and 1990's. The reason for this guess is that this period has been a turbulent time of downsizing and destruction of long-standing strong organizational cultures , leading to increasing anxiety among workers as to the security of their jobs. A feeling of security is a basic tenet of a motivated workforce.

Management authors tell us that job satisfaction is at least partially determined by mentally challenging work, fair rewards, supportive working conditions, and encouraging co-workers. The job-personality fit is also very important. While the relationship between productivity and job satisfaction is not clear, studies show that job satisfaction and absenteeism are at least moderately negatively correlated. In other words, as job satisfaction goes up, absenteeism goes down. There is even a stronger negative correlation between employee satisfaction and turnover. Logically, if we like our job, we are likely to stay there.

Motivation Theories

Motivation is one of the most important topics managers and leaders study in the field of human behavior. Everyone wants to know how to motivate their colleagues, bosses, friends, and, of course, employees. The term "motivate" comes from the Latin verb, *movere*, which means to cause movement. Basically, motivation is about causing others, such as employees, to move toward some predetermined objective or goal. Psychologically, motivation deals with others' (employees') needs. Unsatisfied needs cause a tension which leads to a drive to satisfy the needs as soon as possible. This drive leads to research or action and an examination of alternative ways of potentially satisfying the need. The need is either satisfied or frustrated in which case the search behavior continues.

Overall, *motivation* is generally defined as the psychological forces within a person that determine the direction of behavior in an organization, the level of effort or how hard people work, and the persistence displayed by organizational members in meeting their goals. Organizational members can be intrinsically or extrinsically motivated. Intrinsic motivation is a behavior that is performed for its own sake. Motivation comes from performing the work. Extrinsic motivation is a behavior performed to acquire rewards such as a promotion, raise, or an office. Extrinsic motivation source is the consequence of an action. Some employees are motivated intrinsically and others are motivated extrinsically, while most people tend to be motivated by both forms depending on the task, time and other situational variables.

Content and Process Theories

Motivational theories can be grouped under the categories of content and process theories of motivation. *Content theories* of motivation answer the question, "What things motivate people?" Content theories look for external or extrinsic motivators. Process theories of motivation answer the question, "How are people motivated?" Content theories of motivation generally include: Maslow's Hierarchy of Needs, Herzberg's Two Factor Theory, McClelland's Achievement Theory, and Alderfer's ERG Theory. *Process theories* look at internal or intrinsic processes of motivation; what is the cognitive process by which people become motivated? Process theories of motivation includes: Vroom's Expectancy Theory, Adams' Equity Theory, and Reinforcement Theory.

Process theories and satisfaction. Process theories focus on "*how*" people are motivated. These theories tend to identify specific needs or values that are most conducive to satisfaction with one's job. According to experts, process theorists focus on how a person's expectations for specific outcomes associated with their performance, influence his/her performance. Of course, motivation theorists are interested in how individual behavior is energized, directed, maintained, and stopped. Process theories include Adam's equity theory, Vroom's expectancy theory, Skinner's reinforcement theory, Locke's goal setting theory, and they are central in understanding process theories.

Content theories and satisfaction. Content theories are about "*what*" motivates a person. These theories attempt to specify the particular needs that must be attained for an individual to be satisfied with his or her job. Two theories are most prominent in the study of content theories; Maslow's Need Hierarchy theory and Herzberg's Motivator-Hygiene theory. Maslow's Need Hierarchy theory is categorized in a defined order to include physiological needs, safety needs, belongingness and love needs, esteem needs, and self-actualization needs. Maslow's theory suggested that satisfied needs are not motivators. As lower level needs are satisfied, they no longer drive behavior, and, consequently, higher order needs take over as the motivating force. Unlike Maslow, Herzberg's Motivator-Hygiene theory argues that job satisfaction and dissatisfaction result from different causes and that satisfaction depends on "Motivators" while dissatisfaction is the result of "Hygiene factors." Motivators deal with aspects of the work itself, which includes work, promotion, achievement, responsibility, and recognition. Hygiene factors include working conditions, interpersonal relations, company policies and salary, and supervision.

Theories X, Y and Z

A good starting point in the study of motivation is an understanding of Theory X and Theory Y popularized by Douglas McGregor. According to the Theory X model, managers believe that people dislike work and can be lazy. Therefore, they need to be told what to do and how to do it. As such, they need autocratic managers as such a style would best fit with Theory X employees. Managers who apply a Theory X philosophy tend to believe that:

- Work is inherently distasteful to most people.
- Most people are not ambitious, have little desire for responsibility, and prefer to be directed.
- Most people have little capacity for creativity in solving organizational problems.
- Motivation occurs only at the physiological and safety levels.
- Most people must be closely controlled and often coerced to achieve organizational objectives.

According to Theory Y, workers enjoy work and especially crave involvement and meaningful work. Workers want responsibility and thus the correct way to lead is through delegation. Managers who apply a Theory Y philosophy tend to believe that:

- Work is as natural as play, if the conditions are favorable.
- Self-control is often indispensable in achieving organizational goals.
- The capacity for creativity in solving organizational problems is widely distributed in the population.
- Motivation occurs at the social, esteem, and self-actualization levels, as well as physiological and security levels.
- People can be self-directed and creative at work if properly motivated.

While Theory Y is widely believed to be the better operation system, it must be noted that not all workers want responsibility and autonomy.

The Japanese researcher, William Ouchi, researched the cultural differences between Japan and western countries such as the United States and mentioned that the American culture emphasizes the individual, and managers often feel workers follow the Theory X model. However, the Japanese culture expects workers are committed to the organization first and should behave differently than western workers. Ouchi created Theory Z of motivation and it combines parts of both the Asian and Western structures. In regards to Theory Z management and motivation, managers would stress long-term employment, work-group, and organizational focus in order to create a motivational work environment.

Maslow's Hierarchy of Needs

Abraham Maslow was a practicing psychologist who noted through his experience that people have certain categories of needs. Maslow identified five specific levels of needs that were organized in a hierarchy. The needs are as follows starting from the bottom (physical) and moving up to the top (self-actualization): physical, security, social, self-esteem, and self-actualization. Starting with physical needs, initially workers and people in general are motivated by the acquisition of items that assures them of food and shelter. Once these needs are satisfied, the needs of workers "move up" the hierarchy as they become motivated by safety issues. Once satisfied with the security needs, the worker again moves up the hierarchy to the "social needs" level where interpersonal relations are motivational. Many of the social needs like belonging and feeling needed are played out at work where workers spend so much of their time interacting with others who have similar needs and professional aspirations. When these needs are met, the individual becomes motivated by self-esteem which considers such things as recognition, opportunity for growth and autonomy. At the top of the hierarchy, often depicted as a pyramid or ladder, is self-actualization. At this level, the individual is free from all mundane concerns and may pursue his or her dreams, become all that s/he can be.

Maslow's theory is the most popular motivational theory and most other researchers have used it as a stepping stone. Maslow's theory does provide two insights that are important for researchers and managers: 1) It states that not all people are motivated by similar things; and 2) It states that the same person is not always motivated by the same thing since his or her needs change over time.

Herzberg's Satisfiers and Hygiene Factors

In the early 1950's, *Frederick Herzberg*, a psychologist, studied motivation by asking people to relate critical incidents about when they felt most satisfied and motivated on the job and when they felt most dissatisfied. Herzberg found that these questions received two different types of answers. Thus, the two-factor theory of motivation was born. One factor, Herzberg called *hygiene factors* (or "dis-satisfiers") which are things that make people unhappy when they are not taken care of but do not motivate them when they are provided at the expected levels. In other words, hygiene or maintenance factors prevent dissatisfaction but do not lead to motivation. Hygiene factors include a safe working environment, salary, and satisfactory working relationships with peers and superiors.

The other factor, Herzberg called *motivators* ("satisfiers") which are the things that, when present, cause motivation, but when absent, cause a lack of motivation (and not necessarily dissatisfaction). Motivators are such things as the work itself, autonomy, authority, and responsibility for one's job. As can be seen, Herzberg's motivators are equivalent to Maslow's "higher order needs" of self-esteem and self-actualization. Herzberg's hygiene factors are equivalent to Maslow's "lower order needs" of physical, security, and social desires.

Alderfer's ERG Theory

Clayton Alderfer essentially modified Maslow's model by condensing the five levels of needs into three categories: E = Existence; R = Relatedness; and G = Growth. *Existence* needs are equivalent to Maslow's physical and safety needs; relatedness equates to social needs; growth refers to self-esteem and self-actualization. Managers and researchers can compare ERG theory to Herzberg's model of hygiene factors and motivators. Existence and relatedness equate to Herzberg's hygiene factors and growth relates to motivators. Alderfer sees needs as moving back and forth, not just upward in the hierarchy. Because of the recognition of forward movement, progression from lower needs (existence) to higher needs (growth), Alderfer's model is called a "need progression" theory. While Maslow's model generally portrays motivation as moving in one direction, which is upward, Alderfer feels that people move back and forth among these three needs of existence, relatedness and growth as situations change. So, motivation is situational. As such, it is possible to regress from being motivated by growth needs to being motivated by relatedness or existence needs.

McClelland's Need Theory

David McClelland, a psychologist, looked at motivation from the perspective that people have either a high need for achievement, affiliation, or power and that this motivation would result in different behaviors in the workplace. Specifically, McClelland felt that high achievers only made up around ten percent of the population, but that these people were the real high producers in organizations. McClelland found that high achievers had the following characteristics: high achievers love moderate challenge; high achievers seek concrete feedback, they want to know how they are doing and they also want to know that the manager knows how they are doing; and, high achievers want to take personal responsibility for the work, they can be productive but they do not necessarily make good managers as they depend more on their own individual performance.

McClelland felt that high achievement was largely learned in childhood as people model themselves after high-achieving adults. McClelland also felt that managers could have influence over encouraging high achievement by urging people to have specific goals, face challenges, take risks, and enjoy taking personal responsibility for being persistent toward one's objectives.

Vroom's Expectancy Theory

Victor Vroom looked at the internal, cognitive processes that people go through in order to satisfy needs and thus become motivated. Vroom explains that the behavior workers decide to display depends upon what they expect to achieve from that behavior. According to the Expectancy Theory model, the individual effort one is motivated to exert depends on his or her judgment of how well s/he can perform (first level) and what s/he thinks that performance will earn (second level outcome).

According to Victor Vroom, "*Expectancy*" is the probability that the level of effort workers put in will achieve the desired level of performance; "*Instrumentality*" is the probability that performance (first level) will lead to the desired second level outcome or reward; and "*Valence*" is the value of the reward or how much workers want or do not want the second level outcome. The higher the expectancy, instrumentality and valence, then the higher the level of motivation is likely to be for the employee to get the task completed with high performance.

Adams' Equity Theory

John Stacy Adams says that motivation comes and goes for the individual employee at least in part by his or her perception of equity in the workplace. Thus, the individual compares his or her inputs (skills, experience, time on job, seniority, etc.) and outputs (job title, benefits, salary, responsibility) with the inputs and outputs of a "referent" person. Depending upon that comparison, the individual concludes that his or her own input/output ratio is equitable or inequitable. When inequity is perceived, the employee will feel ill at ease and probably try one of two things. First, s/he may reduce his or her own inputs. Secondly, s/he may try to increase his or her own outputs.

Inequity may arise from faulty perception in which case the manager needs to correct the inaccuracy. If inequity exists, the manager needs to examine the situation carefully and find a remedy.

Reinforcement Theory

Reinforcement theory is based on concepts of how people learn. Most people remember hearing about Pavlov's dogs being taught to salivate at the ringing of a bell because they connected the bell with being fed. That type of "learning" is called classical conditioning as it is a trained stimulus-response reaction. The model that describes human behavior is known as "*operant conditioning.*" In this case the expectation of a consequence determines a person's behavior. B. F. Skinner made the concept of "*behavior modification*" very popular in literature and in the work environment. Behavior modification depends upon various types of reinforcement techniques with the basic belief that you tend to get the behavior you reinforce. Literature discusses four basic reinforcement techniques as follows:

- *Positive reinforcement*: A technique used to increase the incidence of a desired behavior. Telling someone they are doing a good job or giving someone a raise are examples of positive reinforcement.
- *Negative reinforcement*: This is also designed to increase the incidence of a desired behavior. If someone walks into the class late and the teacher jokingly chides him or her by saying, "Good afternoon, Yousuf, nice that you could make it..." the student will likely be embarrassed into coming on time next time. On the other hand, the student may love the extra attention and continue to come late.
- *Punishment*: Designed to decrease the incidence of an undesired behavior, punishment does not fit in well with today's values and may breed frustration and resentment. Examples of punishment include scolding someone in front of his or her peers or sending someone home from work. Naturally, there are some incidents which do deserve immediate punishment such as violence in the workplace.
- *Extinction*: This strategy also serves to decrease the incidence of an undesired behavior. Extinction entails simply ignoring a given behavior and hoping it will disappear. It is often an appropriate response for a minor behavioral problem.

There are many other concepts and thoughts that lead to a motivational work environment; goal setting and empowerment are two factors. There has been much research on the usefulness of concrete goals in motivating employees to higher productivity. Studies conclude that employees with challenging, concrete, measure-able goals tend to be more productive than those who do not have these goals. Employees also need feedback on how they are doing as they try to attain their goals. *Self-efficacy* refers to one's perception that he or she is able to do a given task. If a person has concrete goals that he or she accepts, believes they have the ability to do the job, and are receiving adequate feedback from their supervisor or through self-monitoring techniques, then this person is likely to have a higher degree of motivation than when these variables are not present.

Empowerment Value

Empowerment is a key managerial concept and it delegates much of the traditional management authority to employees who are doing the work. One can see how empowerment fits right in with Herzberg's job enrichment theory. Empowerment can be a "motivator" factor for the employees. High achievers love the additional challenge and participation. But, does every worker in every culture want to be empowered and shoulder more decision-making responsibility? Most likely not; therefore, one needs to act according to the situation.

One's value as an individual. A well-known manager (male) started off the yearly meeting with his employees by holding up a $50.00 bill. In the room of 200, he asked, "Who would like this $50 bill?" Hands started going up. He said, "I am going to give this $50 to one of you but first, let me do this. He proceeded to crumple the $50 dollar bill up. He then asked, "Who still wants it?" Still the hands were up in the air. Well, he replied, "What if I do this?" And he dropped it on the ground and started to grind it into the floor with his shoe. He picked it up, now crumpled and dirty. "Now, who still wants it?" Still the hands went into the air.

My friends, we have all learned a very valuable lesson. No matter what I did to the money, you still wanted it because it did not decrease in value. It was still worth $50. Many times in our lives, we are dropped, crumpled, and grounded into the dirt by the decisions we make and the circumstances that come our way. We feel as though we are worthless. But no matter what has happened or what will happen, you will never lose your value. Dirty or clean, crumpled or finely creased, you are still priceless to those who love you. The worth of our lives comes not in what we do or who we know, but by who we are. You are special – do not ever forget it! If you do not add value by serving others due to the challenges you face while doing so, you may never know the lives your service touches, the hurting hearts it speaks to, or the hope that it can bring. Count your blessings, not your problems. And remember: amateurs built the ark...professionals built the Titanic. If your faith brings you to it - your faith will bring you through it as well. So, regardless of the challenges, have and show great enthusiasm about your goals. Mark Victor Hansen, author and speaker, is quoted as saying "Doing what we were meant to do creates fun, excitement and contentment in our lives, and invariably, in the lives of the people around us. When you're excited about something it's contagious." Empower yourself, and always value yourself and your worthwhile dreams; eventually, others will join you. Regardless of your manager's personality or culture, who you are, as a human being in this society, will always make you unique in this world of billions.

Motivation and Dependency[1]

Since necessity is the driving vehicle for innovation, it can also be an important motivational factor for the achievement of one's desires individually and collectively in a society at any given time. Motivation can impact an individual's actions, group behavior, and society's drive toward certain ideals and objectives. The way people are socialized in a culture will inevitably influence their level of motivation toward different ideals, values and behaviors. For example, the people of Afghanistan as well as many other countries, which live in a constant fear for their lives due to political fighting and civil unrest, tend to be more motivated toward the creation of security than most other ideals such as the reduction of corruption. Their need for security and safety must be met first in order for them to eventually strive toward high levels of education and the elimination of corruption in the business environment.

Of course, motivation must come from within each person in a nation in order for them to develop and grow their economy through sustainable production. However, a motivational environment should also be encouraged by such organizations as United Nations, the International Monetary Fund and World Bank. As an example, the country and people of Afghanistan must strategically work to get themselves out of the challenges which have been imposed upon them over the past forty years by various forces in the international community.

Afghanistan throughout the millennia has been a place of rich culture and a junction of people from multiple continents. Despite its diverse history, most people in Afghanistan have been raised during times of constant foreign and civil wars and thus have been heavily traumatized by violence. This has led the country to become dependent on the international community for survival and the prospect of a peaceful future. According to the dependency theory, poverty in developing nations tends to be the result of their long-term dependence

---

[1] Coauthored with Belal Kaifi, Trident University International.

on high-income countries over time. Influence is exerted over Afghanistan by many other nations across continents. According to experts, dependency theory holds that the industrialized nations often control the destiny of the poorer countries such as Afghanistan, particularly in terms of being the ultimate markets for their exports, serving as the source of capital required for national development, and controlling the relative processes and exchange rates at which market transactions occur. Despite much foreign aid, Afghanistan still lacks in many professional and technological fields. This is perhaps normal as well since the benefits of trade between a rich country such as Great Britain or Canada and a poor country such as Afghanistan will go almost entirely to the rich country.

Even though the majority of the benefits are going to the richest countries, poor countries do not have many options if they want to live peacefully with the international community. The good news is that dependency theory usually promises some prosperity, equity, fairness, and justice once the political obstacles to economic transformation have been overcome. In this case, the future does look brighter if the citizens of the developing country are consistently motivated to educate themselves and become self-reliant key players in the global community.

Ultimately, the people of a country must be self-motivated to help themselves if they want to prosper and to be key players in the global community. Furthermore, it has been suggested that the people of each country must realize that capital and technology which often flow from the West do not always lead to development but can at times only deepen underdevelopment as can be seen in such places as Afghanistan and many African countries. Poor countries are often stuck in the cycle of oppression until they are able to put an end to this cycle through entrepreneurship, development and education. Such countries must develop a comparative advantage for themselves to trade with their regional neighbors as well as globally. Gradually, they must strive for escaping the dependency trap since dependency can be a theory of underdevelopment if a poor country remains enslaved by the rich nations of the world. Long-term dependence cannot be sustained.

Summary

Motivational studies are needed to explore value, attitude and leadership style similarities and differences between employees, managers, and senior executives in all nations. Researchers need to explore the roots of motivation by exploring value similarities and differences between respondents born in one nation, but living in another nation. This research could be conducted for each nation and sub-cultures within each country in order to explore the impact of socialization on people's drive and motivation. We also need to study gender roles and its link to motivation in each country. Also, cross-cultural studies of entrepreneurs in each country are needed.

Discussion Questions

1. What is motivation? How are people motivated?
2. Discuss the content and process theories of motivation.
3. Which motivational theories are applicable across various cultures? Discuss at least two by mentioning examples of how they can be applied in two or more different cultures or countries.
4. What is attitude and how does it relate to motivation and values? Discuss.
5. What are values? Do values differ across cultures? Why are values important to motivation?
6. Can values change over time? Discuss and provide an explanation for your thoughts.
7. What can organizational leaders do to make sure their personal and company values are aligned with the expectations of people in the country or culture?
8. What can public sector leaders in poor countries do to motivate their people toward independency from economic assistance of the international community that are often accompanied by rules and expectations which may not necessarily be favorable to the country's sustainable development.

CHAPTER 4

Management by Values

Cross-cultural management can be very challenging. Managers and employees often make unintentional mistakes. As such, they need to be trained and properly prepared with relevant skills for dealing with people in new cultures based on foundational values that are important for the employees, customers, owners and other relevant stakeholders.

Managers, if they are to be effective, must clarify their own values and they should understand the values of their employees, customers, and the local community. Managers must adjust their management styles and orientations in order to match needs of their employees, customers, organizations, and the local community. As such, this chapter explores value driven management practices for long-term decision making and value creation purposes along with management orientations across cultures.

Value Driven Management[2] for Decision-Making

A valuable resource for cross-cultural managers is the book by Pohlman and Gardiner (2000), which offers a comprehensive introduction to *Value Driven Management* (VDM), and the holistic approach to effective long-term decision-making. Value driven management provides a decision-making framework that can be used in a variety of situations with a homogenous or diverse workforce. Value driven management is based upon value theory, which claims that what people truly value drives their actions and behaviors. The underlying theme is to make decisions that maximize value over time for all relevant stakeholders in the long-term.

---

[2] Contributed by Randolph Pohlman, Nova Southeastern University. *Source*: Mujtaba, B. G. and Pohlman, R. (2010). Value Orientation of Indian and U.S. Respondents: A Study of Gender, Education, and National Culture. *SAM Advanced Management Journal*, 75(4), 40-49.

Value driven management is a practical model that managers can use in their daily work life in a variety of decision-making scenarios. Value driven management discusses the concept of value over time and explains that the two key elements of using value driven management in decision-making are: one, understanding the values of the organization and its employees; and two, knowing the appropriate time horizon for decision-making. The basic purpose of value driven management is to motivate managers and employees, when contemplating making decisions or taking actions, to consider the impact of these decisions and actions on the value of the organization over time. This determination can be accomplished only by an examination of the sets of values held by the relevant constituents (or "stakeholder" groups) of the organization. These encompass world, national, societal cultures and subcultures, organizational culture, the values of employees, suppliers, customers, competitors, and third parties (such as unions and government regulators), and most importantly, but not exclusively, the values of the "owners" of the organization.

There are people, processes, and systems within organizations that add and destroy value. There are, for example, employees within organizations who destroy more value than they create, perhaps as a result of being in the wrong position with the wrong types of skills and abilities, or perhaps they are totally incompatible with their organization's means or ends. It is every employee's responsibility to seek out a role that adds value and ensures success; and the organization's responsibility to eliminate value destroyers by placing people in the proper jobs and instituting proper processes and systems. If value driven management is learned well and administered thoughtfully and consistently with today's multi-generational workforce by managers, then the ultimate goals of achieving, creating, and sustaining long-term growth, surplus, wealth, and value maximization can be attained in any national or international organization. Anthony Robbins, motivational speaker and author, said "Deciding to commit yourself to long-term results rather than short-term fixes is as important as any decision you'll make in your lifetime." So, leaders should commit themselves to long-term value maximization regardless of whether they are working in developing economies such as Afghanistan and Vietnam or developed countries such as France and Germany. A starting place can be to understand value driven decision-making and value-based management or thinking. Of course, there are some assumptions regarding value driven management that should be noted (Pohlman and Gardiner, 2000):

1. Value creation is good.
2. What is valued drives action.
3. Knowledge creation and appropriate use leads to value creation.
4. Value is subjective.
5. There are value adders and destroyers.
6. Markets provide valuable information.
7. Opportunity costs affect value.
8. Order is spontaneous.
9. Values can compete or be complementary.
10. For every action there are unintended consequences.
11. All employees are employees.

Value driven management provides a decision-making framework that can be used in a variety of situations with a homogenous or diverse workforce. The value driven management concept claims that what a person values has a great influence over his or her thinking, feelings and behaviors. The stronger the clarity of one's value is regarding a specific concept, such as freedom or family security, the greater its impact on the person's behavior.

A summary of the value theory and value drive management is provided to help managers and professionals cope with today's tumultuous and accelerating pace of change which is causing technical knowledge to double every two years. Since values tend to be more long lasting than trends and work practices, then knowing what a person or group of people value, and what truly drives their decisions and actions, will help managers understand their decision-making processes and how and why people behave the way they do. We cannot really avoid dealing with value-laden issues and questions since today's decision-makers have to focus on creating value for owners and other constituent groups. In today's globalized world, it is a necessity for survival that decision-makers must create value over time or long-term value for their organizations.

Value driven management is about leading, managing, and working in organizations that are creating value. Value driven management provides a fundamental intellectual and philosophical foundation of how to think about organizations, how to operate in an organization, and how to see oneself as a leader, decision-maker, and value creator in an organizational environment. The purpose of value driven management is provide a framework which makes it clear for every person who must make decisions in organizations to see, understand, and deliver the most fundamental result of all: value creation. The goal of value driven management is that in decision-making, one should consider the relevant values of many different stakeholders such as: (1) external cultural values, (2) organizational cultural values, (3) individual employee values, (4) customer values, (5) supplier values, (6) third-part values, (7) owner values, and (8) competitor values. As presented in Figure 4.1, there are many value drivers and professionals can select those that are relevant for their industry and assessment purposes.

Figure 4.1 – Value Driven Management Value Drivers

It is not prudent to employ a single-minded approach to management and leadership in the new world of organization. One of the keys to satisfactorily and successfully working in this new environment is to first gain an understanding of two sides of the new *value equation*: being task-oriented and relationship oriented at the same time. While a national culture can socialize people to be more task-oriented or more relationship-oriented, it should be mentioned that a strong influence can also be the result of where the person works, the organization.

Organizations are made up of people—people who drive the organization and its culture. The culture of the organization is created by individuals who come together to form groups to produce goods and/or services. An organization's culture, then, is the result of what its members choose to make it to be. The organization itself does not initially have values; it is comprised of people who bring their values to their work. These personal values join with and help form the organizational culture. For example, an organization itself cannot be task-focused, relationship-oriented, greedy, evil or altruistic. Only the people it employs can do or be such things, and as a group can create an organization that responds in ways that may be depicted as 'task-focused", "relationship-oriented", "greedy", "evil", or "altruistic". As we have been saying, what people value, causes organizations to have cultures and acquire the reputations they have. One of the critical characteristics of these successful companies is a careful balance between the values, interests, goals and objectives of the organization, and the values of the individuals who work for it and other constituent groups. The value driven management process provides a framework for thinking through and resolving such important problems, and deciding such things as whether an individual is in the right field, the right organization, or in the part of the organization that is a right fit for the person's skills and competencies.

Value driven management looks at the bottom-line issue from a new and philosophical perspective: the organization's bottom line is creating value (including profitability) from a complex blend and conscious integration of various value drivers, including external cultural values, organizational values, individual employee values, customer values, supplier values, third-party values, owner values, and competitor values. A vital component of this process is the new value equation, integrating organizations and individuals. When individuals work in organizations with which they are in synch—where they can use and develop their skills, grow and learn, make contributions, and look forward to going to work—they will not only create value for themselves as human beings, they will usually also create value for their organizations. When managers make decisions based on value driven management concepts, they will focus on the main value drivers which maximize value over time for the relevant stakeholders in the long-term. As presented in Figure 4.2, managers and employees can jointly decide the most important value drivers for the company, reflect on the short-term and long-term consequences of the specific alternative for each value driver, and classify if it will be a "value adder" or a "value destroyer" either immediately or in the long-term in order to determine the total value over time.

Figure 4.2 – Value Driver Decision Chart

VALUE DRIVERS	Short-Term	Long-Term	TOTAL VALUE
Organizational Culture			
Societal Culture			
Customer Value			
Employee Value			
Owner Values			
TOTALS:			

Of course, value driven management should be used within a value driven culture since any stand-alone strategy is not sufficient for sustainable success and competitive advantage. Furthermore, before making a management decision, or taking a management action, all employees must clearly understand the key issues being dealt with as a decision maker. Also, managers and employees should determine which value drivers are the most important to consider in establishing long-term maximization for this situation. Managers and employees should consider each value driver and accomplish the following (Pohlman and Gardiner, 2000):

➢ Identify specific aspects (facts, problems, potential problems, data needs for further analysis, etc.) of the situation as they relate to this particular value driver (you must be very specific and concrete in this step).

➢ Enumerate the potential positive and negative impacts for the long-term on each aspect as well as its short-term effects.

➢ Consider potential actions you could take to turn the particular negative effects of each aspect to neutral or positive ones.

➢ Consider the unintended consequences that could possibly occur and how they could be made less severe or eliminated.

> In the final analysis, consider the value drivers in their totality to determine the action(s) that will maximize value in the long-term.

The focus of business should be on value creating results that are needed, desired, and cherished in society. While achieving positive results is always the goal of organizations, it also includes the avoidance of disastrous, unintended, and unexpected results as we have witnessed over the past few years such as the housing/subprime bubble which caused the near financial collapse of some of the major western economies. The conscious, conscientious and systematic use of the principles of value driven management provides a promising tool kit for result-oriented value creation through a balanced leadership by focusing on tasks and relationships simultaneously.

Value Driven Thinking and Culture

Value driven management is a mindset of what you value forming the foundation of your thinking, feelings and behaviors. Value focused thinking is relevant as desirable personal or organizational values are consciously selected, internalized, inculcated in the organization, and promoted on a regular basis. Eventually these values become a strong aspect of the person or organization's identity which can greatly influence behavior and decision-making. Ultimately, as per value-driven management theory and concept, what you value drives your behavior. For example, if you value family security then you will do everything within your power and ability to protect your children, sisters, brothers, and parents from harm. If you value loyalty, then you are likely to behave as such and expect the same from your colleagues and friends. If you value competence and various abilities, then you are likely to go out and gain the relevant education to acquire such capabilities that lead to the success of your predetermined dreams and goals.

One example of loyalty is the patronage form of "quid pro quo" associations that are influenced by people's cultural conditioning and overall societal values. In patronage relationships, the relationship usually includes a patron and at least one client, and they are likely to be vertical where the patron is in a higher position. The patron rewards the client's loyalty and service, and the client is expected to reciprocate. Such relationships reflect power/social distances between the client and the patron and tend to exist in countries such as Thailand, Cambodia, Vietnam, India, Pakistan, India and Afghanistan which demonstrates values that are usually characteristic of high context cultures. Overall, what you value forms the basis of your management and leadership styles. So, what are values?

Values are defined as assumptions about "how things ought to be" in the society. Values are often held at a preconscious level and may never be fully articulated. Values differ from beliefs in the fact that beliefs are conscious perceptions of things that exist in society, and how people ought to behave. Values can be a part of a specific organization, nation, and country as it creates a specific culture or norm. National cultural values are often embedded into one's subconscious mind during childhood. Consequently, most individuals are unaware of their cultural conditioning. Organizational values are usually taught and learned later in life, either through general education or workplace training. Therefore, these values are often assimilated into one's conscious level and can be changed "easily." So, values influence the cultures of organizations and nations. Global leaders and managers must recognize the influence of culture and be prepared to develop an understanding of it. Behavior is influenced by the person's personality and values gained from their interactions with the cultural forces of the particular society in which he/she was born. The challenge that international managers often confront is to be able to identify when culture is significant and what type of response, if any, is needed to successfully manage a multicultural group. Successful management of a diverse group can substantially improve a company's ability to attract, retain, and motivate employees from different cultural backgrounds thus increasing the organization's competitive advantage. Overall, managers must:

- Recognize differences between values of individuals and people in different cultures.
- Understand that as cultural diversity becomes the norm in one's department or organization, refusing to recognize and manage it may bring disaster.
- Understand the nature of values and cultures, and how they influence behavior in the workplace.
- Learn about specific values and cultures-- the other, and one's own.

- Recognize which values and how cultural factors influence the expression of business structures, systems, priorities.
- Recognize how far structures, systems, values, and priorities of one's culture can be implemented within the other culture.

Conflicting values and cultural norms can create major ethical conflicts and concerns. Ethical dilemmas involve choosing among alternatives that lie in the gray area of right and wrong, including conflicting loyalties, tradeoffs between principle and practicality, and external pressure to succeed. Ethical lapse usually involves choosing an unethical or illegal action and global managers must avoid these, especially when they value honesty. Managers can test the ethics of a specific decision or message in a number of ways, including asking the following questions:

➢ Does it comply with the law?
➢ Is it fair to all concerned?
➢ Whom will it benefit or harm? If so, how much?
➢ How would you feel about receiving it? Would you be embarrassed? Would you feel good?
➢ Have you checked it out with others who are knowledgeable on the subject?
➢ Would you feel well if your decision was shared with your best friends and professional colleagues?
➢ Would you feel happy if your decision was shared with others in the community on the evening television news?
➢ Would your mother be proud of you if she heard you made this decision?

Resolving ethical dilemmas can be more difficult and bothersome when one's values are not clear. As mentioned before, a person's values can impact his or her thoughts, feelings and behaviors. Human beings are often acculturated to continue acting based on past conditioning until they formally replace the "automatic pilot" mentality with conscious thinking based on facts. This is why it is important to clarify one's values and think differently using one's head, feel differently through one's heart, and act differently thereby changing one's daily habits. It all starts by thinking about and clarifying one's values. If you can die for a specific cause or value, then that is perhaps a good level of clarity regarding certain principles and issues. For example, if you are willing to go to jail to stay loyal to your friends, then you truly value loyalty and expect the same from others. Of course, loyalty to one's friend and colleagues and staying true to one's values can create a productive and happy work environment for all.

Consistency of Head, Heart and Habits

Effective management is about creating harmony and consistency in one's head (thoughts), heart (feelings), and habits (behaviors) about people of diverse values, backgrounds and cultures. It is fair to say that diversity and ethics-related issues are likely to, and should, impact a person's head, heart and habits if they are to lead to long-term peace and prosperity in life. The following thoughts should be noted by all managers regarding the head, heart and habits concept which form the foundation of value driven thinking:

> - *Head.* Head implies continuous cognitive learning about each situation, clarifying one's values, thinking objectively based on current facts, awareness of universal principles, and knowledge generation.
> - *Heart.* Heart implies the consistent controlling of one's feeling, basing it on objective facts, and aligning it with universal values. It means basing one's feeling for long-term impact, rather than short term satisfaction of personal desires that are linked to revenge, vengeance, payback, or retribution.
> - *Habits.* Habits should be linked to one's objective feelings and universal principles. It means ensuring that one's day-to-day behaviors are aligned with one's universal principles of right and wrong, personal or professional values, and knowledge-based and goal-oriented feelings.

The value driven thinking concept claims that what a person values is likely to have a great influence over his or her thinking, feelings and behaviors. The stronger the clarity of one's value is regarding a specific concept, such as freedom or family security, the greater its impact on the person's behavior. For example, most people value life and, thus, will not harm, hurt or kill another person under normal circumstances. However, soldiers and police officers will exert sufficient force on others or even purposely shoot people to prevent them from hurting innocent citizens. This does not mean that they do not value life, it just means that, as part of their professional responsibility and obligation, they value the security and prosperity of the community's citizens more. As such, they will do what is necessary to prevent thieves from stealing or thugs from hurting people in the community. However, if a person values life in all of its forms and has determined that there is no cause for which he or she will take another life, then this person will not even "kill" a fly or a mouse regardless of the consequence. Such was the case of Mahatma Gandhi who was willing to die for certain causes that enhanced life for humanity, but he was very certain that there was no cause for which he was willing to take another life. Living a life of such clarity and vision as that of Mahatma Gandhi and Martin Luther King Jr. are the objectives of value driven management practices. This is also why it is so important to clarify one's own values and understand the values of others in one's department, organization, community, and culture. Such understandings and value clarification can lead to higher performance and synergistic teamwork among diverse individuals while preventing conflict, stress and many other negative externalities that seem to exist in today's diverse places of work.

Global Orientations

Global managers and leaders know that there are different ways that international professionals lead their operations. As such, an understanding of ethnocentric, polycentric, regiocentric and geocentric management orientations are a necessity for global management. *Ethnocentric* orientation is when the individual is home country centered. *Polycentric* orientation is when the individual is host country centered. *Regiocentric* is when the individual is focused on regional headquarters or regional basis. And in the *geocentric* orientation, the individual is world oriented.

In *ethnocentric* management orientation, the approach is basically "what works at home, will work here." One example of this is individuals who choose to open restaurants that are successful in their home country, into a foreign country. Due to cultural differences, a company that mandates particular work shifts may not be successful in other cultures with a polychronic time orientation where a linear view of time is not such a high priority. If a manager was successful with this approach in Canada, and then began operations in Mexico, mandating employees to arrive at 7 a.m. may result in discharge or termination if the employee does not comply. The Mexican worker may arrive to work at eight or so, due to this polychronic view of time, and the company would not be successful. In fact, in this situation, the culture believes this way and people are conditioned toward this orientation. Therefore, it would not be one individual who would arrive late; all employees of the culture may arrive very early or a few minutes late. This would occur due to cultural differences conflicting with the ethnocentric orientation. The manager would be wise to reconsider the approach in this particular example.

In *polycentric* management orientation, managers believe the foreign market to be too difficult to understand. They remain host country centered. An example is Pepsi Cola. They operate in joint ventures in other countries. Basically, they bring individuals from other countries to their headquarters, train them, and then allow them to work however they choose to accomplish the goals of the company. In this orientation, the company probably finds this approach easier and safer, but they fail to learn much about other cultures, or grow in their knowledge of world diversity.

In *regiocentric* management orientation, the company believes the regional managers are best able to organize operations within the region. Regional offices are at various locations, and report to a regional headquarters, and then to headquarters. An example may be an automobile manufacturer. Foreign automakers establish companies within the European Community, and they do not generally micromanage these foreign facilities. They rely on the regional offices to monitor production of the cars, and then report back to headquarters.

In *geocentric* management orientation, the management style focuses on both local and worldwide objectives. The management style is interdependent. An example of such a company is Whirlpool; they were able to create a refrigerator from European insulation technology, U.S. manufacturing and design, and Brazilian affiliates. Therefore, in the geocentric management style, resources can come from virtually anywhere locally, or in the world.

Through these four types of management orientation, companies can clearly change from one orientation to another, depending on the needs of the company. A company's main objective is to ensure success and survival of the organization. Therefore, a successful company would utilize whichever style of management orientation offered the greatest potential for success.

1. *Ethnocentric management* is where the home country management style is imposed on the host country. The assumption is that what works at home should also work overseas. This style of management is not well suited or applicable to the global world today. The management team has to diversify and adjust in being flexible to accommodate the host country's culture and employees' norms and social relation in the workplace.

2. In *polycentric management*, the foreign market is "too hard to understand," so host-country managers are relatively free to manage their own way. Competition is focused on a market-by-market basis. This type of management style is used by such franchises as McDonald's, Domino's Pizza, Kentucky Fried Chicken, Pizza Hut, and Burger King.

3. *Regiocentric management* is the style most parent organization use when they feel that the regional insiders best coordinate operations within the region. The assumption is that the regional workers know the market and their market better than others. Similarly, these employees can serve an entire region for economies of scale purposes instead of having many representatives in various countries.

4. *Geocentric management* is a highly interdependent system that speaks in terms of the global village. The focus is at once both worldwide and on local objectives. Some franchises operate based on the geocentric management orientation. They focus on being a worldwide business first and then they regionalize in groups.

One should remember that the management orientations discussed above are not mutually exclusive. Therefore, they can all take place at one time within the same organization for its different departments or product lines. Many organizations often begin with the ethnocentric mindset or polycentric and gradually develop a more regiocentric or geocentric framework.

Summary
The essence of management is to make sure an organization's resources are efficiently used in successfully achieving the stated short-term and

long-term goals. Of course, the achievement of this objective becomes more challenging when managers deal with different individuals, governments, suppliers, and cultural expectations across the globe. Therefore, value driven management strategies become an essential component of their skills and success. The chapter has covered some of these concepts that are essential in value drive management as well as in effective decision making when values differ. Managers must be aware that differences in ideology, culture, economic and political systems affect organizational, operational and managerial decision making in diverse countries.

Discussion Questions

1. What is value driven management? What is its overall purpose? Does it focus on short-term or long-term?
2. Can value driven management practices work in a cross-cultural work environment? Why or why not? Discuss.
3. Which management orientation best matches a new company entering into foreign countries? Discuss.
4. Are there certain business practices that an expatriate must remember when doing business with professionals in other countries?
5. How can national values become a part of people's personal values when they are socialized in that country or culture?
6. How do national values differ from organizational values? Which set of values tend to be a stronger driver of a person's behavior? Why and when?
7. Can national and organizational values be contradictory? Discuss.

CHAPTER 5

Influencing and Leadership

Leadership must be continuous as it involves a regular feedback loop of unlearning what does not work, changing the status quo, and relearning as per the current needs of an employee or the organization. The primary goal of leadership is to provide a better vision of the future and improve performance. This improved performance has an obvious direct impact on the organization's profit and competitiveness. In order for managers to become effective leaders, they need a repertoire or toolbox of influencing skills. This chapter discusses the art of influencing others as managers and leaders either in the workplace or in the community.

Influence and Persuasion

Influencing or persuading is defined as the art of moving people to action toward a predetermined course or vision that is of value to everyone involved. Influencing is different from manipulation as the later often does not consider the development of a long-term relationship or trust with the other party. According to researchers, *influencing* is defined as the art of persuading others over whom we have no position power or any direct authority.

In today's management climate, organizations are flatter, technology-driven, and made up of more self-directed teams. In order to be effective and successful, there is the need to learn techniques that will permit goal achievement with the assistance of others through skillfully applied methods of influence. These approaches should incorporate a thorough understanding of the influence situation, a clear appreciation for the needs of the other(s) over whom influence is sought, a determination of the type of influence energy needed, gaining command of the communication style of both parties, and creating an influence strategy. Perhaps most importantly, effective influencing is about developing and maintaining positive relationships or rapport with one's colleagues and employees.

Influencing is the ability to achieve goals through the willing and committed work of others. It is an essential skill-set in today's workplace considering the erosion of vertical hierarchical structures that have resulted in more collaborative and team-oriented organizations. Even someone with authority to dictate actions would be better served utilizing influencing skills to encourage the individual's willing investment and commitment in an action. Although there are many skills that can be learned, it is essentially leading or managing employees and coworkers as whole human beings rather than any stereotype. If an organizational culture is imbued with influencing practices, the organization itself will benefit as a collaborative, team-oriented and accountable workforce develops. Tension is reduced and work can be more enjoyable for each effected employee. In attempting to gain approval and successfully implement a program or change, influencing skills utilized throughout the process will engender greater success. Dr. Paul Hersey and Dr. Ron Campbell's 2004 book states that leadership is the activity of managers and in influencing people to strive willingly for group objectives.

There are at least two ways of getting another person to do something. One might force people to do something, in essence, taking the decision making authority away. Or the other person will make the decision, because one grants them the authority or one "sells" them on the idea. The inability to successfully influence others to behave or perform tasks that accomplish one's goals may mean failure to accomplish organizational goals as well. The inability to influence others often creates organizational stalemate and frustration. Getting to know the other person is possibly the most important and most difficult concept in influencing someone else's behavior. Facts are necessary to determine what is important to the other person. More importantly, developing and understanding context for this interpretation of the other person's wants and needs is critical.

Managers often influence their employees to be great performers and model associates. Employees, on the other hand, influence one another, as well as their superiors and customers. Simply stated, influence is the ability to move others to action. Influencing allows individuals to get certain results from others without destroying their relationships. Influencing is important to individuals seeking results whether or not they have legitimate authority. Effective influencing skills allow people to the get work done faster, as well as reduce conflict and stress, while demonstrating that one is a team player and a flexible professional. All of these objectives lead to a more effective work performance.

Within organizations, individuals can be put in a position of having to influence "up," "down," or "laterally" to accomplish a goal. They may be attempting to influence another individual or an entire group. The influencer may seek to motivate an individual to complete a specific task. He or she may have a new idea to develop or strategy to implement. An organizational change may need a champion to become successful. In each of these scenarios, it is essential for the individual who wishes to exert influence to be cognizant of not only his or her goal, but the goal and mindset of others who he or she needs to influence. This allows the individuals exerting the influence to plan the most persuasive strategy. They then must look to use the right actions and communication style to accomplish their goal. Influencing skills are particularly necessary in the current work environment because, modern organizations tend to be flatter, more collaborative, team-oriented in their decision-making, and less overtly dependent on a formal chain of command. Good influencing skills by managers are rewarded through stronger working relationships with employees. Given the importance of the manager-employee relationship in the retention of employees, developing good influencing skills in their managers would greatly help organizations with employee retention. As highlighted before, managers can get their work more efficiently when they exert influence, and it would serve them well to learn good, effective influencing skills.

The leader empowers others to take action when he/she feels it is necessary. Through empowerment and collaboration the leader is able to tap into the employee's motivation. Effective leaders do not rely so much on position power as they do on personal force which comes through their relationships and as such they align the individual's goals with those of the organization. Effective managers and leaders become influential through training; as a result, their leadership effectiveness is raised to new levels through the appropriate use of their skills.

The "Push" and "Pull" Behaviors

There are perhaps thousands of ways that people are influenced by various factors in the society as they go through a socialization process from birth till death. Of course, the socialization influence during one's early childhood years tend to be very influential and long-lasting in life. While many elements and factors that influence people during their childhood years tend to be out of their control, some of these elements are under their full control during adulthood. As an adult, one must take full responsibility for his/her behaviors. Furthermore, as an adult, one can condition himself/herself to take ownership of certain behaviors that, when consistently repeated, will bring one more influence over others.

Researchers usually discuss two key behaviors that tend to drive the success of one's influence: Push energy and Pull energy. When you are trying to impress another person about a product or service that you are offering, then you are using the Push strategy for influencing him/her. *Push behaviors* require that you assertively state your point of view and get your ideas heard by the other person. One can use Push behaviors by being assertive (not necessarily aggressive) and making suggestions. On the other hand, when people are drawn to you or your products and services because they believe in you or the product, then this is the power of Pull energy. *Pull behaviors* require summarizing, clarifying and actively listening by asking questions to draw the other person into the discussion, topic, or interaction. Pull behaviors, when used consistently with one's associates, can lead to better understanding, rapport with others, a high level of trust, and more commitment on the part of the employee. While one can assert and suggest for Push behaviors, summarize and ask questions for Pull behaviors, the combination of Push/Pull behaviors can take place by offering incentives for others to be drawn to what is being said or sold, while making the process easier for them to get it. Managers can use Push behaviors when they know what they want, have good reasons with which to make a case, and when they believe a direct approach is needed. managers can use the Pull behaviors when they want to build a relationship with their employees, when they want commitment from others, and when additional information is needed to complete a task or achieve the end-result. Furthermore, managers should use the Push/Pull strategy when they want to achieve extraordinary results and have rich interactions. Depending on the situation, managers can be assertive, make suggestions, summarize, clarify, actively listen, ask questions, and offer incentives to influence their colleagues and employees.

Power: Forms and Sources

Power is generally defined as a leader's potential for influencing others who may or may not necessarily be working as direct reports; as opposed to the definition of leadership which is a leader's attempt to influence others. Power is an important topic in leadership because power has the potential to influence; it is the "horsepower" of making leadership work. According to Hersey and Campbell (2004) and other experts in the behavioral sciences fields, as previously mentioned, there are many types of power including the following:

1. *Referent power* uses high levels of communication and support and is based on good personal relations with the follower.
2. *Legitimate power* allows the leader to induce compliance and influence behavior by virtue of the leader's position within the organization.
3. *Position power* is the extent to which managers are willing to delegate authority to subordinates, and this power must be earned on a day-to-day basis. Because managers already have legitimate power, that power tends to flow down in an organization once confidence and trust has been established by a subordinate, and that subordinate is ready to take on additional responsibility.
4. *Coercive power* can be helpful in dealing with people of very low job readiness. This power base reminds people of the consequences of failing to progress.
5. *Expert power* is associated with individuals at high levels of readiness. Because these people are both willing and able to do their jobs without close supervision, they will award a manager power for having high levels of skill and knowledge.
6. *Reward power* can increase the effectiveness of the leadership. The willingness of subordinates with low to moderate levels of readiness may be enhanced by the leader's access to rewards for desired behavior.
7. *Personal power* is the extent to which followers are committed to their leader. Personal power flows up in an organization from followers, as it is not inherent. In order for one to establish

confidence and trust in their managers, they must sell up and influence managers by using personal power.

8. *Information power* means the leader has pertinent data that can provide information to maintain and improve performance of the follower. The leader can clarify and explain issues and the follower will have their questions answered, thus improving confidence levels for independent decision making. Information power is where the leader has access to information and is able to provide this knowledge to improve the follower's performance.

9. *Connection power* comes into play as the subordinate begins to develop readiness, but is still concentrating on avoiding punishment. If a person perceives the manager as having strong connections, the person may respond out of a desire to solidify a connection to the manager for personal gain.

The definition of a leader is a person who attempts to influence the behavior of people or a group. Power is the leader's actual potential to influence others. The most desirable situation is to have both personal power and position power.

Personal power stems from the followers and flows up the organizational hierarchy. It is not an innate quality and can vary day-by-day. It is the way the followers feel about the leader and their willingness to follow that leader. On the other hand, position power is delegated by the leader's supervisors and flows down the organizational chart. Leaders receive the authority to distribute sanctions, punishments and rewards. Both sources of power can be taken away, with position power removed by supervisors and personal power removed by followers. When effectively managing down, leaders must influence direct reports and staff members with both personal power and position power. Many experts see personal power as enabling commitment and loyalty, whereas position power commands respect and compliance. Overall, personal power is more valuable toward maintaining better interpersonal relationships. In fact, personal power is used to accomplish the act of influencing followers through managing down as well as the act of influencing supervisors through selling up. When trying to influence executives and supervisors, the leader relies only upon his or her personal power. This is especially useful when the leader has little or no position power. He or she must establish a good rapport with his or her associates and develop mutual trust and confidence. The amount of personal power gained will impact how much position power is granted. Broken down further into as many as seven bases (coercive, connection, reward, legitimate, information, referent, and expert) by Hersey and Campbell (2004), there is no single best type. Effective leaders must diagnose the situation; reviewing the task and evaluating the employee's readiness level. Next, the leader selects and applies the appropriate leadership style along with the correct power base to influence behavior. A comprehensive model can be used to determine appropriate power and style per the follower's readiness levels. Studies have shown that referent and expert power strongly influences employee performance and satisfaction, while legitimate and expert power induces employee compliance. Many variables affect the leader's selection of a power base, so he or she must become familiar with the situational use of power.

Subordinates must prove to their managers that they have the requisite skills necessary for them to receive power and authority. Although there is no best type of power, the most favorable situation for leaders is when they have both personal and position power, which constitutes an interaction-influence system. Additionally, expert and legitimate power is most important for compliance, but expert and referent power are strongly related to follower performance and satisfaction. One thing is for sure, power is perception and in order to influence followers, one must use their power or risk losing it.

To increase their internal power, managers also need to continuously develop their own information and level of confidence through intrapersonal communication and believing that they can succeed. Dr. Marshal Goldsmith, an executive coach, believes that coaches need to internalize the following four concepts (Personal Communication on July 2005 in Escondido, California; Hersey and Campbell, 2004): I choose to succeed, I will succeed, I have succeeded, and I can succeed.

"*I choose to succeed*" is a belief successful people tend to have. Many successful people do not like to be manipulated or controlled. By taking matters into their own hands and deciding to succeed, the person is in control of his/her own destiny. Thus, people will have a deeper commitment to becoming successful and pleasing themselves. When people have personal commitments in their own success, they take ownership, and work hard towards achieving their goals. Each person must make his or her own magic and success. One must make a personal commitment to oneself and not necessarily always rely on outside sources for achievement. Once one owns the decision to succeed, one will not give up in the face of adversity and work even harder to achieve goals.

"*I will succeed*" is an unflappable sense of optimism that many successful people personify. This type of self-talk increases confidence in overall ability, and this confidence is contagious. Many successful people believe the people around them can be successful too, just by virtue of affinity. Successful people tend to be very busy and face the danger of over-commitment. If one believes it can be done, and one sets his or her mind to it, anything is possible. Success is contagious and once you achieve something, the feeling permeates, and makes you want to achieve over and over again.

"*I have succeeded.*" Successful coaches often have a positive impression of their past performance. High achievers not only believe that they have achieved results; they tend to believe that they were instrumental in helping the results get achieved. This tends to be true even if the positive outcomes were caused by external events that they did not control.

"*I can succeed.*" Successful managers and leaders tend to believe that they have the internal capacity to make desirable things happen for themselves and their people. They see opportunities where others see threats. This comfort with ambiguity leads people with high self-efficacy to take greater risks and achieve great returns. In addition, they do not feel like victims of fate. They believe that they have the motivation and ability to change their world; this is why they will find external control and manipulation very distasteful.

For example, with regard to a college degree and academic success, one can say the following: I completed the college program because I chose to be successful in my career and as a personal goal. I know I can succeed because I have stuck with it regardless of the obstacles I have experienced throughout the process. I know I will succeed because I have not given myself any other option. I know I have succeeded because I know I will not give up and continuous effort will eventually lead to my success. I must see success and live it in order to experience it. Every effective researcher, manager and coach must say "I believe I am successful, I act successful and I leave no room for anything else. Success is inevitable." Some wise people tend to say that if you believe you are a good person, then you will be. So, be one, even if you have to fake it at first, eventually it will be a part of you.

According to Marshal Goldsmith, Paul Hersey, and Ron Campbell, successful coaches and managers can do many things to become even more productive. The following are some of their suggestions: Most successful people's positive view of their performance can make it hard to hear disconfirming information from others about themselves and their performance. Successful people should receive input on important self-selected behaviors as perceived by important, self-selected raters who are highly respected. After receiving input from respected peers, select one or two important areas for behavioral improvement in the coming months and year. To increase commitment, involve respected colleagues in the behavior change process by asking them to observe the change, provide feedback on the progress and help with the behavior change.

Successful people can become more productive by seeing the connection between their behavior change goals and their personal goals. In moving closer to doing this, successful people need to let go of the past and focus on the future, while envisioning a positive future that will enable them to achieve their goals. They should learn to be a supportive coach not a cynic, critic or a judge. This will allow them to move beyond setbacks and encourage them to participate in the process of change. Finally, successful people need to develop a follow-up process that provides an opportunity for ongoing dialogue with colleagues. This is important so the executive does not fall back into the same behavior pattern. Additionally, successful people should regularly seek "feed-forward" feedback. The "feed-forward" feedback exercise with one's colleagues and other coaches can provide suggestions for the future which is where success lies. To summarize, give and receive feedback that focuses on the future from those around you in all levels. Also, be open to a learning and growing environment and let go of the past when it doesn't apply or work in new situations.

Situational Leadership Styles

There are many academicians and practitioners that study, write about, and conduct research on the topic of leadership to discover the "best" traits and styles of leading others. Experts agree that while there is no one best style of leadership, successful leaders are those who can adapt their behavior to meet the demands of each unique situation. The experienced leader can use many complex and subtle means to exercise his/her influence and stimulate those he/she leads to creative and productive efforts.

Leadership can be defined as the process of influencing an individual or a group of individuals while providing an environment where personal, professional, or organizational objectives can successfully be achieved. Leadership, as a performance management vehicle, is the process by which one person exerts influence over one or more individuals and inspires, motivates, and directs their behaviors toward the achievement of individual, group and/or organizational objectives. The individual or person who exerts any form of influence that guides behavior toward a predetermined objective is considered to be a leader. Effectiveness, in the context of leadership, is doing the right things for the right reasons at the right times. Effective leadership can greatly enhance and increase the ability of the individual, the group and the organization to successfully meet both its current and prospective challenges as well as opportunities in the areas of gaining a competitive advantage, fostering ethical behavior, providing a motivational work environment, and recruiting and retaining a diverse workforce. A person's leadership style is formed by the specific ways in which he or she chooses to influence other individuals. A person's leadership style shapes the way that this individual approaches the various functions of management, which are planning, organizing, leading, and controlling. All individuals working in professional organizations have their own personal leadership styles that determine how they lead others and how they perform the concomitant management functions.

In the behavioral perspective of leadership, there are two clusters of leadership behaviors discussed that focus on the people or tasks. First, *people-oriented* behaviors include showing mutual concern, trust and respect for subordinates. People-oriented leadership tends to result in higher job satisfaction among subordinates, as well as lower absenteeism, grievances, and turnover compared to using task-oriented style. Also, job performance tends to be lower than for employees with task-oriented leaders. Second, *task-oriented* leadership styles generally include behaviors that define and structure work roles to ensure that everyone follows company rules in order to reach performance capacity and meet the established standards. Task-oriented leadership can result in lower job satisfaction as well as higher absenteeism and turnover among subordinates. Behavioral leadership scholars conclude that some people are high or low on both styles, others are high on one style and low on the other, and most individuals are somewhere in between in the continuum.

Situational Leadership Theory (SLT), developed by Drs. Paul Hersey and Ken Blanchard, states that effective leaders vary their style with the "readiness" of followers, and matches the "readiness" of the follower to one of the four leadership styles, which include telling, selling, participating, and delegating. So, the leader's effectiveness is highly dependent on whether the person's leadership style is appropriately matched to the situation and the readiness of the follower. It must be acknowledged that some situations have leadership substitutes which identify contingencies that either limit the leader's ability to influence subordinates or make that particular leadership style unnecessary. Effective leaders adapt their styles to fit a broad range of individuals and variables impacting their situations. Effective leadership is adapting one's behavior to the performance needs of the person or persons. Effective leaders diagnose, adapt, and communicate based on the readiness of their followers in the workforce and other situational variables. Dr. Hersey defined a person's *readiness* level as their ability and willingness to perform the task at hand and this definition considers two types of readiness: job and psychological. Knowing a person's (follower's) readiness level and effectively adapting one's leadership style to match the readiness level is an important element of making sure the job gets done successfully. As such, situational leadership applies to professionals in business, government, the community, volunteers, religious leaders, as well as to parents, and others who have a need to influence the effort of others.

Situational leadership proposes that individuals can change their leadership style (behavior) depending on the situation and the readiness of the follower. Leaders can and do change their styles depending on with whom they are working. The situational leadership concept is based on the interactive interplay among direction (task behavior) provided by the leader, socio-emotional support (relationship behavior) provided by the leader and the readiness of the follower on the specific task that needs performing. According to the model, there are four readiness levels:

1. R1- followers are unable and unwilling to perform the task.
2. R2- followers are unable but willing to perform the task.

3. R3- followers are able but unwilling to perform the task.
4. R4- followers are able and willing to perform the task.

The situational leadership concept attempts to keep a balance between high tech (task behaviors) and high touch (relationship behavior). Once the followers' readiness is determined, a manager or a leader can choose from the four leadership styles suggested by Hersey and Blanchard's model that focus to some extent either on task behavior or relationship behavior. The four corresponding leadership styles (telling, selling, participating, and delegating) that match these readiness (R) levels are as follows:

1. *R1- matches best with "Telling," high task-low relationship.* The manager or the leader defines the roles needed to the do the job and tells followers what, where, how, and when to do the tasks.
2. *R2- matches best with "Selling," high task-high relationship.* The manager or leader provides step-by-step and disciplined guidelines to get the job done while being supportive.
3. *R3- matches best with "Participating," low task-high relationship.* The managers, or the leader, along with followers (employees and/or colleagues) jointly decide how to get the job done with the required quality standards.
4. *R4- matches best with "Delegating," low task-low relationship.* The manager or leader provides little directions and little support to the followers since they know how to get the job done and they are very willing to do it independently.

Of course, there are perhaps thousands of situations that could use many different leadership styles. The situational leadership model has four leadership styles to keep it simple and easy to understand, so it can be applied by individuals of different skill levels and competencies. In each situation, the model encourages managers to match the style with the followers' level of readiness thus providing the most appropriate amount of task behavior and relationship behavior for the specific task on hand. Dr. Hersey (Personal Communication at NSU, 2012) provides the following recommendations for each of the four leadership styles:

- Style one or *telling* is best when attempting to influence low levels of readiness. Alternative words that describe the telling style are guiding, directing, and establishing.

- Style two or *selling* is best when attempting to influence low to moderate levels of readiness. The leader attempts to get the follower to buy into doing the task psychologically. Alternative words that describe the selling style are explaining, clarifying and persuading.
- Style three or *participating* is best when attempting to influence moderate to high levels of readiness. The key is to encourage the follower to participate and get involved. Alternative words that describe the participating style are encouraging, collaborating and committing.
- Style four or *delegating* is best when attempting to influence high levels of readiness. This is where the follower has almost all of the decisions for both decision-making and implementation of the activities to get the job done. Alternative words that describe the delegating style are observing, monitoring and fulfilling.

As the readiness of the follower (person performing the specific task) increases in terms of performance, the leader should adapt by reducing task behavior and increasing relationship behaviors. As the follower becomes totally ready by showing successful performance, the leader should reduce both task and relationship behaviors to the lowest level possible. Overall, managers apply this model similar to medical practitioners who deal with patients that complain about a pain in parts of their bodies. The medical doctor must first diagnose the cause of the problem and then prescribe the right medication to alleviate the problem or pain. Dr. Hersey says that a prescription without diagnosis can basically amount to malpractice. Similarly, a manager or a leader must first diagnose the follower's level of readiness with each person in his/her team, which can include many personalities, and then act with an appropriate leadership style. Diagnosis, or assessing ability and willingness of the follower to see what leadership style is needed, should be followed by matching an appropriate leadership behavior and then implementation of the leadership style to make sure the job gets done with the required quality in the allotted timeframe.

Leadership Orientation Survey

Regardless of cultural differences and orientations, managers, local and international, need to concern themselves with more than just profits or "making the bottom-line numbers" at the end of each week, month or year. Managers need to be effective leaders by being concerned with the required tasks as well as their people.

Leadership is the process of influencing an individual or a group of individuals while providing an environment where personal, professional, and/or organizational objectives can be successfully achieved. To determine your leadership orientation with regard to task and relationship tendencies, complete the Task and Relationship Style Questionnaire at the end of this chapter and the results will show your use of various task and relationship behaviors.

Summary

Leadership is about helping employees and colleagues strategically perform at their highest capacity. In other words, leadership is about managing performance and helping people become successful in what they are doing and what they plan to do. It should be noted that an important aspect of leadership and management is to effectively influence others. Influencing is basically working with other people to get the results you want, but without destroying the relationship, and it is almost always necessary when dealing with people over whom you have little or no control. Influencing is all about the relationship and communication with the other person or group; it is about identifying the specifics of the situation on hand, determining both parties' goals, using the correct behavior that relates to push, pull and push/pull energies, and attuning to their communication style.

According to experts, successful leaders and managers, if they are to become even more productive, they can let go of the past and focus on the future; they can be a supportive coach, not a cynic, critic or judge; they can develop a follow-up process that provides an opportunity for ongoing dialogue on selected behaviors with selected colleagues; and they can practice receiving feedback from respected colleagues about their performance and in order to get suggestions for the future.

Discussion Questions

1. What is "influencing"? What role can it play in organizations? Give an example. Influencing, which considers the development of trust and relationship as defined in this book, requires understanding one's own goals as well as the other party's. Why is it important to consider both of these factors when influencing others?
2. What is a "push" strategy and how does it differ from "pull" strategy? Discuss using an example for each.
3. What are some important ingredients for effective leadership and why? Give an example of each.
4. Discuss examples of when each style of situational leadership can be applied.
5. What style of leadership is appropriate for a new employee who is trying to learn a new task and is highly motivated about it.
6. What is the role of influence in situational leadership styles? Discuss an example for each of the four styles.
7. What are some best means of increasing one's level of influence with colleagues and employees? List five strategies that might work with both groups.
8. Should managers be task-oriented or relationship-oriented? Which would produce better results and why? Could there be a link between culture and a person's orientation toward high task or relationship behaviors? Discuss.

Task and Relationship Style Questionnaire

One of the most widely used leadership theories around the world today is situational leadership, which was founded by Drs. Paul Hersey and Kenneth Blanchard in the 1960s. *Leadership* is the process of influencing an individual or a group of individuals by using various amounts of task or relationship behaviors. Peter G. Northouse (2007, p. 65) provides a useful instrument, known as Style Questionnaire (p. 85), which can be used to obtain a general profile of your leadership behaviors regarding task and relationship orientations. The Style Questionnaire can be completed by oneself as well as one's friends, peers, bosses, and/or employees for comparison purposes. The results can show one's use of various task and relationship behaviors.

To determine your personal leadership characteristics, circle one of the following options that best describe how you see yourself (or the person that is being evaluated) regarding each statement. For each statement, you can indicate the degree to which you (or the person being evaluated) engage (s) in the stated behavior. A rating of 1 means Never and a rating of 5 means Always with the person demonstrating the specific behavior.

You can choose to complete this survey online at the following link: http://www.huizenga.nova.edu/survey/TROSI

Table 2.7 – Task and Relationship Style Questionnaire

Questions	Never...............Always
1. Tells group members what they are supposed to do.	1 2 3 4 5
2. Acts friendly with members of the group.	1 2 3 4 5
3. Sets standards of performance for group members.	1 2 3 4 5
4. Helps others feel comfortable in the group.	1 2 3 4 5
5. Makes suggestions about how to solve problems.	1 2 3 4 5
6. Responds favorably to suggestions made by others.	1 2 3 4 5
7. Makes his or her perspective clear to others.	1 2 3 4 5
8. Treats others fairly.	1 2 3 4 5
9. Develops a plan of action for the group.	1 2 3 4 5
10. Behaves in a predictable manner toward group members.	1 2 3 4 5
11. Defines role responsibilities for each group member.	1 2 3 4 5
12. Communicates actively with group members.	1 2 3 4 5
13. Clarifies his or her own role within the group.	1 2 3 4 5
14. Shows concern for the well-being of others.	1 2 3 4 5
15. Provides a plan for how the work is to be done.	1 2 3 4 5
16. Shows flexibility in making decisions.	1 2 3 4 5
17. Provides criteria for what is expected of the group.	1 2 3 4 5
18. Discloses thoughts and feelings to group members.	1 2 3 4 5
19. Encourages group members to do high-quality work.	1 2 3 4 5
20. Helps group members get along.	1 2 3 4 5

Scoring Guidelines for Task and Relationship Style Questionnaire.

To determine your scores for the leadership styles questionnaire, do the following:
1. Add the responses for the odd numbered items to determine your score for task-orientation behaviors.
2. Add the responses for the even numbered items to determine your score for relationship-orientation behaviors.

Task and Relationship Orientation Scores

Task Orientation Scores: _____   *Relationship* Orientation Scores: _____

The scoring interpretation for the Style Questionnaire is as follows (Northouse, 2007, p. 87):

- 45-50   Very high range
- 40-44   High range
- 3-39   Moderately high range
- 30-34   Moderately low range
- 25-29   Low range
- 10-24   Very low range

High task behavior scores basically means that the leader engages in more top-down communication by explaining what the follower is to do, as well as when, where, and how each function is to be accomplished. High relationship behavior scores basically means the leader engages in more joint communication with followers while providing socio-emotional support. Of course, the degree to which one engages in more task or relationship oriented behaviors should depend on the variables present in the situation; some of the situational variables can include the difficulty of the task, the importance of the job, the time available to get it done, and the readiness of the follower to successfully complete the task without much input. Effective leaders stay in control by managing through a balance of both task and relationship oriented behaviors, as appropriate, to make sure the objectives and goals are accomplished.

CHAPTER 6

Problem Solving and Time Management

For the twenty-first century firm, the true sustainable advantages and a long-term competitive edge come from the success of each individual manager and employee within the organization. In order for the cycle of productivity and development to continue, the business leader's goal should be to create managers with the requisite skills to compete effectively in national and global markets by focusing on what is important and by managing priorities.

This section provides more information about problem solving, time management, goal setting, and change management skills for managers and employees if they are to effectively learn, think critically, innovate, and to create value for their organizations and themselves. Having effective change management and problem solving skills are a good start toward independence and empowerment. Furthermore, effective management is a continuous process of learning, developing, influencing, and character building through the creation of a trusting relationship as well as effective dealing with stress, change and conflict in a timely manner.

Problem Solving Approaches

All of us 'communicate' in some way since our styles and manners are cultural. The professional leader learns the language and technique of professionalism. As long as we live, there will always be problems, so it is important that we master this skill. There are two principle factors to consider when there are problems; we must learn how to accuse effectively (i.e., how to make the proper statement about the problem) and how to react or respond to accusations.

There are some other general rules to remember for effective communication and problem-solving and the following are some of them:

1. Avoid the invitation to fight.
2. Remember that people's memories are constantly distorting and their perceptions of events are real to them.
3. All human beings have faults and also strong opinions. There are faults that you will have to accept, but there are other faults that may have to be discussed. You must also agree to disagree!
4. Avoid unfair techniques, such as;
   - Blaming the person for something they can't help.
   - Silence.
   - Switching the subject.
   - Analyzing as if you were a psychiatrist.
5. Don't make assumptions or try to 'read' the other person's mind. Always test your assumptions with the other person.
6. Be positive about long-range intentions and sincerity and respond positively.

You must develop a 'mind-set' of professionalism and learn from your mistakes. Effective communication for problem-solving is just one of the many techniques for effective communication, growth enrichment and maturity. The key is to practice effective communication at all times.

Communication is the key to success; whether it is individual, group, electronic, motivational or within a large organization. We all need to convey messages and receive information in order to function as human beings. We now know that to be successful and to lead people within teams, groups and organizations, effective communication is imperative.

Understanding and Solving Problems

The workplace has many challenges due to its fast-paced requirements and changing rules in order to remain competitive. Such complex changes require a competent workforce that can anticipate and proactively solve problems. Educated employees should be developed to think for themselves when it comes to tackling and solving problems to speed up the process in better serving the organization's relevant constituencies. The following are some relevant considerations for developing your problem solving skills.

Do We Really Have Problems? You know that you have been in the corporate world too long if you think that you never have any problems in your life, just "issues" and "improvement opportunities." In reality, most issues and improvement opportunities are problems that need to be taken care of accurately, productively, and urgently in order to remain rational, sensible, and competitive. Herman Melville once said that "a smooth sea never made a successful sailor" which means that through determination to constantly become better and make meaningful contributions we can overcome these issues and become better managers. Without these issues and opportunities, our lives would be very boring and repetitive. As a matter of fact, most managers spend close to eighty percent of their time solving problems. Yet, most of these managers were not taught how to solve management problems. They had to learn through *heuristics* - trial and error.

Defining the Problem and Its Owners: One can define a "problem" as the gap between the real and the ideal in goals while attempting to overcome challenging issues and improvement opportunities in the daily work environment. Furthermore, we can define problem owners as those who have unmet goals and objectives. Issues and improvement opportunities can be looked at as problems and problems can be seen as opportunities for improvement in order to maintain a positive attitude and outlook on life. Some problems are opportunities to simply improve while others are opportunities for turning wrongs into rights. Solving problems quickly and accurately is an art and a science that needs structure, practice, experience, intuition, and discipline. Solving management dilemmas and problems is no different than solving any other difficult problem. Often a problem exists when there is a discrepancy between what is actually happening and what should be happening. The first thing you need to do is determine exactly what the problem is and who owns it. A question that can guide one in determining who owns the problem is to ask, "Whose needs' are not being met."

Process or People Problems? Researchers have found that about eighty to eighty-five percent of problems are process or systems related, and about five to fifteen percent are people related. Only fifteen percent of associate's performance problems are due to lack of training; the other eighty five percent are due to lack of feedback, task interference, and negative consequences. So, find out the source of the problem and then plan for the appropriate solution since training people on communication or motivation may not be the solution to process related challenges. Neither is empowering untrained people to resolve challenges that are beyond their abilities and/or level of comprehension.

Convergent and Divergent Approaches to Problem-Solving: The *convergent* approach is the structured, logical, purposeful and deliberate method of solving problems. Most scientific researchers use this method to analyze the problem and find solutions to them in a formal way. This way others can follow the same procedure and get the same results. The advantages are consistency and standardization while the disadvantages might be "red tape" and eliminating the human factor, which can be disastrous at times. The *divergent* approach is the creative, innovative, customized, situational, and spontaneous method of solving problems. It states that no two situations are alike and each situation may require different ways of solving the problem. What works for one person may not necessarily work for another person under the same circumstances. According to experts, creativity diverges from the straight-and-narrow path that convergent thinking requires one to follow. Advantages of the divergent approach are the human factor and situational attention while the disadvantages can include cost, uncertainty, and lack of direction. The convergent approach integrates divergent thinking to problem solving in dealing with problems that take a significant chunk of a manager's time and effort. Regardless of which approach is used, a manager should:

Focus on what is important: It is critical to separate what is urgent and important from things that are urgent but not important. Pareto's Law states that eighty percent of the results flow from twenty percent of activities. So, some activities have much more impact than others and one should focus on these high leverage activities. The Pareto principle tells us that eighty percent of problems are caused by twenty percent of subordinates. Obviously we do not want to spend eighty percent of our time with twenty percent of our associates that constantly keep causing problems. This will cause managers to keep putting out fires and there will be no time to plan for future important activities. Proactively focusing on what is important will reduce the need for putting out fires, and increase one's time to appropriately *plan* future strategies; *organize*, train, and prepare people as well as resources to get the job done; *lead* people in the right direction, and *control* the unpredictable circumstances as they arise.

Delegate appropriately: Appropriate delegation means fully preparing people to the point where they can competently do the job without needing anyone's help. Most people cannot let go of things they feel comfortable doing and things that they enjoy doing. However, as a manager you cannot keep doing all the tasks by yourself and be successful. J. C. Penny once said, "the wisest decision I ever made was to let go when I realized that I couldn't do it all by myself anymore." Proper delegation requires mutual understanding between the manager and the associate with regards to the desired outcome, guidelines and boundaries of what to do and what not to do, resources available to accomplish the desired outcome, responsibility and accountability for the successful progress of the task, and the consequence of effectively performing the task. If the way a job is being done is too complex or time consuming and if you think there might be better ways of doing it, then delegate the job to the laziest person in your department and soon you will discover the easiest way of getting it done.

Listen empathically: There are four methods of communication which are reading, writing, speaking, and listening. According to most workshop participants, listening is the most important of all four methods. Ironically, it has also been the most neglected one in the education and training arena. Most people do not receive much training in listening and consequently need to improve their listening skills. It is a skill that almost everyone can improve upon to help eliminate misunderstandings. Managers should listen empathically with their eyes and heart for more than just words. The highest level of listening is empathic listening, listening with the eyes and the heart for *feelings* and *emotions*. It is a way of seeing things from the other person's perspective, the way he or she is seeing it. Empathic listening requires you to avoid autobiographical responses while trying to understand the message. Autobiographical responses also discourage people to open up and tell you their feelings and thoughts.

Do not take other people's monkeys. Bill Oncken, in his article co-authored with Donald L. Wass and titled *"Management Time: Who's got the monkey?"* published in *Harvard Business Review* in 1974, stated that a monkey is a problem or the next move a person needs to make when the dialogue breaks. Problems are like monkeys and taking too many monkeys can rob you of your valuable discretionary time. Often managers seem to run out of time while their subordinates seem to run out of work. This is because managers are taking their subordinates' monkeys for various reasons. Oncken and Wass suggest five rules with regard to taking care of monkeys. First, monkeys should be fed or shot; otherwise it wastes the manager's time and resources. Second, the monkey population should be kept below the maximum number that the manager can handle during a given period of time. Third, monkeys should be fed by appointment rather than having to hunt for them. Fourth, monkeys should be fed face-to-face or person-to-person over a telephone rather than email and written documents. Fifth, every monkey should have a scheduled "next feeding time" and an assigned "degree of initiative." Effectively following these rules will reduce a manager's problems and allow him/her to spend more time focusing on what is important. According to Oncken, the best way to reduce procrastination and increase the urgency and importance of a project is to delegate it to subordinates.

Avoid becoming an automatic answering machine. Managers can and do face problems many times daily and they must provide answers to them accurately and quickly. The repetition of solving these problems and experiences can cause managers to automatically respond and solve the employee's problems without fully listening to his or her concerns. Consequently, this tendency can cause anger, resentment, feelings of not being heard, not being part of the team, and dissatisfaction on the employee's part. Some managers carry this tendency to their home lives as well and try to be problem-solvers. This tendency can ruin personal relationships and cause bad listening habits. There are many conscious and unconscious habits that can be very disturbing to employees and becoming an automatic answering machine is one of them. Many of these habits are unconscious and stem from the natural tendency to solve problems quickly because of the mindset that "we are managers and it is our job to provide the answers." This mentality has been reinforced by the fast-paced work environment and the managers' expertise and experience. While managers may have total familiarity with most problem situations because of repetition and the nature of an employee's job, the employee does not know this and may think the manager does not care about his/her problem. While some of these habits are unconscious and routine, others are purposeful, some are trivial, some are therapeutic, and some are caused by the personality traits of the manager.

Using IDEAS to Solve Problems

The IDEAS model is a structured (convergent) problem solving process for identifying and solving a problem. Instead of waiting for a solution to pop into your head from up above, the IDEAS model can help get you to the best solution one step at a time with available resources. IDEAS helps you think critically and creatively to investigate the problem, develop alternatives, examine and evaluate proposed alternatives, accept and administer the chosen alternative, and survey the results for success of current and future opportunities. Edward de Bono, the guru of creative thinking in his 1991 book "*I Am Right You Are Wrong?*", wrote that "the most effective critical thinking is actually creative thinking - the ability to generate alternative solutions. There is a need for attention to thinking that is productive, constructive, generative, and creative. Reactive thinking and problem solving will not equip people to improve society." This is why a manager needs to proactively focus on planning and preparing others in order to avoid putting out fires and solving problems. The IDEAS model helps you solve significant problems and the following are the five steps of problem solving:

1. Identify and Investigate the Problem. Once a problem has been identified, the problem-solving process begins. It is important to make sure the right problem has been identified. So, the first and foremost important step is to *define the problem* statement accurately and clearly. Solution imagineering is the second step to identifying and investigating the problem. *Solution imagineering* involves mentally seeing the problem solved and its prospective results accomplished. The accomplished results can clarify the objectives of solving the problem. This can also be accomplished through brainstorming or "Six Hat Thinking" principles. The third step is to *investigate the real cause* of the problem. Often, the real cause of the problem is hidden underneath the surface. Just like an iceberg has its major parts under the water and its tip above the water, real causes of the problem can often be hidden under all the symptoms. A cause-and-effect diagram can be used to brainstorm and diagnose the real cause of the problem. Always measure twice and cut once because if you are solving the wrong problem, things will get worse. You cannot climb to the right place if your ladder is leaning against the wrong wall.

2. Develop Alternatives. Most people are able to form a solution to general problems based on their intuitive senses as soon as they come in contact with the problem. The truth of the matter is that most often solutions are based on past experiences and developed paradigms instead of facts surrounding the current issue or problem. While one may intuitively have the solution in mind, it is best to generate several other alternatives through brainstorming or "Six Hat Thinking" which is another form of brainstorming for creativity, formality and discipline. The main purpose of this step is to generate ideas, and the first rule of any brainstorming session is not to evaluate ideas as they are being generated.

3. Evaluate and Examine Alternatives. Upon successful generation of several workable alternatives, one must evaluate and examine them for cost and benefit analysis as it pertains to all stakeholders. One must analyze them, and then attempt to evaluate their benefits with regards to all stakeholders and check their alignment with one's personal and professional values. After summing up the values and costs, one may determine whether to pursue an alternative or keep searching for better solutions. There are many roads that can lead you from here to your destination. However, the shortest road is the *"straight path"* which you should travel.

4. Accept and Administer an Alternative. The chosen alternative should solve the problem efficiently, productively, and with the least cost being imposed on the stakeholders. The alternative that respects everyone's rights and maximizes the benefits to everyone involved should be chosen and implemented. Implementation takes time, resources, planning, budgeting, and organizing all the related elements. The way a solution is implemented can make all the difference in the world because a solution is no better than the worst action taken to implement it. Implementation requires proper planning, organizing, control, and execution. Remember, implementation is an *IMP*ortant *LE*adership ele*MENT* because knowledge by itself does not produce anything. It is properly applied or executed knowledge that produces results including power.

5. Survey the Results and Suggest Improvements. Once a decision is implemented, it is very important to follow through and examine the actual results. This can serve as an educational experience and as a confirmation tool to make sure the original root cause of the problem is eliminated. Upon close examination of the results one should take proper action and do what is necessary.

Always make a decision and proceed. It is through convergent and divergent problem solving techniques that managers discover new opportunities, alternatives, and better methods. However, it is through determination, persistency, and decision-making abilities that managers get results and make things happen. We live in an imperfect world and our decisions need to be made in a timely manner with the available information. Because of deadlines, problem solvers will inevitably need to make decisions through "*satisficing*" with the limited information in the allotted time, and they will need to become effective problem-solvers and coaches.

Trust Building Traits

There are many leadership traits and characteristics that are important for effective problem-solving and performance management. However, such traits as trust are mandatory as they can make or break a person's career and level of influence with others. The commonly cited leadership traits and characteristics that shape people as leaders are the following: humility, energy, intuition, vision, perspective, passion, conviction, and learning. While these traits and characteristics are very important for effective leadership, they cannot make a person a leader unless he or she has developed a high level of trust with his or her followers. When trust is high, employees are more likely to voluntarily disclose current and future problems to their managers along with possible solutions.

Managers need to build trust by showing confidence, caring and acceptance. So, trust is having faith and confidence in the ability of those whom you interact with on a daily basis. The best way to build trust is to consistently demonstrate compassion, courage, and honesty in all your interactions for the right reasons and at the right times. A person of integrity and high character is trustworthy and influential. S/he can become a great role model and do many great things for others by being compassionate, courageous, and honest. You build trust by doing what you say you would do (DWYSYWD) 100% of the time. Consistency is the key to building trust by always DWYSYWD. If you read DWYSYWD backwards, it still says "Do What You Say You Would Do."

Trust is a building block for effective communication with one's friends, colleagues, employees, vendors, and suppliers. The flow of communication between you and everyone you come in contact with is greatly affected by the level of trust that exists between you and them. If the trust level is high, you have an environment that supports open and honest communication. It is up to you, as a leader, to help build an environment of trust with everyone around you. When people feel comfortable and safe from being judged prematurely and incorrectly, they are more willing to open up and speak their minds. If the trust level is low, then the opposite becomes true. So, you can make or "break" the level of trust between you and your friends, colleagues, and peers through your character. Remember, who you are as a person communicates much more loudly, persuasively and eloquently than anything you write, say or do. To become a person of strong character, you need to be consistently compassionate, courageous, and honest in all of your dealings with people.

Change Management

The fast pace of today's work environment has created many workaholics who might be successful professionally but personally they have a "bankrupt" life since they have forgotten about effectively balancing their time with family members. The fast pace of today's work world has caused changes in people's eating patterns as well. Instead of eating meals jointly with family members, friends and colleagues many families and individuals have been conditioned to eat in between work or other activities. As a matter of fact, according to a USA Today survey in August 2005, the most popular places to eat on the go were in front of the television set (60% of the respondents), in the car (42%) and at work (40%). Fifty years ago, most traditional cultures did not encourage people to eat by themselves since eating was a social time for family members to talk and converse with one another. Because of such interpersonal conversation opportunities, there was little need for psychiatrists and psychologists which are highly in demand today by many individuals because they are the only professionals who will listen to one's modern day problems, provided that they are paid. In previous centuries, when children and teenagers faced a difficult task they usually approached a family member for advice.

Dynamic change is a constant in today's work environment. Some of the commonly addressed sources of change for businesses can include changes in leadership, management, organizational structures, products, services, customers, customer demands, and location of where the firm produces or offers its products. Change is natural and expected within our lives. It is the nature and dynamics of change that can become stressful or cause conflicts, resistance and fear in us. The problem therefore is not change itself, but unplanned change. As human beings we like to plan and be able to manage our every aspect of life and living. Planned change is the catalyst around which we approach life; our education, training, socialization, communications, etc. Usually, we choose to react to change only when it arrives, and this is where conflict and resistance become major issues. We must prepare for change and then we will be better able to manage it within all contexts.

Conflict is inherent in all human affairs and, like change, it cannot be avoided; it can only be dealt with, and managers and leaders must become aware of this fact. Our differences as individuals serve to perpetuate change and conflict; our language, ethnic and social differences, etc. Knowing this fact, life then is best seen as a process of adapting to change and dealing with conflict, and the best way we can approach this is by effective change management, conflict management, and problem-solving skills.

Due to the changing demographics of the business world such as more competition and the introduction of new technologies, organizations are discovering that traditional tactics of management are no longer enough to remain competitive. As such, change management is coming to be recognized and practiced as an effective tool to increase morale, performance and the bottom line through the success of each individual associate.

Time Management: Important and Urgent

Someone once said that "there are two days in the week about which and upon which I never worry. Two carefree days, kept sacredly free from fear and apprehension. One of these days is Yesterday... And the other... is Tomorrow". Many individuals spend a large percentage of the days and nights worrying about either the past or the future and achieve very little in the present. The past is gone but it can offer learning when one reflects upon it consciously for a limited amount of time. The future has not come but one can plan for it accordingly.

However, actions must be taken in the present and these actions should be geared toward what is important in one's life.

In effective time management, activities can be categorized and understood as important, urgent, not important, and not urgent. The following definitions and concept are foundational in time management and effective decision-making.

◊ *Urgent* – Urgent is defined as activities that have the appearance of needing immediate attention.

◊ *Important* – Important is defined as all those activities that contribute to life's goals and mission.

Activities that are important will always produce better outcomes in the long-term. However, some activities are both important and urgent so they must be completed first. Activities that are neither important nor urgent can be left alone if they do not hinder your mission in life. Properly planning for doing what is important leaves no excuses for not achieving them.

Focus on the Important

It has been said that a person who does not make a choice actually makes a choice. Hopefully, choices are directed toward actions that lead one in the direction of what is important in one's life. A burning "why" will almost always find an efficient "how" in order to get to the predetermined destination. In the business perspective, the "why" deals with leadership while the "how" aspect deals with management tasks. One must know where and why before determining how to get there because going in the wrong direction will waste time, resources, and kill one's morale.

While focusing on the "big rocks" during one of his seminars, Dr. Stephen Covey set up a bucket and asked a volunteer from the audience to take a smaller bucket of small rocks and several large rocks labeled things like - self-improvement, big project at work, vacation time, family, etc. The small rocks represented the small fires or emergencies that we are hit with every day at home and at work. The instructions for the volunteers are clear and simple - you must fit all of the large rocks and all of the small rocks in the large bucket. Several volunteers attempted the task, each time placing some small rocks in the bottom of the bucket and then carefully selecting the most important large rocks, cramming, shoving, and pushing, trying to fit all of the rocks. Most participants tend to miss the key concept of the exercise which is really the moral of the presentations: You will accomplish a lot more in your day, your week and your life if you start with the "big rocks" first and leave the remaining empty space for the "small rocks." As expected and planned, all of the rocks fit into the large bucket when you place the large ones in first and pour the small rocks into the gaps and holes between them.

The same exercise can be conducted a little differently using the same concept of "small rocks" and "big rocks." A professor stood before his "Principles of Change Management" class and had some items in front of him to demonstrate effective time management. When the class began, wordlessly, he picked up a very large and empty glass jar and proceeded to fill it with "*colorful golf balls.*" He then asked the students if the jar was full? They agreed that it was. So the professor then picked up a box of pebbles and poured them into the jar. He shook the jar lightly. The pebbles, of course, rolled into the open spaces between the colorful golf balls. He then asked the students again if the jar was full. They agreed it was. The professor picked up a box of sand and poured it into the jar. Of course, the sand filled up everything else. He then asked once more if the jar was full. The students agreed with a unanimous --yes! The professor then produced two bottles of water from under the table and proceeded to pour the entire contents into the jar effectively filling the empty space between the sand. The students laughed.

Now, the professor said, as the laughter subsided, I want you to recognize that this jar represents your life.

◊ The *colorful golf balls* are the important things -- your family, partner, health, children, friends, and your favorite passions such as your job/profession--things that if everything else was lost and only they remained, your life would still be full.

◊ The *pebbles* are the other things that matter like your hobbies, your house, and your car.

◊ The sand is everything else -- the small stuff! If you put the sand into the jar first, then there is no room for the pebbles or the golf balls. The same goes for your life. If you spend all your time and energy on the small stuff, you will never have room for the things that are important to you. Pay attention to the things that are critical to your happiness.

Play with your children. Take time to get medical checkups. Take your partner out dancing. Play another 18 holes of golf and a game of tennis or racquetball every now and then. There will always be time to work, clean the house, give a dinner party, and fix the disposal. Take care of the golf balls first -- the things that really matter. Set your priorities. The rest is just sand. One of the students raised her hand and inquired what the water represented. The professor smiled and said, I'm glad you asked.

◊ The *water* is a symbol and a reminder for enjoying, relaxing and taking time for you and for nourishing all of your roles in a balanced way. It just goes to show you that no matter how full your life may seem, there's always room for enjoying a couple glasses of cool water with your friends to satisfy your thirst and cleanse your system!

Water is the symbol of flexibility, and it makes a powerful statement as an ending to this quick demonstration of making sure that one's big rocks are clarified, planned and scheduled. Actually water is both flexible as well as adaptable to its surroundings as it can be fluid, solid ice, or it can become moisture and simply evaporate in thin air. All mission-oriented individuals need to remain flexible as well as adaptable in their daily activities by taking advantage of the wonderful opportunities life brings their way each and every day.

Many time management experts use this philosophy when setting goals, writing an action plan, and prioritizing tasks. If needed, we should force ourselves to remember to work on the "big rocks" a little bit each day - otherwise we would become bogged down with small emergencies and never feel as though we have accomplished anything. Education is usually a "big rock" when we are trying to gain competency in our professions, and many competent professionals continue to hone their time management skills because they don't want important "small rocks" like some of the "big rocks" to get pushed aside from time to time. What is important is that you don't ignore "big rocks" for very long. Just like trees, "big rocks" such as your relationships need constant nourishment and development if they are to sustain and grow. As you know, after all is said and done, no matter how famous or important a person might be, the size of his/her funeral is going to depend a lot on the weather. Nonetheless, it is important that you focus on the "big rocks" before inviting others to your funeral!

Conscious thinking, deep reflection, prioritizing according to one's mission, and planning improves time management skills which is all about managing the needed activities in the allotted time. Most of us have experienced the difficulties of balancing available time with the many commitments and opportunities we would like to fulfill. Each day, managers are bombarded by a multitude of tasks and demands in a setting of frequent interruptions, crisis and unexpected events. It can be easy to lose track of objectives and fall prey to what experts identify as "time wasters." For many of us, time is probably dominated by other people and/or by nonessential activities rather our own "big rocks." Through the personal benefits of improved focus, flexibility, coordination, control, and planning everyone can become better time managers.

The organizational culture of most competitive firms tends to be fast paced and they usually require immediate solutions to problems. However, thinking of good ideas and creative solutions requires time. This is also true of our own lives. We need to take the time and see what makes sense for our purpose in life and how many hours we should devote to important tasks (big rocks) each week. Many of us might be wasting valuable time because we have a hard time determining what is important and eventually stop trying. Think, for a minute about meetings. How much time do professionals spend or waste in meetings? How many times have you thought to yourself after an hour-long meeting, we could have accomplished everything covered in a total of 15 minutes? The same is true for bureaucratic rules and regulations. How many hoops do we have to jump through in any given day? If these bureaucratic rules aren't followed to the letter, will it really make a difference? What happens sometimes is that we confuse what is important with what is urgent. Think about the busy lives of famous people who have accomplished great things. Did they have more time than other individuals or were they devoted to a cause that was important to them? If you are working toward a cause that is important, then it doesn't matter how many hours you work on it because it should be enjoyable to you!

The average person spends too much time on many mundane things on a daily basis because their urgency-driven world works that way. While that may be true for most of us in different stages of our lives, it is important that we take time to appreciate others and be thankful for what we have in life. As stated before, it is best to remember that yesterday is the past; tomorrow is the future; and neither of these times can be of much use to us at the present time. However, our time right now is a gift called "present" and we should make the best use of it while we have it because once it is gone, it is gone forever and it becomes part of the past.

Set Personal and Professional Goals

The person determined to achieve success in his/her life soon learns the principle that progress is made one step at a time toward predetermined goals. Soccer, football, or basketball games are won one play at a time and the team with one more point usually wins. Similarly, a business grows bigger one customer at a time and a person grows and achieves his/her wildest dreams one goal at a time. In other words, every big accomplishment is a series of little achievements toward a bigger purpose in life. Such life purpose must be converted into realistic and practical actions that can be taken each day. Otherwise, the life purpose without realistic actions may only become a good intention that is never implemented. Do not become a "Mr. Meant To" as expressed in the following little (anonymous) poem.

> Mr. "Meant To" has a comrade
> And his name is *"Didn't Do,"*
> Have you ever chanced to meet them?
> Did they ever call on you?

> These two fellows live together
> In the house of never win,
> And I am told that it is haunted
> By the ghost of *"might have been."*

Meaning to do something worthwhile and doing it in a timely manner can produce good results and happiness. Actions alone may not bring happiness, but there is no happiness without action. It has been said that the road to hell is paved with good intentions (Mr. Meant To). Let us twist this a bit and say, "The road to *achievement* is paved with good intentions." We call good intentions "goals." You have heard it before that if you don't know where you're going, any road will get you there.

So it's not enough just to "start out" in your career; you have to know where *you're* going as an individual and as an organization. Dr. Ken Blanchard, author of the *"One Minute Manager"* and *"Situational Leadership"* said "Set goals big enough that God will be proud." You need to have a purpose and you need to have a mission that can be converted into specific goals. For example, in soccer, there's no point in carrying the ball forward until you know where the goal is so you can score.

At many of the organizations, they usually tell new hires right from the beginning that they have to let their managers know what their career aspirations are. Do they want to stay in a technical field? Do they want to be a specialist or do they want to be a generalist? Do they want to get into management and formal leadership positions? Managers must know where their goal line is—and they have to know their employees' goal lines—so that they know who to give the ball to, when to pass the ball and with what type of further training.

Yet talk is cheap. Everybody talks about goal setting. Most firms have corporate mission statements and objectives, department goals, and sales quotas; what is their value if they are not put into good use? An old proverb from India sums it up like this: "No one was ever lost on a straight path"; and you'll have to admit it, some companies have gotten lost in the global race for quality products because they are looking for short gains or perhaps their "goal line" is not clear to everyone on the team.

About 90 percent of all new products launched in the U.S. are failures. However, such experiments with new products lead to understanding and learning what to do and what not to do. An Indian Philosopher by the name of J. Krishnamurti said "You must understand the whole of life, not just one little part of it. That is why you must read, that is why you must look at the skies that is why you must sing and dance, and write poems, and suffer, and understand, for all that is life." The same is true for our professional lives and one must keep attempting to set new goals toward higher goals. Our success rate as an individual and as an organization can be enhanced if we're always looking for ways to improve those odds by determining the "goal line." So why don't *people* set goals as frequently as corporations? One answer to this question is "fear." Not having goals covers up for failure. We don't have to face failure if we have no yardstick. If we don't do much, nobody—including ourselves—knows. People without goals drift to the sidelines and eventually disappear. The most important thing about a goal is to have one. Effective goals focus one's attention toward his/her purpose and mission in life. A major element of being or becoming an effective goal setter involves understanding how adults learn best and what makes them stay focused. Dr. W. Edwards Deming, business consultant and author, said "Learning is not compulsory. Neither is survival." Adults understand this concept and learn about their professions because they want to use the learning to achieve their personal and professional goals.

You too may like the story about an older man who was trying to lead a contrary donkey down the road. A passer-by stopped him and commented on the way the donkey was behaving. "Oh, I can make him do anything I want him to with just a kind word," the owner said. "Doesn't look like it to me," the other sneered. "Sure, I can," the owner said. Whereupon he climbed off the donkey, picked up a two-by-four beside the road, and clobbered the animal on the head, then explained to the onlooker. "I simply have to get his attention first." While abusing an animal is never a good thing, "clobbering" (ourselves or animals) may not be necessary if we proactively determine our mission in life so we can have appropriate goals to achieve them. Goals get our attention. Losers stay busy doing things. Winners and successful people concentrate on planning before they ever make a move. For people who don't give attention to long-term goals, the future is any time after tomorrow; but the future has a habit of suddenly becoming the present. Twenty years from now, you don't want to be trying to determine what you want to be when you grow up. To repeat: Goals make one focus. So, what are the characteristics of effective goals?

Well, *first*, good goals are set by choice, not default. Good goals require planning as Ben Franklin said "Proper planning, early to bed, early to rise - Makes a man healthy, wealthy and wise." Proper planning requires that you set the long-term goal at the outset of any project. John R. Noe, in his book *Peak Performance Principles for High Achievers,* sums up the experience like this: "By the time we are ready to make the big decisions; the options have been narrowed by our little choices along the way. If we do not clarify our goals, our lives will be controlled by haphazard decisions." As you can reason, "not deciding…is deciding." In goal setting, the same is true.

The *second* characteristic of a good goal is that it's a big goal— one worthy of your efforts. If you intend to succeed beyond your wildest expectations, you have to have some wild expectations. A few people wake up every day to go out and slay dragons but most are satisfied to chase lizards day after day. If you're an "average" performer, don't set your sights on "above average." Look at "excellent." Whatever the average might be, look at what your colleagues would term a "reasonable" goal, and then double it. That would be worth working for and worth achieving. Consciously or unconsciously, you always get what you expect. So the secret to success, at least for some individuals, is to raise your expectations and to set goals worthy of your personal time and effort. Don't let the "fear" that you won't reach big goals keep you from setting them. Just keep in mind that FEAR is an acronym that stands for **F**alse **E**vidence **A**ppearing **R**eal (FEAR). The author and management consultant Peter Drucker says the following about goals and objectives: "Objectives are not fate; they're direction. They are not commands; they are commitments. They do not determine the future; they are means to mobilize the resources and energies of the business for making of the future." Oliver Wendell Holmes agreed: "The greatest thing in this world is not so much where we are, but in what direction we are moving." Unless you set big and worthwhile goals, you'll never move beyond your current abilities.

The *third* characteristic of a good goal is that it has a completion date. Goals are dreams with deadlines. Always put a deadline on your goals, because deadlines wake you from your dreams to bring you to the reality of achieving them. Sleepwalkers don't get around very well—at least not without bumps on the shins. One of the authors of the bestseller *Thriving on Chaos,* Fred Brooks, a System 360 Chief Designer at IBM, had this to say about the lack of setting corporate goals: "How does a project get to be a year behind schedule? One day at a time." So, set five-year goals, ten-year goals, six-month goals, and so on. Without deadlines for their achievements, goals are simply good intentions and "pie-in-the-sky" plans.

A *fourth* characteristic of a good goal is that it is followed up by a plan of action or a strategy. Someone once said that "Even if you're on the right track, you'll get run over if you just sit there." You have to put the "how-to" to the goal. If you plan to switch careers, what new training will you need? Where can you get it? What college or corporate course? Goals do very little good without plans of action to bring them into reality. Successful companies have elaborate plans. You wouldn't dare to go to work for them if they didn't. "Buy low, sell high. Collect early, and pay late," are all general strategies. Sounds good in theory, but we'd be in trouble if we depended on a paycheck from companies that didn't have a more complete game plan than that. Without plans, the only way businesses run are downhill. The same is true for individuals and organizations. We need specifics to be successful.

A *fifth* characteristic of a good goal is that it can be broken into specific short-term steps and completion dates. Maximum achievements are the result of minimum steps. A big house is built with one little brick and nail at a time. A suit is sewn one seam at a time. A business is built one employee at a time. Similarly, high school is completed one year (short-term goal) and one course at a time (current goal).

Sixth, good goals are written goals. Committing them to writing makes them real. You can review them, modify them, and commit their accomplishment quality levels and dates to others. They're constant reminders of where you've decided you want to be at what point in your life.

Finally, good goals generate excitement. The late Malcolm Forbes said, "Men who never get carried away should be." Don't be afraid to show your commitment—some might even call it fanaticism—about reaching a goal. If you're kicking and screaming about reaching or not reaching a goal, at least we all know you're alive. Let us summarize good goals. How to set good goals:

1. Set them by choice, not default.
2. Set big goals.
3. Add a completion date.
4. Develop a plan of action.
5. Set short-term steps and interim completion dates.
6. Write goals down.
7. Get excited about the stated goals.

If you don't start by taking the first step toward your goals, it is certain you will not arrive or achieve them. The author Tyrone Edwards said "People never improve unless they look to some standard or example higher or better than themselves." If you do not set higher goals and standards, then effective and efficient improvement may not be possible.

The best opportunities in one's life are those that we create. Goal setting provides the opportunity to create an extraordinary life.

Remember, you can resolve and effectively manage many of life's problems by creating your future through setting goals and then working to achieve them. Effective managers and leaders realize that:

1. The best way to determine your limitations is to go too far.
2. The best way to find out how far you can go is to go too far.
3. To find out "how far", you need to go too far.
4. When you have gone "too far", stop and examine your goals realistically to see how much further you may want to go!

Summary

Effective management is about problem-solving and developing trusting relationships with employees so people can jointly clarify expectations and departmental goals thereby leading to specific action plans for their achievement. Management is not an innate skill, but rather it is learned. It occurs through one's life personally and professionally. Effective management is the process of letting people know that what they do matters to you and to the organization. Furthermore, it is about letting them know that you are there to help them be the best they can be as their success is important because it matters to you. It is also about being sincere, specific and to the point about both good and poor performance so employees can take personal responsibility for their achievements.

To be effective problem-solvers, leaders and managers must always be mentally, physically, socially, and spiritually in good shape if they are to proactively deal with change and be a good role model for others in society. Manager your time effectively and set clear goals. Keep your mind sharp by learning something new each day and each week. Keep your body in good shape by exercising three to four days every week for about thirty minutes each day. Keep your spirits high by reading motivational books, enjoying the present through appreciation and living in the moment, and by having a good sense of humor.

Discussion Questions

1. What are some common problems and challenges that managers face on a regular basis in their departments? Focus on obstacles that they might face on their day-to-day basis.

2. What are some problem suggestions for busy managers? List five principles that you think are important to understand and practice when it comes to problem-solving.
3. What is the role of "trust" in a relationship with employees and colleagues? Discuss through examples.
4. How can one build trust with his/her employees and colleagues? List five suggestions.
5. What can managers do to effectively manage change, stress, and conflict in their personal and professional lives? Discuss and focus on both their personal lives as well as their professional workplace when working with their employees.
6. What is time management and why is it important for managers?
7. Should you focus on "urgent" activities in your life or "important" activities?
8. What are the characteristics of effective goals?
9. Why should companies and managers have specific goals? Discuss and provide examples.

CHAPTER 7

Ethics and National Culture

The study of ethics and social responsibility is important for all global managers and employees. By understanding ethics, morality, and social responsibility, one can be better prepared to gain a sustainable competitive advantage while avoiding unethical and illegal activities. The negative implications associated with certain behavior in one country may mean quite the opposite in another; and thus the global business person must be not only aware of the law but also must be culturally competent.

The practice of giving "gifts" and making transfers of value to foreign government officials is one particular area fraught with legal and ethical perils. Most people might agree that corruption is an act that is conducted with the intent to give one's business an unfair advantage in obtaining a government contract and to unduly influence a government official to violate an official duty. Bribery is one very deleterious, and sad to say, prevalent form of corruption today. This chapter discusses ethics, social responsibility, and socialization in a global context, with an example of socialization from Vietnam. The chapter discusses the legal, ethical, and practical ramifications to corruption, which practice, especially bribery, seems to be associated with both developed and developing economies.

Ethics and Morality[3]

Every safe building stands on a strong foundation. Similarly, every sustainable business should stand on a foundation that has strong values, legal compliance, and high ethical standards. Values are rankings or priorities that a person establishes for one's norms and beliefs. Deeply held values can drive behavior. Moral values are

---

[3] Contributed by Frank J. Cavico, Nova Southeastern University.

generally held to be intrinsic. Accordingly, if one views morality to be an intrinsic value, then one must be moral regardless of the circumstances and consequences. Ethics is the theoretical study of morality.

Ethical theories are moral philosophical undertakings that contain bodies of formal, systematic, and ethical principles that are committed to the view that an asserted ethical theory can determine how one should morally think and act. Moral judgments are deducible from a hierarchy of ethical principles. Morality, therefore, properly and accurately should be understood as a development of the ethical, which is part of the philosophical. Major secular and reasoned-based ethical theories are ethical egoism, ethical relativism, both stemming from the ancient Greeks, the Utilitarian theory propounded by the English philosophers Jeremy Bentham and John Stuart Mill, and the Categorical Imperative of the German philosopher, Immanuel Kant. Ethical egoism is a doctrine that asserts that one should advance one's self-interest. That is, an act that supports or promotes one's self interest is a moral action. Of course, the ethical egoists would say that there are limits to this doctrine. Accordingly, one should take a long-term view of the advancement of one's self interest, and thus be prepared to undergo some short-term pain and expense in order to maximize in the long run one's self-interest. Similarly, even if one has a big ego and is very powerful one should not treat people in an arbitrary, capricious, and disrespectful manner. Why should one be "nice"? Because it generally will benefit a person (and a person's business) in the long-run by treating people (such as employees) well, co-opting them, and making them part of your "team." Thus one should act as a general rule in a beneficent manner when dealing with people because it is in one's self-interest to do so. So, regarding the proposed payment of a bribe to a foreign official to secure a contract with a foreign government, if it is in one's self-interest to pay the bribe, as perhaps one's company desperately needs the contract to ward off bankruptcy, and since the bribe is really only a "commission" to the government official, and thus (hopefully!) any legal difficulties can be "circumvented," then if one is an ethical egoist one might pay the bribe. Ethical relativism is a societal-based ethical theory that maintains that whatever a particular society believes is moral is in fact moral for that society. One, therefore, does not have to be a philosopher to make moral determinations under this theory. Rather, one just needs "sharp" eyes and ears, or perhaps some good local counsel, to discern what the societal moral norms are in a particular country. And if is an accepted practice morally to pay foreign officials to "get things to happen," then pursuant to this ethical theory by all means make the payment as this would be a moral "bribe," at least pursuant to ethical relativisms. "When in Rome, do as the Romans," as the old saying goes!

Utilitarianism

Utilitarianism is a consequentialist-based ethical theory, as is ethical egoism, but the important distinction is that the Utilitarians want one to consider the consequences of an action not just on oneself bur rather on all people who are directly or indirectly affected by the action. The next key feature of the Utilitarian theory is to predict the reasonably foreseeable good and bad consequences that would stem from putting this action into effect. Are the consequences good or bad? Does the action cause pleasure (in the sense of happiness and satisfaction) or pain? Or, as is usually the case, are the consequences mixed? Then one must determine if the good consequences outweigh the bad consequences. If so, the action is moral. And if the obverse, that is, the bad outweighs the good, then the action is immoral. Note that there still can be bad consequences and a moral action pursuant to this ethical theory if the overall good consequences outweigh the bad. "The ends justify the means," as the old saying goes. And at least everyone got "counted" and their pain was registered (though outweighed), so Utilitarianism is at least an egalitarian ethical theory in that respect. In a bribery scenario, to do a Utilitarian analysis, one would have to examine the consequences of paying the bribe on all the stakeholders affected, including the company, its shareholders/owners, employees, suppliers and distributors, the person paying the bribe, the foreign government official paying the bribe, the host government and society, the home country government and society, and the competition. Then one would have to decide what the consequences, particularly the adverse legal consequences for paying the bribe as well as the negative financial consequences for not paying the bribe, would be for the stakeholders individually and finally overall. If there are more reasonably foreseeable good consequences for paying the bribe then the bribe is moral.

Kant was diametrically opposed to Utilitarianism and actually he found it reprehensible to have an ethical theory that could morally legitimize pain, suffering and exploitation. Disregard consequences, declared Kant, and instead focus on the form of the action and whether the action passes a formal test, which he called the Categorical Imperative. "Categorical" meaning that, according to Kant, his test was the supreme principle in ethics; and "Imperative" meaning that after one rationally determined what is moral or immoral using his test one had to command oneself to do what is right and not do what is wrong. There are various formulations of Kant's Categorical Imperative. One oft-cited and prominent part to the Categorical Imperative is the Kingdom of Ends test. For an action to be moral it must pass this Kingdome of Ends test, which requires that the action, regardless of any consequences, treat people with dignity and respect and as worthwhile "ends" in and of themselves and as human beings, and not treat them like things, instruments, tools, or mere means. Any action that is demeaning or disrespectful of a person would be immoral according to Kant, even if produces greater good consequences overall. The ends definitely do not justify the means under Kantian ethical philosophy. So, if in a bribery scenario if anyone is disrespected, perhaps the payer of the bribe who is a company employee who is set up as the "fall-guy" if the bribe creates legal difficulties or bad publicity, or maybe the people in the host country who are going to get an inferior product at a high cost that is being foisted on them because of the bribe and now have even more corruption in their society, then the bribe would be immoral.

Social Responsibility

Social responsibility, however, is *not* part of ethics, *not* an ethical theory, *not* an ethical principle, and is *not* a means to determine morals, morality, or moral precepts. As such, it is important to keep the concept of social responsibility distinct from morality and ethics, which are philosophy based, as well as legality, which, of course, is based on the law. The traditional purpose of business, moreover, is the profitable production, distribution, and sale of goods and services, albeit in a legal and moral manner, but not, traditionally at least, social welfare or philanthropic endeavors. Yet, today, since the issue of the social responsibility of business is frequently raised, business is forced to concern itself with the "social" dimension of its activities. That is, business today, is expected to act not only in a legal manner, but also in a moral manner, and when a business reaches a certain size and stature to be "socially responsible" business too.

At a basic philanthropic level, social responsibility may be defined as a business taking an active party in the social causes, charities, and civic life of one's community and society. The sustainability approach to corporate social responsibility is premised on the idea that a company must remain economically viable in the long-term, and that in order to be viable the company must take into consideration other stakeholders beyond the shareholders. Social responsibility and perceptions of being and acting ethically, at least to some reasonable degree, may be in the long-term self-interest of business. A corporation cannot long remain a viable economic entity in a society that is uneven, unstable, and deteriorating. It makes good business sense for a corporation to devote some of its resources to social betterment projects. To operate efficiently, for example, business needs educated and skilled employees. Education and training, therefore, should be of paramount interest to business leaders. A corporation, for example, can act socially responsible by providing computers to community schools and by releasing employees on company time to furnish the training.

Business is part of society and subject to society's mandates; and if society wants more "responsibility" from business, business cannot ignore this "request" without the risk of incurring society's anger, perhaps in the form of higher taxes or more onerous government regulation. An example of "smart" social responsibility concerns Microsoft's "wellness" efforts to help its overweight employees. The company, which already provides free medical coverage to its employees, now has created a weight management benefit for employees. The software company will pay for 80% of the cost, up to $6000, for a comprehensive, clinical, weight loss program for employees. The program, intended for employees who are obese or clinically overweight, includes up to a year's worth of sessions with a personal trainer, behavioral and nutritional counseling, support groups, and medical supervision. Microsoft in the long-run expects to obtain a return on its health care investment for the formerly obese and overweight employees due to cost savings from less prescription drugs and fewer doctor and hospital visits. Similarly, Johnson & Johnson has invested substantially in employee health through its Wellness & Prevention program; but the company has received an excellent return-on-investment, because the program has been estimated by the company to have saved $250 million in employee health care costs over the past decade, with the savings representing a return of $2.71 for every dollar spent.

However, a socially responsible firm must also be a realistic one. That is, socially responsible and environmental efforts must be sustainable economically and should have some relationship to the firm's business. Employees should also be engaged directly in the company's social responsibility activities so as to engage them, inspire them, motivate them, and thereby enhance morale and productivity. Moreover, a firm's social responsibility program does not have to be a multi-million dollar effort; rather, something as simple as an employee social responsibility "suggestion box" or as straightforward as a recycling or energy saving program will do to promote employee involvement as well as to promote and give credence to employee social values. Nonetheless, despite the size, a firm's social responsibility efforts should be publicized widely within the company, for example, in company newsletters, as well as externally, for example in company annual "social responsibility" reports. Being socially responsible, therefore is a smart and sustainable business strategy, especially in a human resource context. One major benefit of being a socially responsible firm is that its employees are inspired and energized, thereby helping the company to retain employees.

Socially responsible business leaders and managers should always include social responsibility goals in their corporate articles and bylaws as well as mission and vision statements. Moreover, the authors long have argued that it is in the long-term, egoistic, self-interest of the corporation to be a socially responsible one, and thus to be active and engaged in community, civic, and charitable activities. The objective is to simultaneously produce economic value for the company, but also value for society as a whole by helping to solve societal needs, particularly by improving the lives of the people (and potential consumers) who live in the communities where the company does business.

The Business Sustainability Continuum

The term "sustainability" also has emerged, along with social responsibility and corporate governance, as important subject matters for business today. Sustainability, of course, encompasses legal, ethical, moral, and social responsibility values, and also is related in to corporate governance. In order to better illustrate as well as explicate the values of practicality, legality, morality, and social responsibility and their relationship to sustainability, let us explore the Business Sustainability Continuum (BSC) model which has four components.

This Business Sustainability Continuum (BSC) model presents a continuum where start-up businesses often focus on meeting their bottom-line break-even points and legal requirements in order to stay in business. As these firms grow in term s of their market share and revenue, these businesses begin to see the importance of their actions being seen as ethical and socially responsible for all relevant stakeholders in the community. Furthermore, intense local and global competition forces firms of all sizes to strategically act in an economic, legal, ethical, and socially responsible manner.

Figure 7.1 - The Business Sustainability Continuum (BSC)

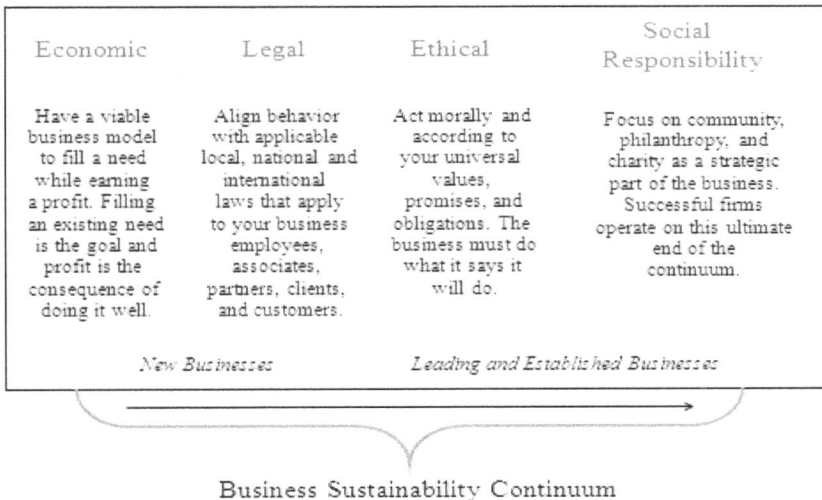

Economic	Legal	Ethical	Social Responsibility
Have a viable business model to fill a need while earning a profit. Filling an existing need is the goal and profit is the consequence of doing it well.	Align behavior with applicable local, national and international laws that apply to your business employees, associates, partners, clients, and customers.	Act morally and according to your universal values, promises, and obligations. The business must do what it says it will do.	Focus on community, philanthropy, and charity as a strategic part of the business. Successful firms operate on this ultimate end of the continuum.
New Businesses		*Leading and Established Businesses*	

Business Sustainability Continuum

The BSC illustrates that the continual success and "sustainability" of the business can only be achieved by an adherence to four core values:

Economic dimension indicates that a business obviously must have a viable business model which fulfills a need and enables the business to make a profit.

Legal, indicating that this profit must be achieved in legal manner by aligning the conduct of the business with all applicable local, national, and international law.

Ethical, indicating that since there may be no law or "gaps" in the law; nonetheless the business must act in a moral manner and also must act in conformity with its values, promises, and obligations.

Social Responsibility, indicating that the business must focus on the community and engage in civic, philanthropic, and charitable endeavors as part of the business' overall strategic plan.

Sustainability will help the business, but also help the business help governments solve pressing social problems. Accordingly, adherence to these "sustainable" values will enable the business to achieve success and to sustain that success in a continual manner, thereby benefiting the business, its shareholders, the communities where it does business, and all the stakeholders affected by the business, including society as a whole.

The BSC model can be used to assess and evaluate business decisions and viable alternatives prior to implementation in order to determine which options are sustainable over time and more likely to lead to long-term value maximization for all relevant stakeholders. Besides business decisions, organizational rules and norms can also be assessed using the BSC model to make sure the stated policies and guidelines are economical, legal, ethical, and that they lead to socially responsible conducts over time.

Social responsibility is a very important and relevant topic for business today. Moreover, business leaders are expected to lead by values – legal values, moral values, and now socially responsible values. Cognizance of, adherence to, and dealing with the value of social responsibility have become imperatives for business leaders today. The view today is that business should pursue profits, of course, but also that business should strive to achieve social objectives, such as philanthropy, too. Social responsibility, therefore, should now be incorporated into business values, missions, and models by business leaders. Moreover, as the authors have emphasized throughout this work, social responsibility clearly possesses instrumental value, because it can be used in a smart, shrewd, and strategic sense to help the business achieve and sustain successful performance. Social responsibility, therefore, is more than just "mere" or "pure" charity; rather, in a modern business sense, social responsibility is an integral strategic component in the company's endeavor to achieve and to sustain larger traditional business objectives. Yet, concomitantly and also propitiously, society as whole is benefitted by these social responsibility activities. So, in essence, corporate social responsibility, along with the values of legality and morality, are "smart" business and "good" business and "sustainable" business – for business, business stakeholders, and society.

Ethics and Communism [4]

Ethical decision-making and socially responsible behaviors are becoming more important today than ever before, as such good conduct often leads to more satisfied and productive employees as well as consumers, who enjoy a better quality of life. And thus under ethical egoism, a business would prosper by having contended, loyal, and productive employees, as well as satisfied consumers. However, in Vietnam the doctrine of ethical relativism emerges as a particularly salient ethical theory, especially since some experts assert that Communist values may establish certain ethical norms for Vietnamese society and thus support Vietnamese in their moral decision-making.

The gradual shift of economic power from the West to Asia and to China more recently presents a new and distinctive challenge to Western domination over global development discourse. China and Vietnam have discarded many of the original basic tenets of communism and they have been the world's two fastest growing economies over the past two decades. Moreover, by late 2008, amazon.com's ranking of book sales revealed that the book of communist theory, Marx's Das Capital, had become a best seller. There is renewed interest in communism in both theory and practice.

Communist China was not only showing the rest of the world how a country could have impressively and continuously high economic growth rate, but also was using some of the results of this growth to invest in Western countries. China is the largest socialist country and world's second largest economy behind the United States. The Chinese model might be increasingly attractive even in the worst global economic crisis since October 1929. China rapidly growing influences the rest of the world. China has a hybrid system; and its own name in Chinese as 'Zhongguo' - the Middle Country. Also, Chinese culture differs from that of the Western countries. Chinese culture has mainly been conceptualized as Confucianism, collectivism, and communist ideology. The Chinese Communist Party's (CCP) ideology,

---

[4] Contributed by Phuong Ngo Thai, Flinders University. *Source*: Ngo, T. P., Mujtaba, B. G., and Fisher, G. (December 2012). The Influence of Communism on Ethical Decision Making. *Proceedings of ICIIIM 2012 Conference*, Bangkok, Thailand. December 14-14, 2012.

namely, Marxism–Leninism, Maoism, Deng Xiaoping Theory, and the theory of Three Represents, is a major source of influence in Chinese organizations, shaping management practices throughout the country. Communist ideals help constitute moral character, including: (a) commitment to abiding by the law and to avoid corrupt practices, (b) positive attitude toward the Chinese Communist Party and willingness to follow party dictates even when they conflict with one's own personal views, and (c) positive attitude toward party political workshops held during working hours. China's case indicates that communism, as an institution or an ideology, has moderated the Confucian influence on Chinese leadership.

As the sole representative of the Vietnamese government, the Vietnamese Communist Party (VCP) is in a position to create and control its state-authored Vietnamese culture, which clearly is related to ethical precepts, norms, and practices. The VCP uses its power and Vietnamese culture as an expedient resource to assist in resistance to outside influence and preserving Vietnamese ideologies and principles and institutions governing routine social life. Communism has served the VCP with an ideology that placates dominant Party and state interests while retaining a concentration of power within the state. Unlike other political parties, the VCP is today arguably as strong as ever in the national culture, and it has and continues to enjoy broad legitimacy across large segments of society.

There are many studies investigating the impact of national culture on ethical decision-making. Culture has both a direct and indirect impact on ethical decision-making. National culture influences an individual's intention to behave ethically. It is clearly an important determinant of moral decision-making. Different cultural backgrounds thus may affect an individual's moral decision making. In the case of Vietnam and based on personal observations, it is proposed that communist values can be a significant variable influencing Vietnamese ethical decision-making.

Communism Defined

Is an individual's perception of business ethics a function of communism? To answer this question, it becomes readily apparent that we must first define communism. It is important to discuss this upfront before reviewing the literature although it is not easy to define communism in simple terms.

With the emergence of mixed economies in most countries around the globe, there is little agreement as to what communism is in the modern era. Webster's New College Dictionary defines communism is a social system often characterized by the common ownership of the means of production and sharing of labor and products. Some researchers define communism as any relationship that operates on the principle of from each according to their abilities, and to each person according to his/her needs. Based on concept of belief, communism requires a more general commitment to a socialist ideology that favors social equality, cosmopolitanism, and scientific-technological progress. It refers to a specific commitment to Marxist-Leninist ideology as articulated in Soviet or East European regimes.

Communism originated from Karl Marx and was further developed by Vladamir Lenin after the Russian Revolution. One function of the Communist Party is to socialize the population in various ways, and this includes control of the education system, control of the mass media and direct communication with the citizenry during election campaigns. In countries such as China, the Communist Party has played major roles in the shaping of each country's national culture. The Chinese government's policy indicates clearly the desire to cultivate a Marxist ideology and communist ethics in its youth. A ruling party's ideology and accompanying rhetoric can have a major impact on citizens' perceptions. Chinese people are able to accept communism as a guiding force in their lives. In communist countries, it is believed that individuals who have been indoctrinated in communist ideology are less likely to behave unethically. Accordingly, based on the above discussion, it is proposed that individuals who have experienced communism and have been heavily indoctrinated in its moral philosophy may behave in a more moral manner.

Ethics, Communism, and the Vietnamese Culture

With a population of nearly one hundred million, Vietnam is the 13th most populous country in the world. Vietnam represents a collectivist and oriental culture. The individual is seen at a lower level than the collective group (the family, school or company). Strict guidelines are designed to protect the reputation of the group. Vietnam has been dominated by ruling elites, initially colonial forces, followed by the monarchy, which was succeeded by the Socialist and current

Communist Party leaders. For example, banks in Vietnam operate mainly on the strength of relationships. Vietnam has no state religion. However, there are three major religions which have a profound impact on Vietnamese behaviours, namely Confucianism, Taoism and Animism. In 2003, Vietnamese religious communities had about 20 million people of different religions. Most Vietnamese Buddhists belong to the Mahayana branch. The Theravada branch exists in Vietnamese ethnic communities living in the Mekong Delta region. Business ethics is a relatively new issue in Vietnam, and the field began emerging after market-economy reforms, when Vietnam started to join in the internationalization and globalization process.

Previously, in the centralized planned economy, all activities were conducted by the Government under the Communist Party's leadership. Most assets were state owned. Most employees were working for the State. They followed the higher authority's direction. Managers had little power to play their leadership role. They were only instruments of State policy. The discipline and salary system were simple and unified. It is easy to recognize the subordinate–superior relationship in organizations and the strict bureaucratic and hierarchical management system in society. The paternalistic approach in management continues to play an important role in various governmental, public and private corporate organizations. One of the distinctive features in the Vietnamese society is the use of "indirect speech," resulting from the importance of "saving face." People try to avoid ambiguous or embarrassing situations by setting up formal rules and codes of conduct, and rejecting inappropriate and deviant behaviors.

Along with the economic reform and open-door policy and joining the World Trade Organization, the Vietnamese cultural-socio-economic environment has undergone some significant changes. It respectively leads to a transformation in ideology and a sense of value. The move towards a market-oriented economy from a command economy and Confucian cultural philosophy has resulted in the mixture between collectivism and individualism. For instance, Vietnamese employees lean towards individualism through a stronger emphasis on personal performance-based rewards rather than being rewarded for loyalty and group performance. The context of Vietnam is linked to modernization, advance technology and the influx of Western management. This transformation has led to an adaptation to Western values and behaviors which are often considered as having more freedom and more publicity than in other Asian cultures. Under pressure of globalization, the Vietnamese mass media mentions business ethics quite frequently, but the understanding of the issue is still very vague and undeveloped; no official definition of business ethics has to date been offered.

Vietnamese Communist Party

Vietnam is a long lasting social communist country where one single Communist Party was established more than 80 years ago. Vietnam has a formal structure of a tripartite state with legislative, executive and juridical branches but with significant involvement of the VCP as a real decision making power. Vietnamese Communist Party memberships account for 3% of the population. They are in key positions in all government agencies: The National Assembly, Ministries, and Supreme Court. The Party's Central Committee with a current representation of 160 members who are high-ranking leaders in the government system is a forum for strategic decision making.

The Vietnamese Communist Party has a monopoly of power, a tremendous control over society and a strong impact on the public administration system. The political system is ruled only by this one single party – the rule of the Vietnamese Communist Party. 'Polito-bureaus and the Central Committee, which center on the General Secretary of the party, have all of the ultimate power of decision because a single party commands the hierarchy of authority in all legislative, judicial, and governmental aspects'. Communism has strict laws and enforcement according to the Party's charter. The party organizations play leadership roles in all state activities to implement party policies. Citizens belong to mass organizations appropriate to their status such as the quasi-governmental Vietnam Fatherland Front, the Vietnam General Confederation of Trade Unions or Ho Chi Minh Communist Youth League. Party members leading such organizations educate and mobilize the masses through regular study sessions to implement party policies.

During the period of the centrally planned economy, the VCP directly controlled all state governance activities. After that, the transition into a market based economy decreased the role of Party and gave more power to the Government and the legislative institution. However, those bodies are far from autonomous since almost all of the state leaders are Communist Party members. The Party's Central Commission for Organization and Personnel appoints the Government's senior personnel management and the National Assembly instead of the Prime Minister and National Assembly. Due to the high level of involvement of the Party in top personnel the state helps Party member government officials to comply completely with the Party's principles. The Party's ideology and mind-set play a crucial role in shaping public opinion and social issue. The Communist Party of Vietnam has adopted Marxism-Leninism and Ho Chi Minh Ideology. The spirit of communism is "for the people, from the people and of the people". Communist Party members are recognized as high-ranking members who play exemplary roles in their daily work, and when faced with major issues. They often place the Party's interest above personal interest; the Party's interests are supreme. For Communist Party members, communist ideologies play an important role and are strong determinants of an individual's values and ethics.

Communism seems to have become a very powerful force in the life of Vietnamese. It is apparent that communism has become a very significant variable in attempting to understand the psychology of Vietnamese. This suggests that communism influences the understanding and explanation of the behavior of Vietnamese. Hence, being a member of the Communist Party would have a positive impact on ethical perceptions and ethical behavior. The VCP introduced market socialism in the late 1980s. It is clear that the Party desires an additional layer of cultural and economic supervision during the period of rapid changing economy. While the VCP creates national economic, political, and cultural dictums, it is up to local governments to make sure that national cultural ideology is woven into the fabric of local policy and their constituents' lives on an everyday, mundane basis.

Government continues to give Vietnam's state-owned organizations preferential treatment for accessing real estate, exempting tax or restricting private competition. Unlike other neoliberal state governments, the VCP still controls the national marketplace in order to protect its economic interests, and developing profitable industries by tagging them with a label of "cultural importance". The VCP's cultural narratives have been constructed over time. In the "Đổi mới" (renovation) era, the VCP still frames national culture on the basis of "Vietnameseness" (as opposed to "foreignness") by creating a state-wide tension between foreign cultural interlocutors and the enduring strength of a state-authored Vietnamese culture.

The presentation of the VCP's Vietnamese culture is important and associated with market reform policies. The VCP has created an economy in which the cultural discourses of equitability, caution, and community play a role in drawing attention away from the state's predatory economic actions, actions which create solvency for state-owned enterprises and challenge private, non-state businesses. Vietnamese culture is almost unique and different than other Asian socialist countries including China. It is because the VCP keeps control power during reform process. 'The nature of the Party in Vietnam may differ from the conventional stereotype of iron control'. The VCP maintains its rule through a system of checks and balances around the principle of consensus. One other main difference between the Vietnamese culture and others is in terms of managing religions. In most communist countries, religions and religious activities were strongly discouraged, closely monitored or even formally banned in Albania in 1967. However, in Vietnam, religious institutions are recognized and co-opted for nation-building and state-affirming purposes. Communist Party policies respect the people's right to freedom of beliefs and religions, clearly state rights and duties of religious individuals and religious organizations. Furthermore, Vietnamese religions and beliefs can be seen as a strong indication of the ideological orientation of the VCP. Nowadays, political leaders usually praise Vietnamese religious organizations for its achievements and contribution to the development of the whole economy.

Like Maoism in China, Ho Chi Minh ideology symbolized the nature of Vietnam's modern cultural identity. Ho Chi Minh, a creative Marxist ideologist and humanist, is an exemplary modern communist of wisdom and intellect. Profoundly and completely believing in socialism and communism, Ho Chi Minh ideology reaches epochal heights. With his understanding of the Vietnamese people's lives and destiny, he devoted his life to the salvation and development of his nation and people. Ho Chi Minh's ideology is a result of the creative application and development of Marxism-Leninism in the conditions of Vietnam. Ho Chi Minh's ideology is in close association with socialism which was developed from a practical viewpoint on development and renovation. That is reason at its 7th National Congress (6-1991) the Vietnamese Community Party affirmed to take Marxism-Leninism and Ho Chi Minh thought as the ideological foundation and lodestar for its action.

Ethical decision-making is a process by which individuals use their moral base to determine whether certain issues are right or wrong. That moral base can be societal-based, of course, as per the ethical theory of ethical relativism. Differences in ethical norms and ethical decision-making may mean that underlying value structures differ across groups and countries. Ethical standards and ethical decision-making is influenced by national culture. National culture influences the individual's intention to behave ethically. Vietnamese culture is created and influenced by the Vietnamese Communist Party which helped the economy grow sustainability over the past few decades. Based on the aforementioned discussion and the apparent gap in the literature, it is proposed that communist values affect ethical decision making. Individuals with a high commitment to communism tend to recognize the ethical issues or problems more so than their counterparts. With the increasing roles of communist countries in the global economy, individuals may increase their perceptions toward ethical behavior which should enable them to make more moral decisions. One area that may require ethical decision-making is the subject matter of bribery, for example, when a U.S. business person attempts to bribe a Vietnamese government official to secure a contract or vice versa.

Challenges of Corruption

Conventional wisdom says that almost all people expect, respect and strive for an equitable and fair form of democracy. We tend to think we know what it is, until asked, "So what is it"? To illustrate, a thoroughly democratic acclamation in China is the Maoist party promise of riches first and democracy later; France changing its constitution to provide more democracy in accordance to the laws of the European Union; and Iraq drafting a democratic constitution to replace the laws once created by the one party system. Democracy has become the solution to freedom, but has it also become the solution to corruption or the inducement of corruption?

Corruption has been in existence since the birth of humans, where it has progressively worsened. What is true is that most people do not want corruption and bribery in their culture; yet such behaviors and actions might be part of their society due to economic realities or unstable governments. So, corruption is not just a cultural or moral issue but also an economic and political concern too. The idea to combat corruption has also been around, but the notion of executing anti-corruption efforts has just remained a notion in many cultures. However, one knows that strong organizational and national cultures can have a strong positive influence on ethical behaviors. There are several forms of corruption, but the most common form that exists around the world today is bribery. Bribery is the act of offering something of value, usually money, in order to gain an advantage, typically regarding obtaining a contract with a government. The emergence of trade and commerce has brought not only globalization, but also corruption. Corruption, moreover, has been deeply rooted in many nations and societies as well as within several people as a way of life. However, the essence of corruption has now spread within the corporate world, where it has become one of the most uncontrollable events despite national laws and treaties aimed at combatting corruption. Corruption is an epidemic, where some of the treatments "prescribed" may not work. This epidemic that exists today, according to experts, comes in various forms, including:

- *Grand corruption:* a form of corruption that exists between the heads of state, ministers and other senior officials. It serves the interests of a small group of politicians and business people.
- *Political corruption:* a form of corruption that involves lawmakers (i.e. monarchs, dictators, legislators, etc.) who seek bribes or other financial rewards for their own political or personal benefit. In return most of these officials provide political favors to their supporters usually at the expense of the public.
- *Petty corruption:* exists when small amounts of money are used to make routine transactions by lower level government officials, such as customs clearance or the issuance of building permits, go more quickly and smoothly. The term "grease money" is also used in this "petty" context.
- *Administrative corruption:* includes the usage of favoritism or bribery between certain individuals and private businesses (i.e. to lower taxes, escape regulations, etc.).
- *Systematic corruption:* a form of corruption that exists throughout all levels of society.
- *Corporate corruption:* a form of corruption that arises among individuals in private business corporations with their suppliers

and/or clients. Most corporate corruption occurs at the higher levels as they are used for private gains, usually at the expense of shareholders; who are most often unaware of these acts.

Corruption is normally seen within the public and private sectors of international business. It can arise from several different situations, including ambiguous laws and regulations, weak enforcement of anti-corruption laws, the opportunity to abuse power; and corruption is very common among the political elite, which can be seen within the political and economic sectors throughout the world. One important anti-corruption law, which also has been formulated into an international treaty, is the U.S. Foreign Corrupt Practices Act, which makes bribing foreign government officials to wrongfully direct business to oneself or one's company a serious criminal wrong. However, the law is vaguely written, and also contains exceptions (that is, legal "bribes") for "facilitating and expediting" payments to foreign officials (that is, "grease money") as well as payments to foreign officials, including travel, lodging, and meals, as well as "good will gifts," that are legitimate and reasonable and directly related to the demonstration and explanation of a company's good and services. The U.S. Department of Justice, which enforces the statute, of course needs evidence of the bribe, which evidence may be difficult to secure overseas.

Different forms of corruption within any nation can hinder economic growth, which is vital and necessary especially for Third World and developing nations. Initially, the notion of corruption begins in the culture, where it grows in its environment and spills over into the nearby societies. In the preliminary years, when trade first began between people of different backgrounds, a breeding ground was created, where bribery also evolved. Bribery is the main type of corruption that exists in most developing nations and transition economies. As globalization evolved, the benefits derived from it increased; however, the spread of globalization resulted in a high growth of corruption on all levels. In fact, through the spread of globalization, industrialized nations began to invest in developing countries through foreign direct investment (FDI), where plant factories were established. High levels of investments continue today through FDIs in several countries, as it is seen as a source of capital for most developing nations and its people. However, the disadvantage of FDI includes most forms of corruption practices. In fact, it seems that local corruption can dissuade foreign direct investment in developing nations, thus deterring multinational firms to invest in other countries. Most international investors who invest heavily in FDI plants and factories in developing countries rarely recognize that their managers are the ones who engage in any form of corruption with the local officials in order to obtain permits, taxes, health inspections, etc. In fact, once the investments have been made, local officials are more than likely to threaten or complicate matters and raise obstacles to success unless they are bribed.

To a certain extent, managers are "pushed" into engaging in the act of bribery due to corrupt local officials; however, preventions can be made if the international managers are willing to work with the long processes from international banks. In addition, during times of crisis, which are very common in developing and third world countries, local corruption may discourage FDI due to international banks helping international creditors bail out of a country faster than international investors; since this will prevent bank loans from defaulting. For example, in countries where there is a high level of political risk, where a military coup d'etat is likely to occur, or in Asia where the currency crisis occurred, international bailouts of creditors took precedence in order to avoid massive defaults. The World Bank, IMF and the Group of Seven (G-7) countries (Canada, France, Germany, Italy, Japan, United Kingdom, and the United States) all provide assistance packages during times of crisis for international creditors, however the same is not done for international investors, which deters investors to be involved in direct investments overseas, specifically in countries with a high corruption rate. Although corrupt local officials are to be blamed most of the time for engaging in any forms of corruption, so too are international investors and managers of direct foreign investment, who are highly prone to initiate bribery or engage in different forms of corruption when conducting business in exploited nations. The critical role played by ethical government officials, international bankers, and managers, especially during times of crisis, to prevent and punish corruption and bribery, will go a long way to encourage legitimate investment and business and thus advance economic development.

Summary

There are several areas in which corruption needs to be reduced and can be reduced, especially where organizations such as the International Monetary Fund (IMF) and the World Bank are largely involved. These organizations are helping nations to be rid of corrupt officials at the national and local levels in order to combat corruption at the international level by providing incentives through monetary aid. There are several ways that corruption can be combated, including having the IMF and World Bank insure that all bank loans are used effectively and efficiently, where other financial institutions can prevent fraud in projects that they finance. International institutions need to fight corruption at the macro level, while at the same time; the national governments must contest it at the national and local levels in order to manage corruption. This can be seen in countries such as Singapore, where there are very low levels of corruption amongst the government officials, citizens, local officials, and MNCs due to the strict enforcement of penalties that exist for such crimes. If other nations followed the example of Singapore, then they too can provide a safe haven for their citizens and international investors, as well as attract high levels of foreign direct investment.

There are other ways to prevent corruption; however, combating it effectively lies in the hands of national governments that must enforce anti-corrupt regulations at the local levels. Until universal policies and regulations as well as moral standards are implemented and enforced, this epidemic of corruption and bribery in business will continue. For many societies today, corruption and bribery are the norm, and worse yet, the moral norm. Yet, fortunately, presently, many public sector officials and private sector leaders are taking appropriate steps to make sure their local and national business environments are fair and ethical for all parties involved.

Questions for Discussion

1. What is ethics? How does it differ from the terms "legality," "morality" and "values"?
2. What is social responsibility? Discuss two examples of companies that are considered to be socially responsible.
3. What is corruption? What causes corruption? Is corruption wrong if one is only using it to get rid of red tape and speed up

the process of getting one's organizational paperwork completed faster? Discuss.

4. Can the national culture be an influence on business behavior in a country? Discuss examples to support your answer.

5. Can communism values increase ethical behavior? Discuss the specifics of your answers and provide examples.

6. Do multinational corporations bribe officials and governments agents in foreign cultures? Discuss the rules for two different countries. Can such bribes ever be moral pursuant to ethics? Why or why not? Provide examples.

7. What distinction does the U.S. Foreign Practices Act make between illegal and legal "bribes"? Provide an example and explanation for each.

CHAPTER 8

Stress Management

We live in work environments that seem to be full of inevitable conflict, change and stress. While workplace conflict, change and stress cannot be eliminated they can and should be managed effectively in order to have a productive workplace. There are professionals and even managers who get frustrated and lose their temper over routine and non-routine issues. Such incidents can negatively impact the morale of the department and lead to much undue stress in the workplace.

While being frustrated, sad, and angry might be a reality of life in the twenty-first century workplace, this chapter provides a realistic perspective on how a person can be driven by emotions during a frustrating moment which can lead to health problems and undesirable outcomes. The chapter provides suggestions on how stressful situations and interpersonal conflicts should be managed through effective people skills, such as the "inside-out-approach," and intrapersonal communication. By offering a model, the chapter emphasizes that instead of reacting based on the emotions during interpersonal conflicts, professionals should respond based on their predetermined personal and organizational values.

What is Stress?

Stress has many meanings to different people. Simply, anything to which the body has to react or adapt to can be termed stress. *Eustress* describes the good or positive things that happen. Eustress is motivating and can initiate creativity and positive mental attitudes. *Distress* describes negative de-motivating stress that can oftentimes place an individual in a situation of inactivity or inertia. There are, inevitably hundreds of definitions that can be found in the literature. The most common may be that stress is defined as a response or as a stimulus. It would appear that the most popular accepted concept of stress is that there is a stressor (which can be anything) that triggers off or has a response to (stress) either eustress or distress.

Stress develops when the pressures and demands in one's life exceed one's ability to cope (distress). When the individual is motivated, creative, and finds balance in the major environments in which they function, the stress becomes eustress. More than 200 million Americans take medication for stress-related illnesses and symptoms. American organizations are losing more than $200 billion each year in workplace accidents, absenteeism, drug abuse, violence, medical insurance, and productivity. In England, the government sponsored a survey in the spring of 2004 to examine psychosocial working conditions in the British workplace prior to the launch of the Management Standards for Stress. Areas such as work, alcohol consumption and ill health, best practices in rehabilitating employees, reducing psycho-social risks, etc. were studied with recommendations.

High levels of distress, or dysfunctional stress, can have fatal consequences such as illness that lead to death, suicide and other forms of violence. For example, during a two-year period in 2012-2013, supposedly there were over 23,000 people killed due to gun violence in the United States. Unfortunately, people might be resorting to such fatal forms of violence due to their exposure to extreme forms of stress, or other mental illnesses. Often, veterans of war go through high levels of stress during their deployment and such prolonged exposures to extreme distress can lead to traumatic illnesses long after the war is over. It has been said that during the last decade when American soldiers have been involved in wars in Iraq and Afghanistan, more veterans have committed suicide in the United States of America than were killed in both of these war-torn countries. So being exposed to high levels of stress can be very dangerous to one's health. As such, everyone needs to effectively manage their stress at home and in the workplace.

The "Cat Kicking" Workplace

We live in a *"cat kicking"* world and office conflicts and stresses should be effectively handled before employees leave for home. If office issues are not handled at work, then a person who is unfairly blamed or "kicked in the behind" by his or her colleagues at work is likely to take it out on other innocent people on the way home or in the house. Have you ever seen a person get mad and lose his or her temper over a minor concern or no issue whatsoever? In such cases, it is clear that there is something deeper that is causing the person's frustration and it has nothing to do with what is going on at the moment. For example, if you are walking in the park to get some exercise and the man coming from the opposite direction says "WHAT ARE YOU looking at?" in a loud and frustrated voice, then you know that your walk in the park is certainly not something that has angered him. There must have been something else that has angered him before this occurrence. Perhaps someone at the office unfairly blamed him for something that he did not even do. Or, maybe he was not given proper credit which he rightly deserves for quality work that he did do. However, now he is taking his frustrations out on others. He might even go home and get into a fight with his wife over a minor issue. Of course, the wife may not understand his anger and will feel sad because she works hard all day long just like him, comes home to take care of the family, and hopefully relax a little before the next day's hectic work schedule but instead gets blamed for no reason by her husband (who happens to be upset from what took place at his office). Now, the wife is upset and stressed…and she may take it out on the teenage children by yelling at them for no reason. The children will be unhappy because they are not clear on why the parents are mad at them when they have done nothing wrong. Thus, they will be unhappy and upset and may just end up taking out their frustrations by simply "kicking the cat" that is innocently walking by and looking for some affection. So, the anger that was caused at the office is now being passed on to others, and there is a snowball effect, even impacting the little cat in the house.

Being frustrated, sad, and even angry at times is a fact of life for most employees in the workplace at one time or another. However, instead of being driven by emotions, as adults, we need to realize and exercise our freedom to choose our responses for the circumstances that happen to us. Instead of responding based on the emotions of the moment, one can choose to respond based on his or her predetermined and clarified values. Consequently, mature human beings do not have to allow daily politics or other office "stuff" to make them angry. Mature individuals who exercise their freedom to choose can determine how, when, how long, and for whom to demonstrate their frustrations in a strategically fruitful manner. Good behavior begets more good behavior. Similarly, good deeds encourage more good deeds.

Therefore, good behavior and good deeds are contagious. Management, as role models, need to be the change that they desire from others. As it is commonly believed that the way others treat us is simply a mirror of our own actions, the "inside-out-approach" focuses on changing one's own conduct in order to attract others toward good deeds and appropriate behavior in the workplace.

Workplace Frustration

The reality of every workplace has been that there are many diverse personalities on each team and department. Perhaps it might be true that some people are more prone to be creative, innovative, opportunistic, or even problematic in the workplace than others based on diversity or homogeneity of their outlook on life. If a person sees the glass as "half full," then he or she is likely to have a positive outlook on life and might trust others by giving them the benefit of the doubt. On the other side, if a person is distrusting of people and believes that this world has scarce resources and opportunities then his or her outlook about the workplace might be that it is "survival of the fittest" in a "dog-eat-dog world," and you must do what you can to get ahead. Therefore, as an opportunistic individual, he or she might choose to get involved in unethical politicking or even backstabbing in a competitive workplace. Of course, regardless of whether the existence of such opportunistic behaviors and individuals are real or perceived, we do know that the true feelings of the "self-proclaimed victims" as well as their levels of stress are very much real.

A frustrated colleague once called during an evening crying, and saying that the secretary in her department is "from hell." When asked what is the real problem? She forcefully replied that "The secretary is the problem, not me." The secretary is a 66-year old accomplished woman who has supposedly been described as a "rude and mean old lady" by several people in the department. The secretary is supposedly the devil of the office, and she is ruining her days and evenings. Therefore, she should quit the job and work elsewhere. This colleague mentioned that she does everything right, and the obnoxious and rude secretary still complains to the boss about her performance and productivity. Furthermore, the colleague reiterated her perception of the issue that the problem is with the "rude" and egotistical secretary who was causing difficulties for everyone in the department by being friendly with the boss and passing on misinformation about each employee's overall performance. Such perceptions and feelings of frustration are real for many professionals in a competitive work environment. If such stresses and frustrations are not handled effectively, they can lead to minor or even major psychological and physiological health problems.

Dealing with Frustrations and Anger

When you think the problem is "out there" (with other people or the secretary), then that very thinking is the problem. The problem is this perception and allowing others (like the secretary) to make you upset. You can choose to ignore others. On the other hand, you can choose to be friends with the secretary. And, you can choose to be pleasant to the secretary. The word "choose" has been purposely emphasized because, between the stimulus and response, human beings have the freedom to choose their attitude toward what others do. Between the stimulus and response, there exists the freedom to choose one's responses. Six hours after work, this colleague was at home and she was still "allowing" or choosing to allow what the secretary did during the day to make her night upsetting and miserable. She needs to realize that she can choose not to be upset by other people's actions, words, and behaviors hours after it happened. She needs to keep in mind that she truly has the "freedom" not to allow the secretary's statements to bother her for hours, nights, and days. In such events, she should step back, take deep breaths, relax for a few moments, and think about why she is being bothered. If it is over a minor issue, then she can choose to ignore it. If it is an issue that needs to be resolved, then she should plan to confront it in the right way at the next appropriate time before it becomes a bothersome issue that ruins her hour, day, or night.

Perhaps, one cannot control what the secretary does, or what one's parents do, but one can control his/her response to it. And, one can control his/her own attitude (i.e., being neutral, being happy, or being upset). Of course, being upset or angry does not produce many positive results....usually it is a wasted emotion, and it can be contagious when one is working with other people. So, this colleague could choose to ignore the secretary and focus on her job or personal goals in the department; and this will be a better use of her time. You will always get better results by exercising your "freedom" to choose. She can choose to quit her job and this might eliminate the problem or stress. However, regardless of the job or industry, there are always going to be some rude individuals with personalities similar to that of the secretary who is supposedly causing her chronic stress. While one can certainly choose to quit a job in order to get away from the real or perceived problem, a better option might be to simply confront the secretary and appropriately deal with the "real" or "perceived" challenges. It might be possible that the secretary is not really the problem. In that case, the employee needs to look in the mirror as everything she receives from others might simply be a reflection of her own behaviors! If this is the case, then she needs to change things from "an inside-out" approach. When she changes her behavior, she might notice that the world responds to her accordingly.

The "inside-out" approach requires recognizing and acknowledging that between the stimulus and response there exists a momentary opportunity when one can choose to act based on emotions or predetermined values. In other words, as visually demonstrated in Figure 8.1, one can respond reactively (based on emotions, feelings, and other variables surrounding the event), or one can respond proactively based on his or her values, goals and long-term strategic vision. Professionals that want to be respected by their customers, employees, colleagues, and superiors should remain cool and calm in stressful circumstances and strategically respond in a proactive manner to achieve their personal and organizational goals.

Figure 8.1 – The Stimulus-Response Model

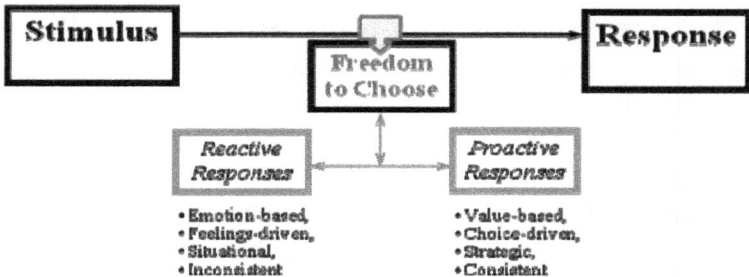

Avoid Being Angry or Upset

In today's competitive workplace, one cannot avoid the realities of being upset or angry at times. It is okay for a person to be upset, angry, or to even cry for a few moments when it is appropriate or when it helps one to feel better temporarily. But too much of it might not be good for one's health, nor will it produce better results. So, it is good to stay focused on the pre-determined goals and things that are under one's control (rather than wasting energy or crying about things that cannot be changed). If you get upset every now and then...this just means that you are a human being with emotions, wants, and desires. It is also a fact that all human beings want to be recognized for their contributions. Sometimes individuals allow other people's behavior to influence their "mood" during the hour, day, night, or even week. There is no reason to "allow" or permit other people to influence you negatively. Never allow anyone, including your superiors, to abuse you verbally or physically. Exercise your rights and know that you can choose, and you have the freedom to choose, your response and future actions. Choose your responses and actions based on your values and goals, not emotions.

It is best to keep in mind that the problem is usually not "out there" or with other people. Often times, the problem is our response to what happens to us. While we cannot always change what happens to us or when and how it happens, the good thing is that we can choose our response to what happens to us. Furthermore, we can alter our personal behaviors and conducts using the "inside-out-approach" in order to be the role models of how we want others to behave. Remember that "It is never the event that makes one feel or do anything—it is how we perceive, judge or evaluate it that makes a difference in the behavior or attitude." Every human emotion is a valid one; the key is how we manage or respond to it—be it appropriate, inappropriate, or indifferent. In every single emotional situation there is never just one way to think, feel, or act.

Be a Professional in the Workplace

Just like most employees, managers can also face complex challenges when it comes to behavior alignment in the workplace, especially when their personal values are in direct conflict with the department's expectations. Professionals must understand that there can be no question as to a manager's responsibility regarding fairness, diversity awareness, and being culturally competent in managing a diverse workforce or "rude" individuals. As a professional manager or agent of an organization, one must treat people with respect and dignity, and ensure that internal customers (associates and vendors) treat each other with respect and dignity. There can be no question as to a manager's responsibility regarding being culturally competent when managing a multicultural workforce or interacting with a diverse customer base. An effective and competent leader and manager must create and maintain an inclusive work environment for all employees by choosing to exercise the freedom to respond based on predetermined values.

Managers have a right to receive training in the area of diversity and understand the organization's expectations regarding cultural competency and behavioral alignment. Similarly, when one's personal values and the departmental expectations are in conflict, managers can use professionalism to meet the organization's expectations and to achieve the goals of having a fair and an inclusive work environment where the natural externalities are teamwork, synergy, and a productive workforce.

Today's associates come from diverse backgrounds and have a variety of experiences and personal values. Therefore, it is important to jointly discuss with everyone and emphasize the relationship between personal inclinations, professionalism, and organizational expectations as well as what to do if there is a conflict between one's personal values and the department's expectations. As taught to thousands of managers, the following definitions can be helpful in understanding this concept:

- *Personal inclinations* are responses based largely on personal feelings and values.
- *Professionalism* (or the bridge between personal inclination and organizational expectations) is about having the requisite skills and experiences in a particular field, industry and profession.
- *Personal alignment* is about adapting one's personal behavior to be compatible with the character and values of the organization. In such a case, one is not required to change his or her values; however, one must align his or her behavior in the workplace to meet the standards established or expected by the organization or agency.

For example, let us say that a manager, due to his or her personal inclinations tends to only believe in a marital relationship between a man and a woman, has attended a diversity workshop. As a result of this training or development, he or she does not have to change his or her personal values. However, since this manager or employee is a professional in his or her field, he or she is expected to behave according to the needed industry standards and expectations to treat each one of his or her employees and colleagues with respect and dignity regardless of their sexual orientation or personal inclinations. In other words, this employee or manager would need to use professionalism as a bridge between his/her own personal inclinations and the expectations of the company when the two are in conflict. Regardless of one's personal view or inclinations, professionals and managers are expected to behave within the law, industry or departmental policies, and the boundaries of fair and ethical treatment of all individuals in the workplace.

Professionalism also implies being focused on the facts of the situation. Effectively resolving conflicts and bringing a successful closure to stressful interpersonal incidents can speed up a team's progress toward achieving its purpose. When dealing with day-to-day conflicts, misconducts, and disagreements, one can use the 4-F model by clarifying and emphasizing the facts, feelings, future expectations, and following up when appropriate.

The 4-F model (facts, feelings, future expectations, and follow-up) provides the facts and expects a change in behavior or the discovery of a new method or process. Discovering the right response in each changing moment requires having an open mind as well as an open heart to see new opportunities and the way things are, and then the way they can be. Change is a choice for learning, creativity, flexibility, and growth; and effective conflict management is the key to bringing about change in an efficient manner. Amid all the change, it is best to remember that flexibility allows one to stretch rather than shrink, and proactively welcoming and embracing change is about choosing a better or pre-determined future. Furthermore, choosing to be synergistic, while involving everyone in the stress and change management process, can transform a "personal" vision into a "professional" vision for everyone in the department or the organization. Being a professional in the workplace also means keeping good relationships with the people you meet and never burning your bridges as you may need to cross over them some day in the future.

If you have ever been given the advice to "never burn your bridges" then it is safe to assume that you know that the "bridge" being referred to is not the relationship itself, but the road back to the relationship. If that road has been damaged the chances of you having the right to return to the relationship are limited if not impossible. Burning your bridges is just like eating too much sugar, it gives you short-term uplift, but in the long-term, it is not good for you. Instead of thinking how horrible the situation or the person has been to you, it might be best to leave the past behind and reflect about your life's important goals and be thankful of the opportunities you have received. Move on and leave the bridges exactly as you found them.

The average person spends too much time on many mundane things on a daily basis because their urgency-driven world works that way. While that may be true for most of us in different stages of our lives, it is important that we take time to appreciate others and be thankful for what we have in life. Yesterday is the past; tomorrow is the future; and neither of these times can be of much use to us at the present time. However, our time right now is a gift called "present" and we should make the best use of it while we have it because once it is gone, it is gone forever and it becomes part of the past.

Summary

A certain level of stress, change and conflict is inevitable and a fact of life in today's workplace. Therefore, everyone should gain the needed skills to effectively manage stress, change and interpersonal conflicts in a professional manner. Instead of complaining about interpersonal conflicts or blaming others for having a "rude" personality, one should reflect on the fact that a person can "choose" his/her responses, and thus does not have to allow other individuals like a rude person who is having a bad day, a politically motivated colleague, or an incompetent teammate to ruin his/her day, night, or week. Just because someone loses his or her temper during a frustrating moment does not mean that this person is "rude" or "mean" all the time. Furthermore, just because someone is older than you and near retirement age does not mean he or she is going to be "rude" or "mean" to his or her younger colleagues.

At times, there might be a few negative and opportunistic individuals who may try to make you feel angry, sad or bad...but you can choose not to fall into their trap. As a professional in the workplace, you can be smarter than them, and exercise your "freedom to choose" an appropriate response; and choose based on your values and goals. Most importantly, choose to be happy, and demonstrate a positive attitude regardless of others' intentions and actions!

Discussion Questions

1. What is stress? Define and discuss examples of distress and eustress.
2. How is stress created and what can you do effectively deal with it?
3. Do we have the "freedom to choose" our response in every situation in life? Discuss.
4. What is professionalism? Provide specific behavioral examples of effective "professionals" in difficult situations in the workplace. How were these difficult situations handled?
5. What does it mean when people say "don't burn your bridge"? Discuss examples and consequences.

Survey: Overload Stress Inventory

The survey is designed to provide a person the extent to which being overloaded with tasks and responsibilities might be a source of stress. For each of the following questions in the inventory, select (or circle) an answer that best describes your agreement or disagreement regarding each statement. Higher scores indicate stronger tendencies toward those elements.

You can choose to complete this survey online along with the task and relationship orientation at the following link: http://www.huizenga.nova.edu/survey/TROSI

Questions	Disagree............Agree
1. I regularly take work home to finish in the evenings or weekends.	1 2 3 4 5
2. I have more work than it is possible to complete at a given time.	1 2 3 4 5
3. I have many important deadlines which I cannot always meet.	1 2 3 4 5
4. More often, I feel less competent on tasks than I think I should.	1 2 3 4 5
5. I do not always have enough time to do as good of job as I am capable of doing.	1 2 3 4 5
6. I am usually given more work than my current qualifications and skills.	1 2 3 4 5
7. Despite the fact that I am usually busy, I often fall behind schedule and deadlines.	1 2 3 4 5
8. Most of my tasks are usually too difficult and/or too complex to complete.	1 2 3 4 5
9. I have too many tasks and jobs needing done all at the same time.	1 2 3 4 5
10. There are many times that I feel overwhelmed by my tasks and assignments.	1 2 3 4 5
Add Total Score for Inventory:	

Interpretation of Overload Stress Inventory:

Scores in the range of 40 – 50 tend to mean *severe* stress from overload. It might be best to take appropriate steps to prioritize and/or reduce the number of stressful tasks and activities you are currently handling.

Scores in the range of 30 – 39 tend to mean *high* stress from overload. Perhaps it is best to prioritize tasks and work on managing those that are direct causes of your stress.

Scores in the range of 20 – 29 tend to mean *moderate* stress from overload. These ranges mean that you might experience the impact of overload at times, but this is normal and tolerable level of stress. You are able to successfully control this level of work and/or overload.

Scores in the range of 19 and below tend to mean *low* stress from overload. Perhaps you have an appropriate number of tasks with properly designed deadlines. It may also indicate that you are managing your time effectively and you feel comfortable with your current workload and responsibilities.

CHAPTER 9

Teamwork and Performance

While all functions of management are critical for productivity and efficiency, one important function of managers is the building and organization of effective teams. High performing teams are made up of members that make work fun and show camaraderie, and they can greatly enhance the long-term value of any department and organization.

According to the experts, high performing teams bring "talent," "difference," and "variety" to the mix, which, when managed effectively, can set the ground for creating a unique competitive advantage for an organization through the firm's human resource asset which is difficult to duplicate for competitors. By becoming aware of today's teams and teamwork and their impact on a company, one can learn effective ways of dealing with prospective complex projects.

Teams and Groups

A *team* is a group of people who are mutually dependent on one another to achieve a common goal. Advantages of working in a team can include the results, how the job gets done, improved communication, organizational learning, and personal satisfaction. Disadvantages of being on a team can include time, individual performance, and conflict, to name but a few.

Teamwork is the coordinated efforts of a *team* working toward a common goal. Because, *T*ogether *E*veryone *A*chieves *M*ore! Of course, it is the performance of each individual that makes or breaks a team. Some say that there is no "I" in "team" and this can provide an inaccurate perception of the responsibility that goes with being a team member. Perhaps, it could be stated as *"Together every individual achieves more"* to emphasize the impact of personal or individual responsibility within the team. A team is different than a traditional group of people working together.

A *working group* relies primarily on the individual contributions of its members for group performance. Working groups thrive in hierarchical structures where individual accountability counts the most such as with individualistic cultures. The following are some common elements of a working group:

- In groups, members usually work toward a common goal.
- Members of groups usually are accountable to managers or higher authorities.
- Leadership in groups is usually assigned to one person or through a matrix structure.
- The culture between members of groups is usually not clear and can cause conflict.

A *team* strives for "synergy;" a magnified impact that is incremental to what its members could achieve in their individual roles. Teams require both individual and mutual accountability. The choice, of remaining a working group or forming a team, depends largely on whether individual achievements can deliver the group's performance aspirations, or whether collective work-products, skills, and mutual accountability are needed. When compared to groups, teams have members who are totally committed to the goal and mission (that they developed or aspired to) for the project. Everyone in the team is accountable to each other. Teams usually have a culture of collaboration that usually leads to trust between the members. Team members agree on a common approach to achieve the performance challenge. Finally, leadership in a team is usually shared between all members and/or, at least those that are highly respected by everyone. Overall, key elements of a team are:

- Limited number of individuals with complementary skills,
- Commitment to a common purpose and performance goals,
- Commitment to an agreed upon strategy, and
- Mutual accountability.

It is estimated that all large organizations will have some type of self-managed work team. Some common forms of teams are functional teams, cross-functional teams, virtual teams, and self-managed teams.

There is always a "learning curve" for each team member through which s/he must climb. However, learning is not enough to become a high-performing team. Each team member's behavior may need to change as well. Behavioral changes can be the most difficult part of teamwork, and it can be very uncomfortable at the outset. The "team performance curve" illustrates how well groups of people perform based on their approach and implementation plans. The following are possible variations of groups and teams shown on the team performance curve (Katzenbach and Smith, 2005).

1. Working group
2. Pseudo-team
3. Potential team
4. Real team
5. High-performing team

A potential team needs a unique blend of actions, events, and decisions in order to move up the curve and achieve high performance as a real team. Real teams do not emerge unless the individuals on them take risks involving conflict, trust, interdependence, and hard work. Real teams learn how to deal with such concerns through frank and open communication. Building the team's performance requires each leader (and team member) to:

- Establish urgency and direction.
- Select members based on skills and skill potential, not personalities.
- Pay particular attention to first meetings and actions.
- Set clear rules of behavior.
- Set and seize upon a few immediate performance-oriented tasks and goals.
- Challenge the group regularly with fresh facts and information.
- Spend lots of time together.
- Exploit the power of *positive feedback, recognition,* and *reward.*

"Team building" can give a powerful boost to the spirit and effectiveness of any group. Well designed and delivered team building programs can lead to better understanding, clearer alignment and much stronger motivation.

Characteristics of Great Teams

Great teams are consciously created to accomplish specific objectives. Great teams require development through various stages of forming, storming, norming, performing, and adjourning. Most researchers and leaders agree that great teams have certain common characteristics. The following are characteristics of great teams identified by Pat Williams, General Manager of the Orlando Magic Basketball team. We were both speaking in Chicago for the same organization as he presented these characteristics at the *Excellence in Management* Conference (June, 1998). According to Pat Williams, great teams have or exhibit the following character traits:

1. *Top talent.* Great teams consist of great talents. Each member of the team is talented in his/her vocation. Furthermore, each member of a great team must be teachable and inspired to learn.
2. *Outstanding leadership.* High performing teams have outstanding leadership. Leadership skills are learned through education, experience, and hard work. Bobby Bowdin, Head Football Coach at Florida State University, once said that "... No one is born a leader. Everyone must work in developing his/her leadership skills." Most researchers agree that leaders have:
   - A vision of the future for themselves and others.
   - Great communication skills and the ability to clearly communicate their thoughts.
   - An optimistic perspective on daily obstacles and situations.
   - Excellent motivation skills and are great motivators or cheerleaders in their organizations and communities.
   - Character traits of integrity, honesty, and a strong work ethic.
   - Competence in their vocation and avocation.
   - Boldness and are able to make decisions based on what they know. And
   - A servant mentality and orientation.
3. *Total commitment.* High performing teams are totally committed to their cause, people, quality, and purpose. They are achievement-oriented and very competitive in nature, because they understand that competition brings out the best in each individual.

4. *Passion for the cause*. Great teams are passionate about what they do, their cause, and achievement. Team members are always upbeat, enthusiastic, and moving. They enjoy what they do and communicate their passion to others.

5. *Think teams*. Great teams have the philosophy of *"less me and more we."* Each member is willing to do what it takes to help the team achieve its purpose.

6. *Empower each other*. High-performing teams are able to feed and motivate each other to accomplish what may appear beyond their capability. Members of great teams constantly build people up. Abraham Lincoln once said "there is nothing stronger than quiet gentleness" and great teams are gentle to themselves and to others. They are also great with their children and family members. Research shows that people, specifically males, want to satisfy their fathers. Research with male prisoners have shown that majority of them have had some type of a dysfunctional relationship or problem with their fathers. Members of high-performing teams are able to positively empower people, both in their personal and professional lives, in a gentle and caring way.

7. *Build trust and respect*. Great teams are constantly building trust among themselves and their colleagues, customers, suppliers, and community members. Team members respect each person as an individual and see something positive in everyone.

8. *Have members with strong character*. High-performing teams are made up of people with strong character who exhibit:
   - Faith in a higher power.
   - Integrity, honesty and maturity.
   - Humility.
   - Influence by positively affecting others. And,
   - Courage in their conviction.

Building High-Performing Teams

Price Pritchett and Ron Pound (1992), in their writings (such as *"Teamwork: The Team Member Handbook")*, offer many practical steps for building a high-performance team that starts with improving oneself and one's team members. The following are some of their suggestions with brief explanations that assist managers in applying the concepts toward building a high-performance team.

Push For High Quality Communication. Communication keeps teamwork alive. It is crucial to the coordination effort. No other factor plays such an important role in building and preserving trust among teammates. Everyone in the group needs to know what is happening and what is going to happen. The information network should connect all the individuals of the team. Teammates should meet, discuss and be involved in very open communication. Encourage members to give their opinions and to discuss their differences. This is the only way the team can achieve understanding, find out the best approach, and end up with "buy-in" by everyone. The individual needs to serve as a "relay person" helping to send information to teammates. Anyone who is left out, gets the information too late, or does not get it at all can destroy the coordination effort. Every member of the team needs to be a quality control person in the communication process, making sure that the data is accurate, up-to-date and meaningful. Any teammate that makes a move based on misinformation can ruin the group's efforts. Be sure to send clear and timely messages. Inaccurate and late messages can cause conflict and disorganization that can limit or damage the group's performance. Remember that accurate, timely communication is the key to high quality teamwork.

Bring Talent To The Team. The essence of teamwork is to be good at what you do. Teams need talented individuals. The more talent you have the more you can contribute. Improve your skills and you will be improving the team. "Strive for continuous improvement-the Japanese call it kaizen- so the team never stops growing." Keep improving your current skills and learning new ones and you can improve the team's scores. If you level off your learning, the potential of the group is not as high. If you are to be relied upon, you must be competent. Master the fundamentals of the job and bring your individual talent to the group. Never stop learning and improving. Give teammates good reasons to believe in you. Keep getting better at what you do.

Play Your Position. Find out the duties, standards of performance, time frames and deadlines you are supposed to meet. Know what is expected of you for your job and/or your assignment. "Play your position." Teamwork, by definition, implies interdependence. Some people in the unit depend on you for their success; if you fail you may cause them to fail. If you are not at your own position you may change the timing of the entire team. Your teammates may have to bail you out, abandoning their own assignments. Sometimes you may need to cover for teammates, however do not get in their way. It is best to support your teammates by playing your own position perfectly.

Turn Diversity to the Team's Advantage. In a team, differences can add depth, create strength, broaden the group and bring balance. Teams perform best when the team members bring a variety of abilities, experiences, personalities, and problem solving approaches. But for diversity to make a difference, you have to take advantage of it. Respect and use those individual differences to improve the team. Do not ignore the person who is "different"– whether that person is you or someone else. Do your part to help the team find and benefit from all of its members. Team members who are in the minority should not hamper the team by thinking that they should be treated differently. When someone decides that being "different" means special treatment, it creates controversy and conflict. Diversity can make teamwork seem more difficult at first, however it produces a more powerful team. Respect people's differences, and use everyone's uniqueness to benefit the team.

Back Up Others Who Need Help. Teamwork is helping one another to get the job done in the best possible way and in the shortest period of time. Thinking as a team will improve overall performance and build morale. Know your teammates' assignments and responsibilities. If you see that someone is having a problem, you will be able to back that person up. Being an effective back up means knowing other members' assignments and broadening your skills to cover for them. Cross training is very important to a team. In an emergency situation, any team member can be used as a replacement of another. In a team, an attitude of helpfulness is a necessity. Your teammates will be more eager to help you if you are willing to help them.

Practice. Practice is an important part of performance since it brings one closer to doing it perfectly. Practice gives you a chance to make errors and then find out what is the best way to correct them. You can learn new ways of doing the job or more efficient ways. The team can assess its weaknesses and its strengths by practicing together.

By practicing, the team should be able to meet challenging situations in the real world with a better understanding.

Be Prepared To Sacrifice For the Team. In any organization, there is always a question of "me versus we." This can sometimes cause conflict among team members, deciding whether the individual aspects of the team are the most important or the group as a whole. Sometimes an individual may have to sacrifice his/her own personal interest for the group. The choice may be a difficult one. Keep in mind your teammates will remember the choice you make.

Help New Teammates Make Entry. Life brings changes to us in many ways. We meet many people, some for only an instant. When new teammates appear, it is important to everyone that they succeed. If there is a high rate of turnover, it is because the team was not supportive enough. New teammates should be welcomed, supported, and taught their important role in the group. This will contribute to the success of the team.

Play Down Yourself and Build Up Others. Always point out the importance of the team members. Make it a habit to point out their strengths. Build up their confidence and you will bring success to the team. When someone compliments you, make sure you give credit to the team. If you are selfish in the accomplishments, the team will suffer. This will alienate the other team members. To keep team members feeling appreciated, you must make sure they feel important. Do not concentrate on you, but the team as a whole. Build up your team and they will praise you.

Spend Time With Your Teammates. Getting to know your teammates is necessary to form a cohesive unit. The more you work together as a unit the better your team will be. It is important to have togetherness for the group to be a real team. Set aside time to find out more about each other. This helps to understand each other better. You will be more able to back one another up if necessary. An informal atmosphere is more likely to increase bonding between teammates. So be sure to spend time with your teammates and you will find the togetherness that makes a real team.

Help Drive Discipline into The Group. Each member of a team needs to have self-discipline. The leader cannot be everywhere at once. He/she should not have to keep everyone in line. Individuals need to hold themselves to the highest standard. Discipline in your work is very basic. Doing what needs to be accomplished, living according to the rules, and making sure to follow the standards. Sometimes this may mean making sacrifices, but it will benefit the team. Coordination of a team needs discipline. Discipline helps the team to perform at the highest level, creating trust, reliability, and dependability. There is pride and accomplishment of a job well done in a team that has discipline.

Make Sure You Make a Difference. Making a difference is doing what counts. On a team, it is important that everyone has an equal opportunity. Others on the team may be more talented than you, however if you try hard enough you may find that attitude is more important than talent. Meaningful results come from making a commitment to the team. Be someone who will be missed if you were not a part of the team.

Give Attention To The Group Process. There are always going to be problems when working with a team. Keep an eye on the team's effectiveness. Is the team using its resources efficiently? Are team members confused, or discouraged? If you find any of these problems bring them to the team's attention. Fix a problem when it is small before it becomes too large to handle. The team process has as much to do with its success or failure as does the talent of its members.

Help Create A Climate Of Trust. Trust is a key ingredient to teamwork. Every member of the team needs to be able to believe and rely upon one another. Your behavior is how the team members will know how much you are committed to the team. Be aware that even small violations of trust can destroy the cooperation within a team. Keeping your word, honoring your commitments, being consistent, and playing fair are ways that you can build the climate of trust.

Strengthen The Leader Through Good Followership. Good followers have initiative. They know what to do without being told and can think for themselves. They are able to lead themselves allowing the person in charge more time for other assignments. The responsibility of the follower is to support and strengthen the leader. A commitment to the team's common goals will support your leader. However, sometimes it may be necessary to argue your point, disagree with your orders or to challenge the leader if you feel they are abusing their power. You may need to do this for the good of the group, do not do it for your own personal gain. Do not blindly follow your leader, it is important to have enough knowledge and commitment to make sure your team is being led in a positive direction.

Be a Good Sport. Play fair and respect others. Forgive your team members' mistakes as they are bound to happen. Admit your own mistakes and do not take the criticism from your colleagues personally. When you are praised share that praise with your team members. Do not lift yourself up at the expense of others. Teammates pay attention to your conduct and your attitude. Good sportsmanship creates harmony. Without harmony the team will not be a success.

Synergistic teams have members that share information with each other in a clear manner while building effective relationships by speaking with each other and listening well. In other words, all the members tend to communicate well with each other. The goal of effective communication is to make sure each team member is clear, concise, and credible in what s/he says to others. Getting your point across and getting the results you want requires that you build credibility, use logic and radiate positive emotional power. Using the power of asking effective questions is a good strategy for building credibility as an effective team member or leader.

Team Evaluation Elements

You can evaluate your team's readiness to become a "real team" or a "high-performing team" by making sure the common elements have been considered and appropriately integrated into the "performance challenge" and teamwork process. The following are some of the common elements for team evaluation that have been used in most large corporations:

1. *Leadership*: The team leader has the necessary team management skills.
2. *Authority*: The authority is clear and consistent with the team's responsibility.
3. *Goals*: The team has a clear set of goals.
4. *Decision-making*: Team members have a real opportunity to participate in key team decisions.
5. *Recognition*: Individual members receive appropriate recognition for their contributions to team effort.
6. *Roles*: Members are clear about what is expected of them.
7. *Boundary Management*: The team does a good job of developing relationships with key stakeholders in other parts of the organization.

8. *Performance Appraisal*: Performance on the cross-functional team is included in each member's performance appraisal.
9. *Team Training*: Leaders and members have been trained in team effectiveness skills.
10. *Team Meetings*: Meetings are well planned and executed.
11. *Communication Technologies*: The team makes effective use of non-meeting methods of communication.
12. *Team Size*: The team is small enough to ensure effective communication and decision-making.
13. *Management Support*: Management actively supports the work of the team.
14. *Co-location*: All key team members work in the same location, if possible – otherwise, use technology to stay in touch.
15. *Customers and suppliers*: As appropriate, customer and supplier representatives are included.
16. *Cross Training*: Members receive technical training in other team disciplines and functions.
17. *Openness*: Members feel free to express their views on key issues.
18. *Conflict Resolution*: Differences are resolved openly, constructively, and quickly.
19. *Cultural and Style Differences*: The team appreciates and utilizes the different styles represented on the team.
20. *Customer Focus*: The team's primary emphasis is on satisfying the customer's needs by getting the project done.

One can use a Likert Scale of one to five with one being "strongly disagree" and five being "strongly agree," to create a team score. Then, add all of the points and the higher the score, the better the teamwork! Of course, synergy results when the team's productivity or results are much higher than the sum of the individual parts if each person had worked by himself or herself on the required tasks.

Summary

Teamwork is about working together toward a common vision which usually means following the leader who represents the common vision held by everyone or most individuals. When everyone in the process or value chain is jointly working toward a common goal of providing the best value for consumers or the country, reaching it will become much easier because of the profound impact of synergy. The following "geese fly in formation" visual literally provides the power of teamwork and synergy.

> When
> geese fly
> in formation
> they travel 70
> percent faster than
> when they fly alone. Geese
> share leadership. When the
> lead goose tires, it rotates back into
> the "v," and another flies forward to
> become the leader. Geese keep company
> with the fallen. When a sick or weak goose drops out
> of the Flight's formation, at least one other goose joins to
> help and protect.

There are many lessons which can be learned from the research conducted on geese and they can be applied with teams in the workplace. For example, as each goose flaps its wings, it creates an "uplift" for the bird following. By flying in a "V" formation, the whole flock adds 71% more flying range than if each bird flew alone. The lesson here is that people who share a common direction and sense of community can get where they are going quicker because they are traveling on the thrust of one another.

Whenever a goose falls out of formation, it suddenly feels the drag and resistance of trying to fly alone, and quickly gets back into formation to take advantage of the lifting power of the birds immediately in front. The lesson here is that if we have as much sense as a goose, we will join in formation with those who are headed where we want to go.

When the lead goose gets tired, it rotates back into the formation and another goose flies at the point position. The lesson here is that it is beneficial to take turns doing the hard task and sharing leadership with them – as with geese, they have an interdependent relationship with one another.

The geese in formation honk from behind to encourage those up front to keep up their speed. The lesson here is that we need to make sure our honking from behind is encouraging and motivational, not something less helpful.

When a goose gets sick or wounded or shot down, two geese drop out of formation and follow their fellow member down to help and provide protection. They stay with this member of the flock until he or she is either able to fly again or dies. Then they launch out on their own, with another formation, or to catch up with their own flock. The lesson here is that if we have as much sense as geese, we'll stand by one another like they do. These are principles of teamwork and synergy which must be demonstrated by everyone in the value chain.

Discussion Questions

1. What is the definition of a team and discuss how members of a team contribute to teamwork?
2. How is a team different from a group?
3. How often should the performance of a team be evaluated in the organization? Who should evaluate the performance of a team?
4. What are some of the characteristics of effective teams? Discuss at least five of them.
5. Discuss the essential ingredients for building a high-performing team.
6. What is the role of a designated leader and/or manager of the department in the creation of a high-performing team?
7. What are some best practices in appreciating team members and acknowledging their contributions to the team and the overall department or organization?

CHAPTER 10

Negotiations

It is commonly assumed that treating others the way one wants to be treated is sufficient for healthy interpersonal relationships, and perhaps this is true to some extent. When it comes to negotiations and different cultural practices, the "Platinum Rule" states that one should treat others the way they want to be treated. In other words, negotiators must also study and understand their counterpart's negotiation styles as well. Today's diverse situations and cultures require flexibility in using whatever is relevant for the person, culture and time. In any case, negotiators must plan and strategize based on a standardized process to effectively prepare for a win-win negotiation process. The chapter expands on a four-step model for negotiations which includes initiating or pre-planning, negotiating, closing, and maintaining the relationship or renegotiating when necessary.

Negotiations Process and Steps

Regardless of the process, steps, or model used, negotiators should always open the negotiation by stressing mutual benefits to all parties involved, being clear and positive, implying flexibility, creating interest in the dialogue, demonstrating confidence and trust, and promoting goodwill. These are the imperatives of successful negotiations. Furthermore, it is best to focus on interests, not demands; keep in mind that demands are what you want and interests are why you want them. Demand tends to be somewhat confrontational and it often slows down the negotiation process. Also, create new options for joint gain by focusing on each party's interests that allow for new ideas to come forth. Overall, the bottom-line is to focus on what is fair for each party; keep in mind that emphasizing fairness can allow and encourage both parties to effectively negotiate and eventually agree on a satisfactory solution.

While there can be many processes to a negotiation model, it is best to simplify all the steps into as few as possible so that it can be easily remembered and practiced. For the purposes of a negotiation model, the main steps to a negotiation can be simplified under four categories which are: (1)-Initiating or pre-planning; (2)-Negotiating; (3)-Closing; and (4)-Maintaining the relationship and renegotiating if necessary. Figure 10.1 presents the model in a visual format. As can be seen from the model, an effective negotiation model provides a process along with some general steps as a guide, and focuses on the future by maintaining a good relationship with all parties involved. An effective model emphasizes a win-win objective with a focus on the creation of a long-term relationship, trust and interdependency.

Figure 10.1 – The Negotiation Model

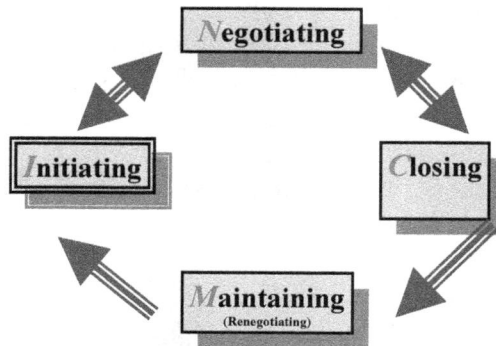

Pre-Planning

Experts mention several key factors in order to prepare for any type of negotiation; and some of these are: 1) define the issues; 2) know the other party's position; 3) know the competition; 4) know the negotiations limits; 5) develop strategies and tactics; and 6) plan the negotiation meeting.

Defining the issue(s). When it comes time to negotiate with an international or local company, you need to first have the objectives of the company clear and defined. These should be based on the interests of the other party in order to start *defining the issues*. The negotiator should define the issues in a clear manner and needs to know what topics are about to be discussed in the meeting or negotiation such as pricing, distribution, agreement condition, and in some cases commission. It is wise to have more than one person in the negotiation research because two heads think better than one.

Knowing one's position. This factor works hand-in-hand with defining the issues. Both parties involved have to work together with the issues or goals of both companies. The tangible goals can include the price, rate, specific terms or contract language in the case of an international transaction. The intangible goals are those that can be suggested to change, for example quality of service.

Knowing the other side's position. This process is like a ladder in which you have to start from the first step to get to the top. It is analogous to a face-to-face meeting process in order to get good results from the final agreement. One best way to research another large company is through the Internet. This tool can help the negotiator in the process of finding much of the information needed about the other company. Analyzing another organization is a long process, and some research methods are needed.

Knowing the competition. This is one of the most important elements of the business world. You start with your "biggest" or fiercest competitor in the market, but never ignore the "smallest" or weakest one because they too are able to make a run or comeback in the market; and they usually have the clients that you want. The best way to know your competitor is to investigate all aspects of their company.

Knowing one's negotiation limits. One must be familiar with the logistic part of the negotiation. Have a standard against which a proposed agreement should be evaluated and this process can make decision-making easier.

Developing strategies and tactics. These two aspects come into consideration in a meeting when all the process and all the hard work pays off. You usually prepare a strategy before any negotiation. Sometimes you do not expect that the meeting will start or finish in a different manner. When this happens, the negotiator needs to use his/her improvization skills. Planning the meeting comes into consideration when determining where the meeting will take place; it can be at your home place or overseas. This is one of the most important aspects of a pre-negotiation because this will determine who has the advantage.

As defined by experts, it is best to remember that *negotiation* is the process of two or more parties that are attempting to reach a mutually beneficial goal through a common course of action or agreement. Of course, relevant individuals from one of the parties must initiate the process. One must also remember that negotiation is a tool, vehicle or instrument by which two or more parties try to reach a "common ground" for win-win objectives. Initiating a negotiation requires cultural competency and sensitivity as well as conflict management, change management, stress management, and effective listening skills.

As part of the pre-planning and before initiating the negotiation process, one must also know his/her counterpart and competitors. Keep in mind that your counterpart is not your competitor. The competitor is the party that is trying to bid for the same relationship with your counterpart or the other party. It is good to assume that your counterpart has studied your competitors and is aware of what they are able to offer or will soon be speaking with them about their offer. Overall, when it comes to competitors, experts suggest that it is best to recognize key organizations, analyze performance records of each, study their satisfaction/complacencies, probe each one's market strategy, and analyze current and future resources, along with competencies of each competitor.

Opening High or Low

When placing an offer the negotiator faces the decision of placing a high or a low offer. If the offer is high there is the risk that the other party might end the negotiation considering this offer unacceptable; and to place the offer too low can result in losing a margin of profits.

An advantage would be to place the offer within the bargaining point of the other party. As such, it is necessary to know their reservation point; but usually negotiators do not have that information to start with. It can be discussed, and through questions, negotiators can get an idea of how far they can go to achieve the maximum possible profit, without having to give their reservation point.

When a high offer is opted, a negotiator has to be very careful not to give concessions right away. The best way to deal with it is through questions and answers, focusing on the disagreements, and after the information is exchanged they can either stand on their initial offer or make a counterproposal that can be based on the information received.

When the offer is low many negotiators do it with the intention of raising the offer once more information is gathered. This is to assure an opportunity to get to the negotiating table. This is a very risky position to take, unless once you have received the information of what the other party wants to have to be willing to make changes and adaptations that get close to what the other party is looking for, and by this you can raise your offer. Different regions in the world have different approaches to the initial offer: "a high initial offer is expected in many countries in Latin America and the Middle East. In highly competitive markets, frequently found in Southeast Asia, North America, and Nordic Europe, opening offers are slightly above the bottom line" (Cellich & Jain, p. 78). This is very important information for negotiators that are dealing in an international arena; they should acquire the necessary information of how business deals are commonly done in the other party's culture, and how proposals should begin. They have to understand that different cultures do negotiations differently than their home country, and gathering that information could help them achieve the most profitable outcome.

It is important to show respect for the other party's culture. This is one of the most important issues in international businesses. People have to research and be informed of what the other party's behavior and culture is, and what they expect from you. When the other party feels that you are interested in learning about them, this is always positive. This application will most likely give successful results; it gives the notion that the party is interested in more than just profits. You have to be patient to get to know the other person and not rush into finalizing the deal. Negotiators have to be careful not to overdo it; this can lead to making the other party feel uncomfortable. There are always limits that have to be set, and even though you want the other party to like you, you cannot expect to get too comfortable with them, you are still doing a business deal.

Making Concessions

Concessions are to be made after the first offer is given. But negotiators are not supposed to give concessions right away; the best way to approach it might be to exchange information by asking what part of the offer is accepted and what are the flaws; with this detail the negotiator can provide information to support their proposal. Objections should be dealt with by questioning; giving both parties the chance to gather information from the other. Once the information needed has been given, the next step is to propose a counteroffer, which can be the original one, or in some cases it can be managed through concessions. When concessions are made parties have to decide how flexible they are willing to be. They can give some concession while expecting the other party to do the same. They have to determine what size of a concession they are willing to make, and be aware of the pattern that concessions are being given by the negotiators. There are several ways to influence the other party to accept your proposal. According published studies, there are several categories, which are reciprocity, consistency, social proof, liking, authority, and scarcity.

Reciprocity. This is defined as the feeling of obligation of one party to make concessions in return for favors. Negotiators take advantage of past or present favors or concessions in order to lead the other party to reciprocate.

Consistency. A negotiator should be consistent with what it has proposed and accepted. It is not favorable if a negotiator agrees on something that they have no intention of doing. What is agreed has to be fulfilled.

Social behavior. This is used in negotiations as a reference point using past behaviors from other sources. A negotiator can use this in order to get a concession, it is important to have proof to support it.

Liking. It is easier to accomplish a negotiation with someone you like. Sometimes negotiators try to influence the deal by making the other party like them. They behave in a way that they know will allow them to be more connected and liked by the other party. A way to achieve this is by presenting them with a gift, or by showing interest in something they know the other party would appreciate.

Authority. When a negotiator shows they have an authority in the subject and decision, this is well seen by the other party. It is important for the negotiator to have the power and authority to give concessions and to discuss the deal.

Scarcity. It is very influential to make an offer seem scarce. People tend to want to acquire things that are considered as unique and rare. If the negotiator makes the other party feel there is something scarce in the negotiation they should hold this information until further talks.

Negotiators have to be concerned and aware that they might face some problems. Sharing information can be beneficial, but both parties have to exchange the same level of information. For example, it is very risky to give your reservation price; that gives the other party the knowledge of how low or high you are willing to go. If negotiators decide to share this information it is important they both respect this agreement. This creates trust between the parties, but will not give a negotiator the desired profit.

When the reservation point is given, negotiators have to be careful because the other party might have lied. This will make the concessions and the negotiation difficult, since wrong information has been given. They might also lie about information rendered to the other party. It is important to ask for proof and documents, or as much data as possible, as well as asking questions to ensure that what has been said will be fulfilled. Making a final offer should take time, and rushing into a deal is not recommended. You have to ensure that the other party is going to comply with what was discussed. Patience is a great quality for effective negotiations. Negotiators should discuss every aspect of the deal to ensure no misunderstandings in the future. Good business relationships will guarantee your company a reputable name and will open potentially lucrative deals in the future. Overall, when negotiating, the following are some general steps to remember and follow:

1. Maintain a positive attitude and negotiate in good will.
2. Focus on developing a relationship.
3. Know your own needs and your counterpart's needs.
4. Be aware of your own and your counterpart's negotiation style.
5. Create a plan with goals and the best way to achieve them.
6. Design and implement a strategy to accomplish goals.
7. Have clear knowledge of the negotiation subject when making first offers.
8. Make the offer.

9. Communicate ideas clearly and precisely.
10. Be sensitive to the other party's idealism and concerns.
11. Know your own and your counterpart's reservation and target points.
12. Exchange information and interests without giving away confidential information.
13. Persuade the other party through logic and rational thoughts.
14. Select wisely between high and low offers.
15. Exchange information and analyze pros and cons of the offer.
16. Propose counteroffers.
17. Be prepared for concession and agreement.
18. Be patience and discuss every aspect of the deal.
19. Always smile and, regardless of the outcome, retain a good relationship.

Long-term relationships and effective networks require maintaining a high level of trust among all parties. Just as it is true in real life between a husband-wife, mother-son, brother-sister, friend-friend, and others to continuously work on the relationship, the same is true for professional business relationships that are successfully negotiated for a common purpose. Of course, a successful negotiation is the beginning of the relationship. If the relationship is maintained with honesty and a win-win attitude, then more business can be gained through this network.

In any case, one must remember that in international negotiations, renegotiations are expected and professionals must handle it with flexibility. Some of the common reasons for renegotiation can include the changing dimensions of international business environment, diverse mechanisms for settling disputes, involvement of government, and cultural differences between nations. Of course, there are some strategies that can be used to reduce the need for another negotiation. Experts recommend that professionals can prevent renegotiation by locking the other party in, balancing the deal, controlling the renegotiation, and building in renegotiation costs.

Negotiation Flowchart
Regardless of the type of an initial negotiation or renegotiations, one must always remember to use effective approaches to clarify

ambiguities in the existing agreement, reinterpret key terms, waiver from one or more requirements of the agreement, rewrite the agreement, and renegotiate with cultural sensitivity.

As demonstrated in the negotiation flowchart (Figure 10.2), before initiating the negotiation, one must gain competency in the culture of one's counterpart as well as in the negotiation process that they are likely to be familiar with and use. Another important point to remember is that one must not begin closing the deal until everyone is satisfied with what has been discussed. Negotiators can use the skills of empathic listening to clarify and/or confirm their understanding. Once everyone has agreed to a mutually-beneficial deal, then the negotiation should be closed. A final and very important point is the learning that comes from the negotiation and renegotiation processes. As appropriate, the negotiating party must assess and evaluate the success of the process once the deal has been closed and after the deal has been implemented. There might be many lessons that can be learned and applied in the future negotiations with the same party or others. If the process has been successful in the long-term, then the team should celebrate this success and further build the relationship and network.

Figure 10.2 –Negotiation Flowchart

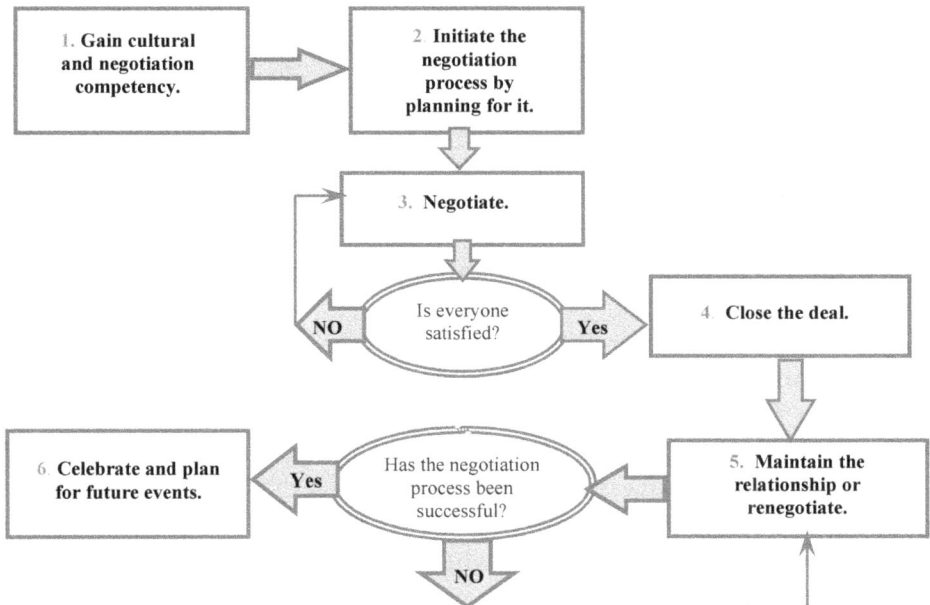

Overall, negotiators must plan and be prepared, they must be patient and respectful, they should know the local language and customs, they should identify key decision makers, they should stay focused on developing a relationship and, finally, they should appreciate cooperation and be thankful for the friendships developed.

Negotiation takes place everywhere, not only between firms but also between friends, family members, coworkers, etc. Because people are naturally conflictive, negotiation becomes vital so differences can be solved peacefully. Negotiation is something that we do constantly, then, there is no doubt that we have engaged in this process more than once in our lives. However, the fact that we negotiate all the time, does not mean that we know how to do it effectively; and at the time of negotiation, effectiveness is what really matters. If negotiators do not accomplish their goals then the negotiation has been useless. Effectiveness becomes even more crucial when poor decisions in a negotiation affect not only one's goals but also that of an organization.

Determine Your Negotiation Styles

Cultures are likely to greatly influence negotiations, because culture, according to Cellich and Jain (2004), "includes all learned behavior and values that are transmitted through shared experience to an individual living within a society (p. 24). The Japanese culture is interrelated. For example, a manager within a company holds prestige over his or her subordinates while in the workplace. This status also extends into the Japanese social arena, where one still upholds the respect for the manager. Also, this culture is upheld by most of its members; implying Hall's third characteristic that culture is shared.   Success in cross-cultural negotiations requires skill and practice to hone one's thinking "muscles" and skills.

To determine your general style of negotiations, complete the questionnaire (Negotiation Style Assessment and Inventory, at the end of this section) provided by Cellich and Jain (2004) by answering the questions based on your opinion and general tendencies when negotiating. The questionnaire is provided at the end of this chapter for you to complete and you will be able to determine your dominant negotiation tendencies which will fall in one or more of the following styles:

- *Dodging (Dodgers)*: Trying to postpone decision-making or finding reasons for not getting involved at all.
- *Dreaming (Dreamers)*: Keeping the major goal in mind; preserving the relationships even at the cost of giving up certain concessions.
- *Haggling (Hagglers)*: Perceiving the negotiation process as a give-and-take game to obtain a good bargain.
- *Competing (Competitors):* Effectively managing conflicts, feeling comfortable with assertive behaviors and being aggressive when appropriate.
- *Problem Solving (Problem Solvers)*: Problem solving requires creativity and flexibility in finding mutually satisfying agreements. It means working toward a win-win solution for the relevant parties.

Figure 10.3 – Negotiation Quadrants and Styles

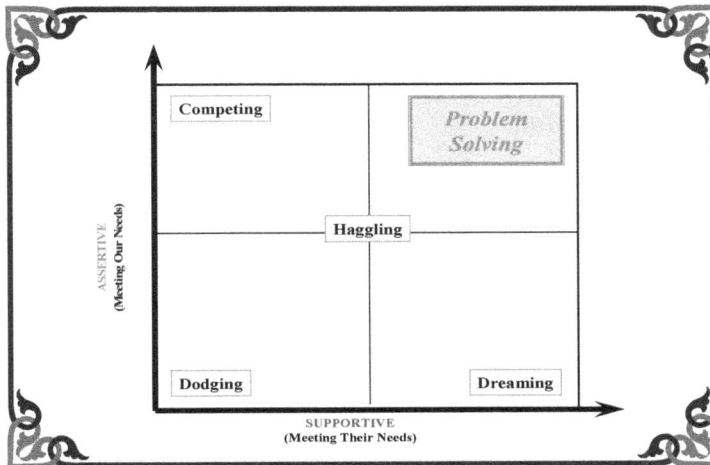

When negotiating, one can be somewhat assertive (from low to high) or somewhat supportive (from low to high) or both simultaneously. Supportive styles focus on meeting the other party's needs, while assertive styles focus on meeting one's own needs. The key might be to make sure there is a win-win solution for both parties; thereby meeting one's own needs as well their needs. Once you have determined your negotiation scores using the Negotiation Style Assessment and

Inventory for the five possible styles; then transfer your scores in Figure 10.3 and circle your highest or dominant style.

Summary

Negotiation skill is a necessity of life and a standardized process can easily be implemented by managers when negotiating with one or more parties. This chapter offered a simple model that managers and global negotiators can use to begin planning for negotiations, negotiating and closing negotiations. Negotiation is both an art and a science. Just like soccer or various forms of martial arts, one cannot become a skilled player without actual practice and the application of various skills that can be gained only through personal involvement. To get some experience with negotiations and "taste" its challenges, it is recommended that managers, expatriates and entrepreneurs attend seminars and workshops that can provide them with practical discussions and simulation opportunities for negotiations. Workshops on negotiations can be an excellent means of gaining practical tactics and skills for effective negotiation planning and execution.

Discussion Questions

1. Discuss the main steps to a negotiation process as presented in this chapter.
2. What are some pre-negotiation items that must be planned in advance?
3. What can one do to initiate and plan for a negotiation?
4. Should a negotiator make the first offer? What are the advantages and disadvantages?
5. Why do some people rush the process of negotiation to close it as quickly as possible? What are the advantages (if any) and disadvantages (if any) of this tendency?
6. What can be done to reduce the need for renegotiations?
7. Why is it important to stay focused on the long-term relationship building process with one's negotiation partners? State five top reasons.
8. Are concessions necessary in a cross-cultural negotiation? Why or why not?

Negotiation Style Assessment and Inventory

The Negotiation Style Assessment and Inventory comes from Cellich and Jain as presented in their 2004 textbook entitled *Global Business Negotiations: A Practical Guide*. It is duplicated in this book with permission from the publisher for educational usage.

Directions: To determine your general style of negotiations, complete the following questions based on your opinion and general tendencies when negotiating. For each statement, you can provide an answer ranging from one to five: 1 (strongly disagree), 2 (disagree), 3 (neutral), 4 (agree), or 5 (strongly agree). Once you have answered all the questions then transfer your scores to the table on the next page to interpret your results.

	Rating (1-5)	Statements
1.		I am not comfortable negotiating.
2.		I push the other party toward my own positions/interests.
3.		I avoid hurting people.
4.		I try to learn the real needs of the other party before making a concession.
5.		I enjoy making offers and counteroffers.
6.		I don't like making difficult decisions.
7.		Before negotiating, I know what results to expect and how to work to obtain them.
8.		When negotiating, I like to make quick decisions to speed up the discussions.
9.		I am willing to lower my expectations to save the relationship.
10.		I encourage the other party to work with me in finding an acceptable solution.
11.		I avoid getting involved in difficult situations.
12.		I make sure I have power over the other party, and I use it to my advantage.
13.		To advance the negotiations, I like to split the difference.
14.		When negotiating, I make sure the other party feels comfortable.
15.		I have no problem sharing information with the other party.
16.		I don't negotiate when I have little chance of winning.
17.		If necessary, I use threats to reach my goals.
18.		I like to compromise to expedite the negotiations.
19.		I make sure the other party explains his or her real needs.
20.		I like to explore innovative approaches with the other party to achieve maximum outcomes.
21.		I like taking risks.
22.		To get what I want, I ask for more than what I am willing to settle for.
23.		I look for a fair deal.
24.		To me, personal relationships are vital to constructive discussions.
25.		I frequently summarize issues we both agreed to.
26.		I dislike dealing with difficult negotiators.
27.		I try to create doubts in the mind of the other party.
28.		To me, negotiating is a game of give and take.
29.		I do not like to embarrass other people.
30.		When I negotiate, I take a long-term outlook.
31.		I avoid getting involved in controversies.
32.		I do not give away information, but I try to obtain as much information as possible from the other party.
33.		I look for a middle-of-the-road solution to close negotiations.
34.		I avoid getting involved in nonessential details.
35.		I enjoy meeting people.

Source: Cellich, C. and Jain, S. C. (2004). *Global Business Negotiations: A Practical Guide*. Thompson-Southwestern. ISBN: 0538-72658-X. Reprinted with permission.

Interpreting the Negotiation Style Assessment and Inventory Score

Directions:

After completing the survey, transfer your scores from the Negotiation Style Assessment and Inventory questionnaire to the following table and add your responses according to the structure of each column.

Dodger		Dreamer		Haggler		Competitor		Problem Solver	
Statement	Rating	S	Rating	S	Rating	S	Rating	S	Rating
1=		3=		5=		2=		4=	
6=		9=		8=		7=		10=	
11=		14=		13=		12=		15=	
16=		19=		18=		17=		20=	
21=		24=		23=		22=		25=	
26=		29=		28=		27=		30=	
31=		35=		33=		32=		34=	
Total=		Total=		Total=		Total=		Total=	

Scoring Example:
If you answered 2 for the first statement on the survey, then you would enter 2 on the Dodger column after Statement 1.

CHAPTER 11

Progressive Discipline

Managing the performance of each employee through fair development, discipline and termination procedures is a critical component of effective management. The creation of an ethical work environment is an important aspect of a manager's responsibility. Such a workplace a work environment can result in high morale, greater satisfaction and increased commitment on the part of the employees.

In any workplace, employee discipline and terminations are realties of work environment. However, these events do not have to be negative as they can be objectively used for an employee's developmental needs. Similarly, terminating employees when they are not the right match for the job is a very important element of success for both parties. Accordingly, this chapter provides a discussion of the employee discipline process in order to make sure employees are treated fairly.

Discipline

Managers should use the formal standards for objectively and fairly interviewing, hiring, developing, and appraising employees. Fairness and consistency in communicating expectations to employees are extremely important in managing their performance and development, especially in a diverse workforce. Through the implementation of a consistent and fair process, managers and organizational leaders can achieve their goals while gaining the cooperation of employees. It also is clear that without a consistent and fair process for developing or disciplining employees, even outcomes that are favored by employees can be extremely difficult to achieve.

Dessler (2001) states that it is necessary for employers to institute appropriate "disciplinary and discharge procedures that will survive the scrutiny of arbitrators and the courts" (p. 248). Dessler writes that three principles contribute to perceived fairness in business settings: engagement, explanation, and expectation clarity (2001, p. 249).

1. *Engagement* requires involving individuals in the decisions that affect them by asking for their input and allowing them to refute the merits of one another's ideas and assumptions.
2. *Explanation* requires ensuring that everyone involved and affected should understand how and why final decisions are made and the thinking that underlies such decisions.
3. *Expectation clarity* means making sure that all employees know the standards by which they will be judged and the penalties for not living up to the standards.

Disciplining employees for misconduct, low performance, or not meeting the stated requirements in a timely manner can be one of the most difficult parts of a manager's job. Yet, a proper and systematic process can certainly make the job easier in order to benefit the manager, the employee, and the organization. Disciplining employees is a reality of life and most managers are likely to face it at one time or another. The purpose of discipline is to make sure employees are behaving according to the written, documented, and stated work-related rules and regulations. An initial step for both managers and employees is to understand that employees have rights and they must be given proper and timely feedback on their performance in the workplace. All employees and customers in the workplace have rights, and are thus entitled to a fair, safe, respectful, and healthy work environment. This understanding can lead to respecting employees for their work, taking lessons about performance management and coaching employees, attending appropriate workshops, understanding the company's rules and policies with regard to discipline and termination, and being an effective manager.

Before moving forward with the discipline process, a manager must clarify the problem. The manager should make sure the performance problem or misconduct statement is clear. One must avoid generalities and never translate performance shortfalls and misconducts into attitudinal or personality problems. Managers should also make sure the problem description is specific, observable, documented, and factual. Also, it is important to proactively answer the "when," "what," and the "impact" aspects of the problem to clearly state the issue. The clearer the problem description, the easier it will be to communicate and discuss the issue with the employee.

Once the problem statement and its description is clear, one can begin resolving it. Overall, with regard to disciplining employees, it is best that managers not jump into making irrational decisions based on emotional outbursts. For effectively disciplining employees, managers should follow a progressive disciplining process in order to make employees aware of their shortfalls or misconducts, so they can immediately begin work on improving it. So, progressive discipline is about effectively communicating with employees about their performance, being fair to employees, and respecting their rights. An effective and consistent appeal process goes smoothly when a progressive discipline process has been followed and implemented by each manager. Many experts and managers recommend using a progressive discipline without punishment process by gaining the employee's acceptance of the documented and expected rules and policies, while reducing the punitive nature of the discipline itself (Dessler, 2001, p. 254). The discipline without punishment process, mentioned by Dessler, includes the following steps:

1. Issue an oral reminder about the standards and the fact that the employee's performance is not aligned with the expectation.
2. Issue a formal written reminder that the performance deficiency or problem must be aligned with the expected standard.
3. Give the employee a paid one-day "decision-making leave." The employee can think whether he or she would like to continue with the job or find another position that better fits his or her desires, skills, and competencies. Upon returning to work, the employee meets with the manager and provides a decision on whether he or she will follow the expected rules and policies to meet the expectations.
4. If the behavior is aligned with the expected standards for the next full year, then all records are purged from the employee's file. Otherwise, if the behavior or performance problem is repeated, then the employee is dismissed.

Progressive Discipline

An effective discipline process allows some flexibility in exceptional circumstances. *Progressive discipline* is a proactive approach to enhancing each employee's performance, letting employees know how they are doing, and being fair in allowing employees to either meet the expectations or find another job. Through a standardized progressive discipline process and proper factual documentation, managers can greatly enhance employee retention as well as the probability of correcting work-related problems and treating employees fairly, while also reducing the chances of legal liability for the organization. A video entitled *Legal and Effective Progressive Discipline,* made available by Coastal Human Resources, provides a six-step process for effectively dealing with disciplining employees (Progressive Discipline, 2005): counseling the associate about the problem, oral warning, written warning, suspension, termination contract, and termination. The general steps and considerations suggested for progressively disciplining employees who are not meeting the expected work-related standards are as follows:

First: Initial counseling session to clarify the problem and expectations. An employee must be effectively counseled immediately (not months later) if his or her performance or behavior is not satisfactory. This initial step is very important and must be properly planned to make sure the employee is treated fairly, and that the expected standards are communicated effectively. Through effective discussion and communication with the employee, oftentimes this initial counseling can eliminate the problem, thereby leading to better or more satisfactory performance.

Second: The oral warning. If the initial step does not eliminate the problem or enhance performance, then the manager must escalate the seriousness of the problem by meeting with the employee and orally warning him or her about the problem and expected standards. For example, a manager can say: "Deena, this is an official oral warning directly related to what was discussed at the initial counseling session about you wearing inappropriate skirts and thereby not following the company's dress code. You must adhere to the company's standards when it comes to proper hygiene and dress code. Your use of strong perfume and the short skirt do not adhere to the company's dress code standards as you can see in the employee manual." It is the manager's responsibility to indicate to the employee what the expectations are and help the employee meet the expected standards. Furthermore, the employee should be reminded of the possible consequences if the performance does not improve or behavior does not change to meet the expected standards. Once the employee clearly understands the problem, the expectations, and possible consequences of continued behavior or status quo, the oral warning session can come to a close. The manager must document this session's material by writing down what was discussed and why, what the expected standards were, and what may happen if the expectation is not met. This should be kept with the manager in case more follow-up sessions are needed.

Third: The written warning. If the problem or performance has not changed through the initial counseling and oral warning, then the employee must be warned officially in a written format. Every detail must be written comprehensively, clearly, succinctly, and with the specific consequence if the behavior is not improved as stated in the written warning. The written warning form must state the problem, the expected standard, and that the employee will be suspended or terminated if the behavior does not change immediately.

Fourth: Place employee on suspension. If the behavior or performance does not improve, the manager can terminate or suspend the employee as agreed upon in the written warning. Suspension is recommended when the manager wants to provide the employee a chance to personally think and reflect on whether the employee wants to continue working with the firm. The suspension must state the problem, the reason the employee is being suspended, the expected standard when the employee returns to work, and the next consequence which will be termination if the behavior does not change or improve as expected. Furthermore, the employee and the manager must jointly sign a new written warning and termination contract—the contract can be signed when the employee is being suspended or when the employee returns to work, depending on the standardized policy.

Fifth: Final written warning or termination contract agreement. Both the employee and the employer jointly agree on the expected standard and sign a contract that if the behavior does not improve immediately, the employee will be terminated.

Sixth: Terminate the employee. If the employee does not live up to the expected standard, then respectfully terminate the employee;

clearly state why the employee is being terminated. Employees must be terminated correctly and respectfully; otherwise, it can cause major morale disruptions in the workplace. The termination of an employee often can be disruptive to the existing employees; therefore, managers must take extra caution to make sure morale and productivity are not impacted too negatively in the department.

The above steps should be handled professionally, respectfully, and privately with the employee. The word "privately" does not mean that a manager should not have a witness. As a matter-of-fact, for steps two through six, it is best to involve another manager or someone from the human resources department in the disciplining session. It is always best to have an objective third party present; however, the third party should be an objective person such as another manager or someone from human resources (preferably not the employee's colleague who works in the same department or division). As mentioned before, disciplining an employee can be stressful and time-consuming. However, effective and progressive discipline can be a great way to let employees know that their performance is not meeting the expectation and they must improve. A progressive discipline process can focus managers on the facts of each situation, objectives or the expected standards, solutions to eliminate the work-related problem, and actions needed to meet the expected standards.

It is important that managers and their firms give employees appropriate vehicles for allowing them to express their concerns, opinions, and frustrations without receiving or perceiving retaliation. Such a process can help managers gather the right information about improving the work environment for all employees, thereby creating an inclusive and safe workplace. One important element of a good work environment is fairness to all employees; or having an effective discipline process to deal fairly with problems and performance deficiencies. An effective discipline process attempts to be fair to employees while allowing them sufficient opportunities to fix the problem. An effective discipline process is accompanied with proper discharge and termination processes.

Discipline without Punishment

Discipline is about correcting behavioral or performance-related problems and misconducts in the workplace. Some managers do not like to enforce discipline when employees are not performing or behaving as expected, and no one likes to be the target of it. This result is probably because most traditional discipline approaches require punishing the employee for behavioral problems. With punishment, some employees learn not to get caught by managers for doing what is disliked, instead of attempting to correct the problem and behaving as expected. While punishing the employee to correct a problem can lead to success in the short-term, it may only gain compliance to please the boss and not necessarily commitment to doing a good job. With the practical "discipline without punishment" concept, managers understand and learn how to handle one of the toughest issues any manager faces in managing employees' behavior. Discipline without punishment is very much like using appropriate situational leadership styles where the manager provides either less or more direction to the employee depending on his or her level of readiness and maturity to perform correctly the specific task. In essence, situational leadership is about disciplining employees without punishment in order to take care of the task at hand, guide or develop the employee to correctly perform the task, and enhance the manager's relationship with the associate.

Every organization is likely to have employees that occasionally show "discipline problems." If these misconducts and problems are handled incorrectly, as explained by the concept of discipline without punishment, and "when discipline is equated with punishment, even a small problem with only one person can ruin the entire team's morale and productivity" (Discipline without Punishment, 2005). When discipline issues are handled incorrectly, discipline has the possibility of causing a "battle of wills," with anger and hurt on both sides. As experienced in the workplace, for long-term purposes, not much is gained with many of the traditional discipline approaches, because most employees do not respond progressively better when they are treated progressively worse for a performance issue or a misconduct.

Using modern approaches and respectful examples, the discipline without punishment scenario provides effective ways to use discipline for a healthy department and long-term productivity. It should be understood that workers do not change their attitudes and personalities, but they can change their behavior in the workplace when asked by the organization and managers. Changing employee behavior is the essence of discipline without punishment since misconducts in the workplace tend to be a behavior problem. Discipline without punishment requires that managers first get the individual to admit there is a problem, and then coach the employee on how to solve his or her misconduct or performance-related problem.

There are many situational variables, such as the employee, the manager, the problem, the environment, the culture, the relationship of the employee with the manager, and other such factors that must be considered when disciplining employees. While considering the situational variables, one should follow a standardized process to help the employee improve his or her behavior and performance in the workplace without hurting morale or causing negative or ill feelings. Discipline without punishment provides four steps for managers to achieve the goal of helping employees correct behavioral or performance-related problems. The four steps offered for discipline without punishment are (Discipline without Punishment, 2005):

1. *Focusing on the problem at hand.* Focus on the issue that is causing the problem and not the person. Stay away from personality related concerns or your likes or dislikes of the person. Discuss the specific work-related problem so it can be fixed. To avoid generalities and vague statements, managers should clarify the specific problem and perhaps write it down before discussing it with the employee.

2. *Gaining the employee's agreement that there is a problem and that it must be changed.* The employee should at least agree to change or that a change is needed. Furthermore, he or she should agree that it is his/her responsibility to correct the problem.

3. *Identifying appropriate strategies for improvement jointly with the employee.* These strategies should either eliminate the problem or at least improve the performance to a satisfactory level as agreed upon.

4. *Following-up to make sure the problem is eliminated and the behavior is improved.* Take correct action as appropriate. When the behavior is improved, this provides an opportunity to further develop the individual and the relationship.

The four steps for disciplining employees without punishment is one effective approach to correcting behavioral, work-related problems in the workplace, without causing too much stress to employees, or personally being stressed each day as the manager of the department. It is understood that the manager is running the department and not the other way around, so managers should not stress themselves. Because some discipline incidents or approaches tend to be negative and cause friction between the manager and employees due to a lack of effective communication, a few managers simply avoid facing the problem until it becomes a huge issue and can no longer be avoided. Such tendencies and procrastination of discussing problems and performance-related issues with employees can cause much undue stress, frustration, and hostility.

Discipline without punishment offers an effective approach to address most behavioral and performance-related problems immediately in a mature, professional, direct, and task-focused manner, while attempting to jointly "brainstorm" on possible solutions that the employee can use to improve the situation. It must be remembered that the problem "owner" is the employee and consequently he or she is responsible for taking care of the problem. Managers can use the situational leadership styles of telling the employee what to do, selling the employee on the solution, participating with the employee on coming up with a solution, or delegating the task to the employee as per his or her level of readiness and maturity for the specific task or issue. Just like effective leadership, disciplining is not always reserved just for poor performers; rather, it is something that managers should do consistently with all employees, when needed, in order to create an inclusive, productive, and safe work environment for all. With this mindset and paradigm, disciplining employees requires effective leadership, management, and coaching skills. Effective managers and leaders know that solving the problem or performance challenge is one immediate opportunity for improvement, while developing the employee and a good relationship with him or her is another major objective for the department's long-term success. Managers must be cautious to not always strive for gaining immediate benefits at the cost of long-term success. Managers should work to enhance long-term performance.

The discipline without punishment approach, when applied correctly, can correct most behavioral and performance-related problems in the workplace without having to resort to progressive punishment or employee discharge and employment terminations. However, when all else fails, one can resort to progressive discipline, which can lead to employee discharge and termination if the problem is not resolved correctly in the required or agreed upon time.

Employee Discharges and Terminations

When employees are not able to perform their tasks and duties successfully, managers must intervene to help and provide them the needed resources so they can live up to the expectations. Since most large organizations give employees about 60 days' notice during layoffs and plant closings, managers should provide sufficient opportunities for employees to enhance their performance. If such efforts do not increase the employee's performance or eliminate the problem, then the employee can be discharged and his or her employment can be terminated with the organization. Dismissal, which must be taken very seriously, should be a last step in the discipline process after all reasonable efforts have been made to correct the problem. It is a fact that dismissed employees may take their cases to court, which can cost the manager and others in the organization much wasted time and resources. Managers should double check and ensure that sufficient evidence exists to justify the dismissal. The best way to handle a dismissal is to avoid it in the first place. In the event an employee is dismissed, it should be done respectfully, and a clear reason should be provided for the dismissal.

While disciplining and dismissing employees is not an easy task for managers, they must be consistent, professional, respectful to the employee, and factual. It is the manager's responsibility to make sure a standardized and consistent process is followed with each employee so it is fair, and that it is perceived as such.

Managers should take every possible step to avoid mistreating employees and wrongfully discharging, terminating or dismissing them. Managers can avoid wrongful discharges when they follow their company's stated rules and policies and when they effectively state their expectations to employees from the outset in the employee's employment process. Once again, it is best to remember that the best way to avoid wrongful discharge claims is to avoid discharges by helping employees meet the stated standards and expectations. Dismissals and discharges can cause much undue stress on both the employee and manager. Managers after run double their usual risk of suffering a heart attack the week after they fire an employee. Studies do conclude that the stress associated with firing an employee doubles the risk of a heart attack for the manager. When a termination becomes a necessity, managers must proceed cautiously and strategically since it can be devastating to employees, even if the employee is warned many times prior to the dismissal. While most employees handle dismissals effectively, some might become disoriented and even resort to violence. Experts offer the following guidelines for managers who are terminating an employee.

1. *Plan the termination session carefully.* Speak with the human resources department to make sure every step is being followed properly and all the paperwork or forms are completed in advance. Do not let the employee know about the termination over the phone. Find a neutral site for the termination session instead of holding it at the manager's office. Also, have the phone numbers for the employee assistance program personnel and security officials ready in case they are needed.

2. *Get to the point.* Inform the person immediately about the purpose of the session and make it quick.

3. *Describe the situation.* Briefly and factually state the reason that the employee is being terminated. Remember to not attack the person...simply focus on the performance problem or the reason he or she is being terminated. Emphasize that the decision is final.

4. *Listen with empathy.* Continue the interview until the employee is reasonable and speaks calmly about the reasons for his or her termination and future steps.

5. *Review all elements of the termination package or the severance package (if any).* The manager or human resources specialist can describe the severance payments, benefits, and other relevant support material available for the employee.

6. *Identify the next step.* Inform the employee what he or she should do next. Let the person know if there is an Employee Assistance or Outplacement Program available to help him or her with resume preparation or to look for jobs outside of the organization.

Some large organizations do offer outplacement services as part of their severance package. Outplacement services could include outplacement counseling, where a terminated person is trained and counseled in securing a new job that is appropriate to his or her needs and talents. The outplacement program is simply a service which can provide retired or terminated employees with suggestions for dealing with the process of securing a new job. Such programs also can offer advice on determining appropriate jobs, resume development, going to employment agencies, and preparing for interviews.

Upon the termination and dismissal of employees, human resource personnel can conduct an exit interview with the employee to gather his or her insights on some of the challenges and problems facing the organization. Exit interviews could elicit information on how the person was hired, oriented, trained, developed, and promoted to various jobs during his or her employment. Furthermore, questions can deal with the fairness of salary, ethics, morale, communication, employment relations, the style of management, the direction of the company, what they liked about their job or organization and what they disliked, and the way their decision to leave the organization or the dismissal was handled.

Summary

Disciplining and terminating employees are realities of life in all organizations, and they are all very important elements of a manager's responsibility. Effective managers attempt to avoid employee termination and discharge by recruiting and hiring the right individuals. Furthermore, through the creation of a motivational work environment, they develop and assist employees in achieving the stated objectives through effective leadership skills, discipline without punishment processes, and progressive discipline approaches. Effective managers are always concerned about the progressive development of their employees, and thus utilize a standardized corrective action process when performance expectations and standards are not going as expected.

Effective managers must be sensitive to the needs of their cross-cultural people and work strategically to make sure all their employees are as successful as they would like to be based upon each employee's qualifications, goals, abilities, and competencies.

Discussion Questions

1. What are some of the common causes of employee tardiness and excessive absences? What can managers do to effectively deal with such issues? Discuss and list five specific actions to reduce voluntary absences.
2. What can managers do to effectively discipline employees?
3. Can employee discipline and termination cases be avoided? Discuss.
4. Why are employees terminated? Discuss some common examples or reasons. What are some guidelines for effective employee terminations?
5. Discuss the concept of Discipline without Punishment? Should managers adapt this process? Why or why not?
6. Have you ever seen managers or heard of managers who terminated an employee in a totally wrong manner as the manager allowed his or her emotions to drive the decision? Discuss personal examples. What could have been done to terminate the employee in a dignified and respectful manner?

Discipline is not something managers do to poor performers. Discipline is something managers and leaders help create for all employees because they deserve a safe, inclusive, and professional work environment.

CHAPTER 12

Coaching for Performance

It is more important than ever today for everyone in the organization to perform at his/her highest capacity. Organizations are faced with increased competition, new markets, competitors from global environments, new and updated technologies, demanding and knowledgeable customers, and at times fewer skilled workers. These variables of skill building and performance enhancement are valid in any industry in the twenty-first century.

Managers, as coaches, work with their employees to achieve more with less, solve attitude problems, and are able to work with and inspire difficult associates to be productive. They are able to do all this by communicating with their employees, listening to them and getting their feedback, developing trust with others, documenting their performance goals, following up on promises and agreements, and by being caring and compassionate. This chapter discusses how managers can serve as developmental coaches when they help employees to enhance their performance in their jobs.

Introduction

In a coaching process to build an employee's skills and enhancing performance standards, managers tend to clearly state the performance problem or their expectation, get the employee's agreement on the problem, create practical solutions to the problem, agree on a specific action plan to solve the problem, and follow up as agreed upon. Effective leaders, managers and coaches understand that developing people for peak performance provides the much needed competitive edge, since the human asset in many cases is the most difficult asset to be imitated by competitors. However, due to the day-to-day pressures of getting more things done faster, some managers may only focus on current production and fail to develop the skills and competencies of their most important asset, their associates.

The objectives here are to understand the vital role of effective coaching and how coaching skills can be used to keep the organization and people competitive. Furthermore, managers and leaders should be able to utilize effective coaching techniques and apply the steps to coaching when working with employees to reinforce and guide everyone toward high performance.

By becoming an effective coach, you will be able to develop the people who serve your customers, promote your products, and manage your systems; and those whom you effectively coach will be on the road to peak performance.

Coaching Benefits and Situations

Due to the changing demographics of the business world such as more competition and the introduction of new technologies, organizations are discovering that traditional tactics of management are no longer enough to remain competitive. As such, coaching is becoming recognized and practiced as an effective tool for managers to increase morale, performance and the "bottom line" through the success of each individual associate. For example, studies have shown that most employees who received coaching in their jobs say that it improved their job performance and professional success. In some organizations where coaching is effectively practiced as a management style, the bottom-line performance is two to three times better than the traditional "command-and-control" type of organizations. Furthermore, it has been proven that employee commitment increases when there is a strong, positive relationship between the manager and his/her employees. These types of relationships are developed best as a result of effective coaching.

It has been noted that about 53% of employees say that they would like more coaching; 60% say that they want better coaching than they are receiving in their workplaces, and 56% say that the coaching they receive is not helpful or developmental. While employees want more, and better, coaching in their jobs, managers need to develop their own personal skills if they are to glean the benefits of a highly productive workforce. Managers need to become better coaches and develop a focused and developmental relationship with each employee.

Effective relationship-oriented coaching creates more knowledgeable and competent employees, reduces errors and rework, and it greatly assists in bringing new changes to the culture. Both effective and ineffective managers tend to know what makes a good coach. The difference lies in being able to transfer this knowledge into successful actions with employees to increase their performance and success.

Simply stated, coaching is about developing a trusting relationship with your people so you can jointly clarify expectations and departmental goals thereby leading to specific action plans for their achievement.

Everyone has benefited, to some extent, from the guidance, assistance and leadership of effective coaches during one's socialization in the society at an early age, at school, at one's initial job, during advancement opportunities, during challenging times, during changes, and during happy times. Effective coaches can be personal or professional at any stage in one's life. When managers think of their past experiences related to effective coaches and other such leadership experiences, most people tend to remember their coaches from ten, twenty and thirty years ago because they made such a positive impact on them. Those who look up to you for guidance and direction (such as your children, employees, students, and colleagues) are likely to have similar positive memories if you use effective coaching techniques with them. Most professional people who look up to you are likely to fall into one of the following three groups with regard to their performance on a specific task:

1) *Below standard performers.* People in this category are not performing at the desired level and need to add new competencies. People in this group might be new in their roles or they might be veterans whose skills are below standard. *Clarify and set the standard for them.*

2) *Satisfactory performers needing new skills.* People in this group have to unlearn old behaviors and learn new skills. Typically, they are performing well today, but their skills will be obsolete or insufficient as priorities evolve and new challenges become a reality. Changes in work demands, organizational strategies, or competitive forces might precipitate the need for a new direction. *Set new direction and expect the development of new competencies.*

3) *"Going beyond the limit" performers.* In this group, you help people reach their full potential. They need to stretch their limits and find fresh applications for their skills so that they do not become stale or restless. You might not notice these developmental needs if people are content within their comfort zone and they are meeting organizational needs. Sometimes you need to stir people up and expose them to new possibilities to get maximum yield from their talents. *Set free and challenge them to new heights.*

Coaching Roles

Effective coaching is a continuous process of conversational collaborations and interactions aimed at assisting others unlock and realize their full potential one task or one skill at a time and at a pace appropriate for the person being coached. The essence of coaching is unlocking people's potential, through stimulating questions, so they can maximize their own performance. Effective coaches keep in mind that imposing their way of accomplishing tasks is not their objective because that is not part of coaching but rather dictating. Effective coaches accept the challenge knowing that the growth and development journey is a continuous process, and that learning how to learn and develop are the real goals for both individuals (coach and the coachee).

Effective coaches play the roles of *communicators* (encourage, inform, praise, raise awareness, and collaborate), *performance leaders* (set clear expectations, serve as role models, empower, help, and challenge), and *catalysts* (vehicles for change, remove barriers, and enable others to reach their full potential). *The Practical Coach* video offers many insights and suggestions on coaching for all leaders. The following are some highlights from this video: Coaching can be the single most important thing you do as a leader or manager; never let good or poor performance go unnoticed; when you see good performance, say it and praise it; don't let poor performance go unnoticed, make it private and positive, and or real personal issues and poor personal habits: first, prepare the teammate/associate, and second, be gentle and to the point. *The Practical Coach* video offers a concept, called the *"Two Minute Challenge,"* that coaches can use with their employees using the following steps:

- First, state what you observed.

- Second, wait for a response.
- Third, remind the person of the goal.
- Fourth, ask for a specific solution.
- Fifth, jointly agree on the solution and its implementation.

Overall, it is important managers follow-up and not let good or poor performance go unnoticed. Perhaps, some of these steps from the *Practical Coach* video can apply to your department or life. Which ones are you able to apply in your workplace or your personal life as a coach? Document them and plan on using them immediately to help improve performance while following the coaching guidelines.

Coaching Procedures and Steps with Associates

Coaching requires that managers describe the performance gap (problem or expectation) to the employee/coachee, get the coachee's (employee's) agreement on the problem or performance gap, brainstorm on possible solutions to the problem or performance gap, agree on a specific action plan to solve the problem or performance challenge, and follow up as agreed upon. In other words, coaches should pursue the following procedures when coaching an employee:

1. *State the problem.* Clearly state the problem, challenge, performance gap, and future expectations.
2. *Agree on the problem.* Both the coach and employee must agree on the performance problem or expected standards. The consequences of status quo should also be discussed.
3. *Develop alternatives to solve the problem.* It is important that the employee comes up with possible solutions. Of course, the coach can ask open-ended questions or provide hints or possible suggestions to guide the employee.
4. *Select an action plan to solve the problem.* The employee and coach should jointly agree on a solution that enhances performance or eliminates the problem. Specific timelines, actions, and standards must be clarified as part of this action plan.
5. *Follow up to make sure the problem has been eliminated.* As agreed upon in the action plan, the coach and employee should jointly assess the outcome and proceed accordingly.

Now that the basics of coaching along with its principles, roles and responsibilities have been discussed, we can discuss the basic steps involved in a comprehensive coaching process. There are five specific steps in the coaching process as you oversee the work done with and through your colleagues and associates. As such, effective coaching requires:

- Planning,
- Supporting others for good performance,
- Communicating and/or setting a time to increase performance,
- Leading others to higher performance, and
- Following up and confirming effective achievement of objectives and expectations.

These five key steps will help you become more effective in getting the work done with and/or through your associates and colleagues. While the steps apply to all people you want to influence or help toward better performance, the following sections will discuss them with regard to one's direct reports (employees) and colleagues.

What is Your Coaching Style?

A person's socialization and background, as well as his or her personality characteristics are likely to heavily influence and determine his or her style of coaching. According to experts (such as Herman Aguinis, 2007, p. 201 in his *Performance Management* book), coaching styles can be categorized into four categories or quadrants: driver, persuader (expresser), amiable, and analyzer.

Driver. The driving style coach tells the employee what to do, how to do the task, and when to do it. Driver coaches tend to be assertive, task-oriented, and get right to the point. Drivers tend to:

- Focus on results.
- Take charge.
- Make quick decisions.
- Like challenges.

Persuader (Expresser). In the persuading style of coaching, managers try to "sell" the employee on what needs to be done so the person would want to do it because of its benefits. They are expressive and assertive. Persuaders tend to also use more body language and stay focused on the beneficial consequences of completing the task successfully and building relationships. Persuaders tend to:

- Create excitement and involvement.
- Share ideas, dreams, and enthusiasm.
- Motivate, inspire, and persuade.

Amiable. Coaches using the amiable style work on getting everyone to be happy. They rely more on their feelings and what the right thing to do might be based on situational factors, rather than always relying on "cold" facts. Amiable coaches tend to:

- Cooperate to gain agreement.
- Provide support.
- Communicate trust and confidence.

Analyzer. Analyzers tend to assess the results and outcomes, while following the established rules and procedures as a consequence for the next step. They coach employees based on the rules and policies that are established in the training guide or a manual. Analyzers are not always assertive, but they are task-oriented and do stay focused on facts rather than feelings. An analyzer coach tends to:

- Focus on facts and logic.
- Act when payoff is clear.
- Be careful not to commit too quickly.

As a coach, it is best to be adaptable and use a relevant style as per the needs of the coachee and other situational variables. To determine your coaching styles, complete the Coaching Style Questionnaire at the end of this chapter. What is your dominant coaching style? Which coaching style would be the best one for you? Which coaching style is likely to be the most effective in your department or industry? Of course, as per the assessment of coaching experts and researchers, there is not one best coaching style.

Effective coaches do what needs to be done as per the needs of their employees and organizations. Effective coaches learn about their employees' needs and work with them on setting new and relevant development goals. In achieving the stated goals, effective coaches may provide direction or tell employees what they need to do, coaches may sell employees on an idea, at times coaches might be the cheerleaders by empathizing with their employees, and, at other times, coaches might want to simply stick to the facts, rules and established procedures. In other words, effective coaches use a style that best matches the needs of the situation, the organization, and the employee at a given time. Ineffective coaches tend to stick to one style at all times and cannot always adapt to use any of the other styles. Coaches that can adapt their styles to the needs of the employee and the situation tend to be most effective. In other words, effective coaches are likely to use a style that best matches with the concept of situational leadership styles. Sometimes, a coach might need to be assertive and, in other times, he or she might need to simply be responsive to an employee's situational needs. The process of adjusting assertiveness as a coach or one's style of responsiveness to the needs of employees, requires both willingness and ability on the part of the coach to successfully adjust his/her behavior to accommodate people whose readiness levels, concerns and expectations are different.

Effective coaches need versatility which is defined as adapting one's behavior to meet the concerns and expectations of others. Versatility requires understanding, appreciating, and adapting to other styles and needs. Versatility can improve work communications and ultimately the productivity of one's employees. Managers and leaders adjust their styles and use various skills to accommodate the needs of their employees. For example, to become more versatile, amiables can take the initiative and express a sense of urgency when appropriate; and they can assert firmness and self-assurance about their ideas on issues. Analyticals can take risk, or be willing to take shortcuts through procedures; they can also make decisions on the basis of intuition when appropriate. Drivers can show patience when others try to express the merits of their ideas and engage in a thorough analysis of situations. Expressives and persuaders can pay attention to details supplied by others and keep their emotions open, but under control. While all people are versatile to some degree in their communication, some individuals are more versatile than others. However, all of us can improve our versatility.

Effective coaches, as suggested by experts and trainers, can use the ASAP and STAR models with employees and customers who are upset or dissatisfied. The ASAP model requires that coaches:

- *A*ttend their feelings/emotions by listening without judging.
- *S*hare their understanding and empathy for each employee's concerns.
- *A*nswer their concerns by presenting ideas/solutions.
- *P*lan action after recognizing the problem.

The STAR model requires that coaches provide:

- *S*upport by encouraging employees to take action and asking questions.
- *T*ime for employees to think about the issue or to discuss it later.
- *A*ssurance or the feeling that one understands the employee's perspective.
- *R*educed risk by discussing solutions and how they can help.

As a coach, to increase your assertiveness by *telling* employees what to and how to do something, do the following:
- Demonstrate a willingness to get to the point.
- Volunteer the information you have to others.
- Be willing to express points of disagreement.
- Summarize the positions you feel others are suggesting.

As a coach, to increase your assertiveness by *asking* questions and gaining employees' approval, do the following:
- Be open to others' opinions, concerns and feelings.
- Acknowledge the value you place on other people's time.
- Demonstrate a willingness to follow the lead of others.
- Ask for cooperation, but do not demand it.

As a coach, to increase your responsiveness by focusing on the *task*, do the following:
- Acknowledge the ideas and points that others make.
- Articulate expected results of taking action.
- Talk about the task; reference facts as well as feelings.
- Try to organize your thoughts in a logical pattern when communicating.

As a coach, to increase your responsiveness by focusing on the *people*, do the following:

- Take the time to establish rapport with your coworkers.
- Reinforce other people when they express good ideas.
- Share your feelings or personal information.
- Allow yourself and others to break the routine while problem solving.

Regardless of the style or styles coaches use, if they are to build trust with their people, they need to consistently show patience, honesty, compassion, and courage. Consistency, in this regards, is the effort and intent to accommodate others' concerns while still being themselves. Coaches should be flexible, adaptable and consistent when it comes to caring for people and organizational outcomes.

Socratic Coaching

Socrates is known for asking reflective questions in order to guide others to think for themselves. Asking good questions is important for one's own personal development as well as for leading and guiding coachees in the right direction. Good coaches will always give support to associates, but when associates are not performing up to the standard for the job, it is necessary to provide effective coaching by asking leading questions to assist them in the thinking and solution generation process. When coaching associates, you help them solve problems they are having with the tasks they have been assigned. Every associate will have difficulties with some task at one time or another. That is why the coach's support is so vital. You will be able to spot an associate who is having trouble and coach them to a solution for the problem.

There are at least two main reasons why people do not like to ask for help. *First*, some people cannot admit, even to themselves, when they cannot do a job. *Second*, others can admit it, but they are afraid to ask for help because they do not want to appear incompetent. These two reasons are very similar, but the reactions when you ask if there are any problems, are very different. Some individuals who cannot admit they need help will answer "No problems here" or something similar. Associates who are afraid to ask for help will be relieved if you phrase your question in a non-threatening way.

When supporting and leading associates, it is important to focus on the work results and not on the person. If the results are not what you expected, ask the following questions: What happened? Why did it happen? What can be done to prevent it from happening again? Never assume that the associate is incapable of doing the work. If you have concerns about an associate's overall performance, talk to your coach and/or mentor when needed, and privately to the associate in a very empathic manner.

Instead of just telling associates the solution to a problem (assuming you have a solution), try asking questions that will help them discover the solution. This method has the benefit of making the associate feel that he or she was part of the solution and, additionally, associates will tend to remember the solution much better, since they reasoned it out for themselves.

There are many common questions that one might ask during a coaching session. What are some questions you can think of that would help in coaching your associates? You might want to think of coaching situations other than work that one may experience. For example, teaching a child a new skill or coaching an athletic team requires coaching skills. Using questions as a coaching tool is particularly valuable when it is necessary to suggest alternate resources to associates who are having difficulties. The resource may include another piece of equipment, a different type of tool or product, and another associate who is skilled in the task.

The one habit that you, as a coach, must guard against is helping an associate who is having difficulties by doing the task yourself. Of course, there will be emergency situations where a coach may do this, but in general, it is not a good idea because it can hinder the employee's development. There are many reasons why coaches should not do associates' jobs and the following are some of them:
- It is not your job.
- The associate will not learn to do the task independently.
- If you consistently do tasks yourself, instead of coaching others, you are not doing your job.
- It is much more time-consuming if you do tasks yourself, rather than coaching associates to better performance.
- Allowing your associates to take responsibility for task completion helps them develop their skills.

- You are responsible for "running" the department and not the other way around. So, don't let the department "run" you!

Coaching Challenge and "The Practical Coach"

Effective coaches encourage, inform, praise, raise awareness, collaborate, set clear expectations, serve as role models, empower, help, challenge, serve as vehicles for change, remove barriers, and enable others to reach their full potential. One should remember that coaching others to higher performance can be the single most important thing one does as a leader or manager. Also, skilled managers and coaches never let good or poor performance go unnoticed. When effective coaches and managers see good performance, they say it and praise it. One should not let poor performance go unnoticed by saying it privately to the employee and making it positively anchored toward future performance. For real personal issues and poor personal habits: first, prepare the teammate/associate; and second, be gentle and to the point in stating the problem that needs fixing. *The Practical Coach* video, as previously mentioned, offers many insights and suggestions on coaching for all leaders. The video offers the *"Two Minute Challenge"* with the following steps: First, state what you observed; second, wait for a response; third, remind the person of the goal; fourth, ask for a specific solution; and fifth, jointly agree on the solution and its implementation.

Perhaps, some of these steps from the *Practical Coach* can apply to disciplining employees without punishment in order to effectively fix problems and enhance performance. A manager's responsibility, as a coach and as a leader, is best fulfilled when he or she maximizes long-term value for his or her department, organization, and the society through the use of available resources and effective discipline management approaches. Effective managers jointly and collaboratively work with their employees to increase each worker's commitment to the job, enhance his or her performance on each task, and maximize each associate's long-term value to the organization.

Summary

Coaching is about specific goal-oriented collaborations and communication to influence others toward successfully achieving their personal and professional goals. Just like any other skill, coaching requires knowledge, patience, and practice. Coaching and enhancing employee performance requires that managers open their mouths and communicate by describing the performance problem or expectation, getting the employee's agreement on the problem, creating possible solutions to the problem, agreeing on a specific action plan to solve the problem, and following up as agreed upon.

Coaching can be seen as an advanced form of communication which can increase employee performance and job satisfaction, improve motivation and retention, reduce stress, and create better working relationships, especially in a cross-culturally diverse workplace.

Discussion Questions

1. What is coaching and how does it apply to twenty-first century managers and leaders? When and where can leaders or managers coach? Can coaching be used in any industry? Discuss how and where.
2. How is coaching different from telling people what to do? Does one need to be a manager to be an effective coach?
3. Is there a relationship between coaching and productivity/performance?
4. How can the questioning method be used by coaches to understand their people and enhance performance?
5. Discuss the characteristics of effective coaches. What are some best practices in becoming the type of leader or coach one wishes to be?

CHAPTER 13

Rewards and Recognition Programs

The support of executives and managers are critically important to the success and ethical implementation of socially responsible performance management and reward systems. To create an environment that supports ethical behavior, it is extremely important to educate executives and managers in the creation of a holistic performance management program as well as in designing and executing ethical reward programs. In order for a reward program to work effectively, high level executives and managers, as well as their employees and colleagues, should also be appropriately rewarded for supporting it.

Proper design and implementation of reward and recognition programs, as part of a comprehensive performance management system, can be productive and it will recover more than just its cost. This practical chapter reviews various aspects of reward programs, as well as the ethical implications of such programs, and recommends guidelines for the implementation of effective recognition programs in a responsible manner.

Reward Systems and Feedback

There is an increasing demand on corporations to develop reward programs that are motivating employees to work harder and faster. These programs usually educate and encourage associates to become more productive, efficient, and valuable individuals in the company in terms of the "bottom-line." However, due to the pressures related to performance and incentives, in some cases, these programs have encouraged unethical behavior as was shown in the case of Sears Automotive associates in the 1980s. Mechanics were charging customers for work that was not required and in some cases for jobs that were not even performed in order to make more money because their bonus was based on sales volumes. Ethics training programs and corporate emphasis on fairness and morality are important elements of a successful campaign aimed at increasing ethical awareness and behavior in the workplace, but it means nothing if the reward systems and incentives are not aligned with the program. A survey of managers and employees from the retail industry, in a Fortune One Hundred company, shows that today people are better prepared to deal with ethical issues and are less tolerant of questionable practices in their firms. Nowadays, committed associates are more likely to speak out or leave the company if their values conflict with that of their firms. So, in order to attract and retain qualified and committed individuals, firms need to have appropriate pay systems that encourage and reward employees to always stay focused on producing quality products in an efficient manner and to always do the right thing.

In order to remain competitive, managers and entrepreneurs need to effectively manage the performance of their most valuable asset, people. Managers and entrepreneurs should be moving toward greater alignment between performance management and company strategies, values, and quality measures. Reward systems should be linked with goal-setting, employee development, competency measures, and team performance. This will decentralize the decision-making down the hierarchy to empower those performing the tasks. This will translate into better reward systems and better morale among employees. In order to create a competitive edge, many organizations are now doing more with fewer employees, so it is imperative that people are rewarded for using effective and ethical problem-solving and decision-making skills.

While most human resource managers agree on the value of effective reward systems, few consider how differences in the quality of reward systems and incentive programs can affect the morale and productivity of each individual. Most reward systems have been written by one individual or obtained from a traditional or generic reward program. These types of reward systems may have serious limitations that may prevent its application to the general population and they can be very costly without producing the desired results for the organization. These rewards may not provide all the information needed to motivate employees to achieve top performance on a continuous basis. A Gallup Poll once found that about 33% of the American workforce would prefer a 20% reduction in their salaries if they could have the option of working fewer hours. Research has shown that those companies that have offered such options, their employees have taken advantage of it. There are many people who would like to live a comfortable life which is normally a balance between work, family, and time for oneself. Many individuals are finding out that happiness does not lie in having money, but rather in a balanced life where one prioritizes his or her time around quality and family oriented life-style. As time, technology, and people's priorities change, so should the corporate reward system.

It is important to continuously monitor the needs and wants of employees. For example, the executives of Tupperware, based in Kissimmee, Florida, are required to take thirty days on the road each year to spend time with their top 15,000 sales people. They try to cover a large portion of their sales force and not just the top five or ten sales people as done by most companies. The chairman and president of Home Depot Inc., headquartered in Atlanta, used to hold a quarterly meeting on Sunday mornings and all 23,000 employees were paid to attend and watch this forty-five minute program via satellite television hookup. The executives would answer questions and go over the growth plans and how employees are to play a part in this growth plan. At Knight-Ridder publications, they have "management coffee breaks." During this time, management would meet with twenty to twenty-five employees for about an hour to have coffee and discuss employee questions and suggestions. It has been said that if two employees are each having a penny and they exchange their pennies, then they will still each have only one penny. But, if these two individuals each have an idea and they exchange their ideas, then they will each have two ideas with the possibility of creating a third or even fourth because new ideas generate more ideas when seen from different perspectives.

In the traditional performance appraisal systems, people are normally put into categories of above average, average, or below average. This format may damage morale in the company and, thus it should be enhanced or eliminated. Rather than waste time and energy on the traditional reward systems, as part of a comprehensive performance management program, managers should consider conducting a formal job analysis that would provide relevant work behaviors and characteristics of the work environment. This information would lead to designing a reward program that would classify, compensate, and evaluate jobs based on individual and team performance.

Immediate feedback on performance can motivate individuals to change their strategy or to become more creative and adjust their methods to become high performing. In parallel with the Pygmalion effect or the self-fulfilling prophecy concept, it is appropriate for managers and entrepreneurs to assume that everyone would like do well and become a contributing part of the society or company. However, people need feedback about their performance; and, if they can see and evaluate their own performance, then they would be able and willing to take appropriate action. For example, people are often motivated to go bowling because they can get feedback instantaneously and that makes them happy. It is difficult to imagine many individuals bowling if there was a curtain between the bowler and the pins where the bowlers could not immediately see their results. This is also true of watching sports on television where viewers can see who wins and who loses as it happens. Not many people watch games that were played weeks ago since they know the results and therefore cannot be part of the game because the outcome is already known to them. So, just-in-time feedback is vital to every individual at every level of the organization and everyone wants to learn about his or her progress and stay abreast of it.

The reward programs should be individually focused because the value of certain rewards varies between different individuals. Bob Nelson, author of "*1001 Ways to Reward Employees*" says, appreciation for your best performing people tends to heighten morale and it enhances corporate image. The rewards should also be matched with each individual as his or her expectations, background, response to public or private recognitions, desire for money or promotion, and desire for peer respect may vary greatly and could be influenced by his or her past.

Why Should Rewards Have An Ethical Dimension?

The answer to the question of "Why should rewards have an ethical dimension" is that because the ends do not always justify the means. Traditionally, most rewards are based on the bottom-line results, profitability and making the numbers look right to meet expected or set targets. This type of a reward system may encourage and promote immoral behavior in the organization. The importance of money and profits become greater than trying to do the right thing. So, managers and entrepreneurs should look at the rewards from all aspects, including the motivation and incentives it provides for accomplishing the monetary results. An example of this would be the Bausch and Lomb's managers and executives who inflated their sales volume of Ray-Ban sunglasses to meet set performance standards or targeted goals. They were sending a large supply of these glasses to customers who did not need them. Some of those customers were sent two years of supplies despite the fact that they did not ask for them.

There are cases where some people have taken advantage of the system because of their passion for the reward. Ron Waver was a thirty-year old football player who played football at the University of Texas under an assumed identity during the 1995-1996 Season. He pleaded guilty of using someone else's identity and social security number to get onto the team. He says he loves football and the rewards are great for doing what you love. So, he did not feel bad about what he did. This is similar to the case of singers' Millie Vanillie. The two singers were using someone else's voice as their own. They became very famous among teenagers during the late 1980s but were finally discovered and their dreams were shattered. They took advantage of the system and betrayed people.

Joseph Jett, a Harvard MBA graduate and former Kidder Peabody bond trader, was named Kidder's "man of the year" and received Kidder Peabody's star employee "Chairman's Award" for 1993. However, in April of 1994 Jet was fired by Kidder and they accused him of faking about $350 million in profits to mask $80 million in losses through the complicated, computerized systems of trading. These fake profits, over a two year period, translated into millions of dollars in bonuses for Jett and other executives at Kidder. Regulators claim that his motive of personal gain led him to fix the numbers and report the fake profits. And as the result of the fake profits, he earned more than $11 million in bonuses during 1992 and 1993. Joseph Jett claims that he is innocent and his superiors were well aware of his trading. He argues that he could not have committed fraud because all of his trading has been documented and it has always been available to his bosses and the auditors. He says "money is important to me only as a symbol of accomplishment" (USA TODAY, May 20, 1996). A main problem with this money mentality is that it is a never ending process and it can go on forever. Success and accomplishment cannot be solely defined by money, because money can be gathered with immoral means which contradict the internal feelings of accomplishment that produce intrinsic rewards. Just because the documents are clear and everyone agrees with an action, does not make the action right. Executives need to set specific guidelines and training programs that help people look beyond the numbers for their purpose and the means of achieving those purposes. In Jett's case the system allowed room for such errors and he took advantage of it claiming he did not do anything wrong. Similar errors have been made by people at Enron, Tyco, WorldCom, and other firms in recent years.

The Department of Justice, in the USA, reported that in 1995 about 5,506 former officers, directors, consultants, and others of saving and loans involved were convicted of fraud in the savings and loans debacle. And of the total number of people convicted, 4,157 were sent to prison. According to Louie Larimer (1996), AT&T, on October 20th of 1995, was accused of bilking millions of customers on their long distance phone calls. They were allegedly billing people for telephone calls that were never made. This lawsuit sought to recover $50,000 for each of its class members. He further states that Dr. James Thompson, a family practitioner, filed a lawsuit against the nation's largest hospital chain- Columbia-HCA Healthcare Corp. The hospital was supposedly paying bribes and kickbacks to the doctors in exchange for their referrals.

On September 25, 1995, Honda Motor Co. and some of its subsidiaries, such as the North America and American Honda, were charged with sending the popular models to those dealers who paid bribes and kickbacks. Michael Monus, former president of Phar-Mor drug chain, was convicted in September of 1995 on 109 counts of fraud. He was convicted because of using phony financial data to lure more than $1 billion in investment. William Aramony, former president of United Way, was also convicted of fraud and misappropriating funds in 1995. These few examples of fraud and immoral acts exemplify the need for effective reward programs that are designed to provide encouragement and support for ethical decisions throughout the company.

Recognition and Rewards

Traditional methods of running an organization have changed rapidly and will probably continue to do so at an even faster pace as the workforce changes. In the past, a majority of the workforce was made-up of males and this has been changing rapidly as more women and minorities from different backgrounds are joining the workforce. It has been predicted that about 5/6th of the new workforce in the United States will be women (2/3 of the new workforce), minorities, and immigrants. This diverse group of workforce requires different sets of compensations packages. For example, in general, when compared to men, more women may prefer to have time off as opposed to working overtime for increased salary or earnings. Also, young adults and new immigrants tend to prefer to work more often for the monetary rewards.

Recognition programs can be geared toward both extroverts, those who need incentives to be motivated, and introverts, those who are motivated because of internal satisfaction of pride in workmanship and responsibility. Human resource professionals should design recognition programs to serve both introverts and extroverts to make the job more fulfilling. Challenging and fulfilling jobs can keep people happy and internally motivated to complete their jobs with commitment and personal integrity.

Many organizations are rewarding people based on a bonus system that can increase or decrease depending on the performance of bottom-line (profits), or sales for the company or individual. In most cases the organization will provide a basic salary and the bonus will be added based on the sales or net profit of the individual or the team. In some cases, these programs can backfire and hurt the company from the unethical behavior of one or more employees. As mentioned before, Sears Automotive used to reward their associates based on their sales volume, so some of the mechanics started overcharging people for supposedly fixing parts of the engine which they did not do. This unethical behavior was discovered by the media which pressured the company to change their bonus programs so it does not allow room for immoral behavior. Another company provided bonus for their management and full-time associates on quarterly basis. They discovered that some managers hesitated to recommend or promote eligible part-time associates to full-time and kept them at their part-time status as long as possible. They did this so they would not have to pay them a bonus each quarter because that will decrease the profits of their departments as well as their personal bonuses. So, the company had to create more policies that would prevent or eliminate this type of discrimination by certain individual managers.

Types of Rewards

Cash awards are good; however the marginal utility of each dollar decreases as the award increases. Cash awards are temporary awards and the affects usually end during the next paycheck or the next month. So, cash awards in general, are not very effective in the long-term, and they are not always very popular either. Most employers agree that they can get more mileage from noncash awards than they can from cash awards. Noncash awards are less costly and they should be given immediately, and more often, to continuously reinforce positive behavior. Research shows that every 12 cent cash award has been costing only 4 cents in recognition by noncash awards. Rewards tend to be about 38% a combination of cash and noncash, 15% cash, and 47% noncash for most large firms.

Table 13.1 – Common Recognition Programs

Recognition Program	Percentage of Firms Using It
Years of service	59%
Going "above and beyond" the job	51%
Customer service	41%
Cost saving	39%
Increased productivity	37%

Today's employers are constantly finding different methods of recognizing their associates. These methods can range from recognizing productivity gains, to customer service and even putting an effort to make a new project or product work. A survey of 213 companies reported using one or more of the programs listed in Table 13.1, and years of service was ranked first among the awards.

Rewarding for Performance

It is extremely important that rewards are perceived as fair and just in the eyes of the beholder or those receiving it. Fairness in pay and rewards appear to be the key factor in providing an environment that motivates people to believe in their superior's actions and policies. It is obvious that each manager would like to reward his or her productive employees, however, surveys show that top performers do not always receive top pay for their efforts and performance. A survey of more than 350,000 government employees showed that more than 50 percent believed that some employee do most of the work while others do just enough to get by or to not get fired. Most of the respondents did not believe that job performance was an important factor in promotion, nor did they believe that the best people rose to the top of the organization. It is true that top managers make decisions regarding pay, rewards and promotions based on employee or team performance, however, it is important that these decisions are perceived as just and fair by their associates.

The scenario of giving high performers more work and avoiding the least performers is very familiar to most supermarket managers. A stock person who completes his or her aisle or work before everyone else is usually asked to help the person who is either a slow worker or is not able to get his or her work done on time. It is a good idea to have high performers work with low performers, however, the high performers need to be acknowledged, recognized, and rewarded appropriately for their contributions. Traditionally, people with seniority are being paid higher than the new associates and this may not be very fair on jobs that do not need experience. It may even have a counterproductive effect on new associates who are high performers. Usually, high performers that are not recognized properly may reduce their standards to match the average standards, meaning they are going to do the minimum just to get by until a better position comes along.

It has been documented that managers spend most of their time with two to five percent of their employees who cause many of the problems. So, not only the average and top performers get ignored by the manager but they also get most of the work that needs immediate attention. In general, most managers would give an important project to people who they can count on based on their past performance. Over time, these high performing people can get frustrated and may even change their performance or leave the company. This is especially true if they feel that their co-workers who are not very productive get the same reward as high performing associates. It is crucial to spend time and effort with low performers to help them get better, but we cannot afford to do it at the expense of others who are doing well. Managers should spend appropriate or evenly balanced amounts of time with each group or individual in the department in order to recognize their contributions or to help them become better performers.

Establishing and Designing a Recognition Program

Designing and implementing an effective recognition program takes time and an understanding of the organization's resources, culture, management styles, and employees. While there are no templates that might fit each organization, managers and entrepreneurs can begin by following the generic steps mentioned in Table 13.2: setting goals, mapping the strategy, developing measurement plans, planning the budget, identifying target groups and awards, identifying ethical dimensions and criteria, identifying a marketing plan, and implementing and improving the program.

Table 13.2 – Steps for Designing a Recognition Program

STEPS	ACTIONS	DESCRIPTION
1	*Set Goals*	What are you trying to accomplish? Begin with the end in mind
2	*Map the Strategy*	Create a task force, set rules and policies, involve representatives from all groups or departments.
3	*Develop Measurements*	How and where will it be measured? Company or department level. Should be simple.
4	*Plan the budget*	Take care of the administrative costs including roll-out process, training, and promotion costs.
5	*Identify target groups and awards*	Identify demographics, delivery time (2 - 48 hrs.), Variety of awards for teams and individuals.
6	*Identify ethical dimensions and criteria*	Is it encouraging the mission? Is it aligned with company philosophy? Is it rewarding the desired behavior? Do the ends justify the means?
7	*Identify Marketing Plan*	How and when is it going to be delivered? Who will be running the program? And who is going to follow-up on the promotion?
8	*Implement and Evaluate the Program*	Follow through, get feedback on benefits and side-effects, can it be made better? How long should the program last? Measure effects such as sales, profits, morale, satisfaction, turnover, and so on.

Guidelines for Reward and Recognition

Since there are many layers of management with different background and experience throughout the organization, it is important for professionals to follow a systematic and flexible approach to recognition and reward programs. It is also important to train managers and supervisors at all levels to reward and recognize their people appropriately and responsibly. While it is important to treat everyone consistently because everyone has the same rights, it is even more important to remember that people have different needs and the journey toward fulfilling those specific needs are the key motivating factors. It is the journey that enlightens people and not always the destination, so people should be recognized for their achievements and they should have new goals to accomplish. Managers should try to match the reward with the individual.

Some managers have used the Myer Briggs survey profile to make better decisions about different task forces, working groups, and teams. They have tried to match the task with the right teams or individuals. Perhaps, similar profiles and strategies can be used to determine the type of rewards that would match individual or team needs and desires. One should also keep in mind the piece rate or pay for performance methods as well. When it comes to goal setting, managers and entrepreneurs should consider SMART (Specific, Meaningful, Achievable, Reliable or Rewarding, and Timely) goal-setting strategies for effectively recognizing and rewarding people. Human resource professionals should always make sure that their recognition and award programs are SMART. Besides having a SMART recognition program, organizations should use the following guidelines to develop, design, and deliver fair reward programs.

Train managers and supervisors about rewards. Research shows that there is about a twenty-five percent misunderstanding between managers and associates as to what is important in the organization. Some managers are afraid to give timely feedback to low performers and that might be why they are performing poorly. It has been said that honesty is the best policy, and honest feedback can create many opportunities for managers and employees. Feedback appears to be the number one motivator and this can be seen from watching sports on television. Some people are watching sports for long periods of time because they are able to receive feedback on a continuous basis. This immediate feedback can reinforce many positive thoughts and may encourage people to become "couch potatoes."

The immediate feedback process can be a great motivator which appears to be true in the case of bowling. What if there was a wall in the middle of the lane and the bowlers could not see the pins falling, there would be no immediate feedback, and the player probably would not experience the same effect as getting feedback immediately.

Figure 13.1 - Management Training Circle

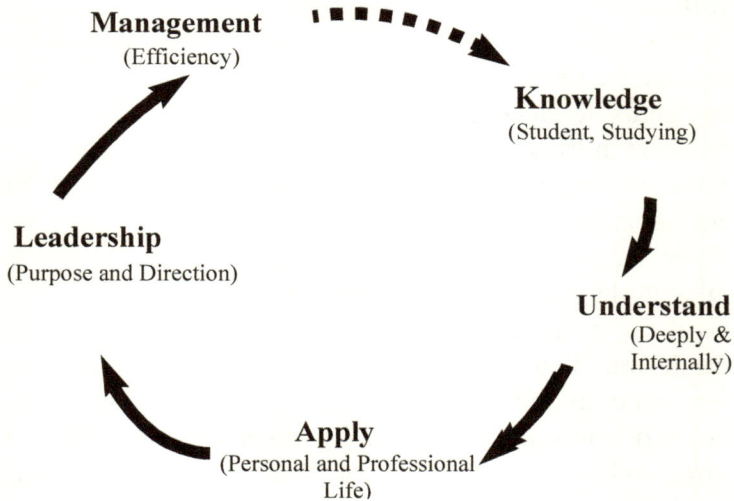

Management
(Efficiency)

Knowledge
(Student, Studying)

Leadership
(Purpose and Direction)

Understand
(Deeply &
Internally)

Apply
(Personal and Professional
Life)

Results and goals should also be communicated to all associates as they become available. These goals should be set reasonably high and should be communicated to everyone on how they can accomplish these results. Rewards should be designed to create and recognize many winners, not just the top performers. For an example, ask a group of people to choose a partner and try to have an eye contest from a close distance. Let them know that the first person who blinks, loses and should sit down; and after one minute see how many pairs are still competing. Normally, there would not be too many pairs still standing up. However, if you tell them that the next contest will be for one minute and all winners will get some type of a reward, this time you will see many more pairs, almost one-hundred percent, who are going to become winners and this is because the first time you did not give them a set time limit or goal. So, communicating the set targets to associates can make a difference as long as they can see the rewards as fair and achievable.

It is also helpful to follow the "Management Training Circle" approach (Figure 13.1) in training the material to the designers, executives, and managers. This approach is based on knowledge, understanding, application, leadership, and management or implementation of a new program. It is an inside-out approach and it starts with each person involved in the design and implementation of a program or reward system. They have to experience and model the program in order for it to be successful. Employees watch what their superiors do; you can lecture them and give them classes, but it is your personal example they will follow. So the executives and the designers need to experience the material firsthand in order for it to make sense.

First of all, the designers, executives, and managers should have the relevant knowledge about reward programs and their purpose. Next, they should dig deeper into the purpose and the logic behind having reward programs. This involves understanding what motivates people, why it motivates them, and how it can help their purpose. Then, they should apply this material to themselves and other small groups for experimentation. The results will provide a vision of leadership that will guide people to their mission, goals, and values. After establishing and understanding their mission, goals, and values, they will be in a position to work on managing the program for efficiency. It is important that leadership or vision of the future precedes management because without a purpose it is extremely difficult and costly to be efficient, especially with people. There are very few things more costly than being on the wrong track or recovering from it. Also, being on the right track involves continuous research and updating, otherwise it will not take too long for one to get run over by others who are speeding down the competitive highway of business.

Create flexible and creative reward programs: It is important to keep the individual in mind when rewarding teams and groups. Reward programs should focus on teams as well as individuals in many different ways. Rewards should be based on win-win-win situations where the company stakeholders, teams, and individuals are recognized and rewarded accordingly. It is critical to match the reward with the employee so the reward can be meaningful to the person receiving it. It is also important to reward and recognize people appropriately as some individuals like to be recognized publicly while others may not want public recognition. However, everyone wants to be a winner and substandard performers can become winners if they are given proper opportunities, encouragement, and guidance. The key to finding the easiest way to get a difficult job done is to delegate the job to a lazy person and you will see the easiest way of accomplishing it. The moral of the story is that anyone can be creative in their own way if they apply themselves and if one looks at things from their perspective or frame of reference.

Clarify standards and expectations to everyone: Without a destination, one can be driving around for days and never get anywhere. With proper destination one can eventually get there, even if they have to stop and ask for directions. It is crucial to have standards and communicate those standards to all employees on a regular basis. Job descriptions and evaluation forms should be designed professionally and they should measure the right elements, those that are geared toward the mission\vision of the department or the company.

Cross-functional training and agronomic: It is essential to consider the work environment and enhance it to reduce boredom and increase creativity and involvement. Repetition can be very boring and sometimes repetitive jobs do not require the person's spiritual mind to be involved one-hundred percent of the time. Studies have shown that listening to music may increase productivity on the job. Sometimes it is helpful to provide job enrichment and cross-train people for different jobs and/or departments. This can reduce cost of overtime, increase morale and job satisfaction, and keep people involved as a team. This would also help to find the right people for the right jobs, especially during the busy times.

Align rewards with company mission and values: It is important that reward programs are on parallel paths with the corporate culture of an organization. All rewards should be geared toward the mission and values of the company. Goals and objectives are short-term strategies that focus people to strive for the purpose or mission of an organization. The long-term purpose and mission of the company should be communicated to all parties and they should not be sacrificed at the expense of short-term goals. It is important to emphasize ends as well as means; otherwise some people will create unethical means of accomplishing the results.

Encourage experimentation and individuality: Managers should be encouraged to try new methods of rewarding and recognizing people to keep them creative, innovative, happy, and satisfied. People get tired of becoming "employee of the month" and getting to park at the employee of the month's parking lot as its reward. So, managers should try to experiment and find out what works in the organization and how it can be altered again and again.

Managers should also be recognized for their efforts regardless of positive or negative results. Some incentives are designed based on good intentions, but they may not work realistically because people abuse the concept. For example, one company recognized their associates for creating "raving fans" and this could be done by going above and beyond the call of duty to satisfy a customer or if a customer wrote a complimentary letter or complimented the manager for having such a great employee. This recognition program got out of control because employees started asking customers for written letters and compliments which defeats the purpose of the incentive. So, even a well-intended reward program may have some "side-effects" that need to be taken into consideration in the designing stage of the program.

Summary

Managers are expected to match rewards with individuals and to direct individuals toward accomplishing company objectives. The difficulty occurs when personal and professional objectives do not match. So, most companies have various types of organizational reward programs that recognize and reward good employee performance.

These organizational rewards should be structured in such a way that it recognizes and enhances performance as well as the efforts of each individual. These programs should convey a message of getting the ends with ethical means. These programs should be concerned with how the results are accomplished and the results should be evaluated accordingly. In order to make sure the reward programs are designed and implemented properly, managers and executives should receive training and education to deal with these issues properly. They should try to set goals that stretch people's performance capability and goals so that employees can accomplish them and get rewarded for it in a timely manner. Everyone wants to become a winner and managers should try to help them become winners personally and professionally. This will create win-win-win situations for managers, associates, and the company. Overall, any reward and recognition program should be a part of an integrative and comprehensive performance management system that is strategically aligned with the organization's mission and vision statements.

224 | Bahaudin G. Mujtaba

Discussion Questions

1. How are rewards and recognitions programs related to company success? Discuss.
2. Why should managers consider the ethical implications of their rewards and recognition programs?
3. What is the role of managers and human resource personnel in the area of ethics and reward programs?
4. What types of rewards and recognitions are typically offered to employees?
5. Mention and list five rewards that the new generation of employees might desire in their ideal workplace? Why would the offering of these rewards create a motivational work environment?
6. What can managers do to create a motivational work environment and an organizational culture in the service industry that encourages high performance?

CHAPTER 14

Communication and Listening

Communication takes place whether it is intended or not. Human beings have communicated for thousands of years and some major miscommunication experiences have been documented in books and cultural stories. Such experiences can teach human beings historical trends and their outcomes. The trends and outcomes will tend to show that most conflicts and challenges have been caused by misunderstandings and/or lack of effective communication to settle ideological or philosophical differences and disagreements around a table rather than battlefields. So, communication skills are extremely important for workforce management in a cross-cultural and peaceful work environment. As such, this chapter explores communication and listening skills.

Introduction

Communication is the process of exchanging information in ways that ensure a mutual understanding of content and feelings; this includes being heard and understood. Effective communication can also be defined as the transfer of information from one person to other(s), without the meaning being changed. Often communication takes the forms of speaking and listening. While speaking is done for the purpose of being understood, listening is the real tool for understanding, learning and growing. Being a good listener sets you apart and helps you become a much better communicator while speaking. Have you ever had someone describe you as "a very good listener?" If so, it is a compliment that says quite a bit about you. Remember, people are like fruit; therefore, human beings are either green or growing (learning and thriving), or ripe and rotting (suffering mental stagnation and atrophy).

Living a life of continuous learning pays a wealth of dividends if people listen and use their learning effectively.

Every person without a hearing disability has been listening to what is said since before he or she were born. Yet, it is one of the most difficult skills of human interaction. Listening is not natural which means that people have to work at it; and furthermore, not listening, like communication, is irreversible. What you don't hear is gone and you may not get the opportunity to listen again. So, as a professional, you should learn to communicate in a manner that builds trust, teamwork and consensus with others whom you directly and indirectly influence. Through effective communication, you can develop the requisite skills that result in effective two-way communication, which is critical to a participative management in today's diverse and global environment of business. Furthermore, as you read this chapter, try to examine some of the obstacles to effective global communication and learn to facilitate supportive communication with diverse individuals and groups in a cross-cultural work environment.

Effective Communication

The bigger the global or multinational firm the more communication challenges they are likely to face. As such, global managers and expatriates must proactively prepare for effective communication with everyone in the value chain. Synergistic teams have members that share information with each other in a clear manner while building effective relationships by speaking with each other and listening well. In other words, all the members tend to communicate well with each other.

Communication is simply exchanging information. *Effective Communication* is sharing information with others in such a way that they understand what you are saying. The goal of effective communication is mutual understanding. In a team environment, the goal of effective communication is to make sure each team member is clear, concise, and credible in what s/he says to others. Getting one's point across and getting results requires that one build credibility, use logic and radiate positive emotional power.

Building trust and credibility takes time, and just like a strong character, they can be chiseled over time by consistently showing courage, honesty, and compassion in dealing with others.

One should always consider the basic elements of communication when encoding messages. The basic elements of communication includes the message, the sender, the receiver, the medium for communication, the language of the sender and receiver, the environment, and perceptual filters of all individuals involved.

Effective communication and listening skills are critical for managers of a culturally-diverse workforce. Associates have the right to know how they are performing and managers must clearly convey their progress to them on regular basis. Managers and team leaders should give continuous feedback to associates. Managers and team leaders should provide effective feedback to associates, based on the thoughts generated from factual observations and analysis of their performance. One should remember that effective feedback is clear, specific, timely, practical, and sincere. It is best to make individualized feedback regarding performance private, positive and performance oriented.

Effective communicators prepare the individual for the occasion where the performance is an issue, by letting them know, that "we need to discuss your performance because it is important." During the session, effective managers and leaders do not "beat around the bush"; they get right to the point. They do not get "side tracked" and stay focused on the performance issue until they get a specific commitment and plan from the individual to improve it. The manager can end the session by summarizing the performance issue/challenge, repeating the expectations, reviewing the specific plan which the employee created, and wishing the individual success with it. Of course, the manager needs to follow-up to make sure the expectations are met.

Listening and Communication

While many individuals in the workplace believe they are effective listeners, very few actually are listening well. Knowledge of the facts and listening are not necessarily the same since one can get the facts without being a good listener. Listening requires more than just one's ears as it is an active process of hearing, processing and matching what is heard with the sender's non-verbals and tone of voice. Many decades ago, the research of Albert Mehrabian showed that 7% of communication tends to be through the words (what one speaks), 38% is the vocal (how one speaks), and 55% is through nonverbal.

In order to become aware of the active listening process, at the basic level, managers should understand that hearing, listening, and effective listening are different terms and concepts since their definitions vary. For example:

- *Hearing* is the process of receiving sound waves through the ear and brain. Hearing does not equal listening because listening is more than just hearing.
- *Listening* is the active process of mentally interpreting sound waves in the brain. People focus their hearing upon stimuli they wish to attend to and must interpret them into meaning and action.
- *Effective listening* is purposefully paying attention to and desiring to understand the other person's point of view. Effective listening requires giving and receiving feedback. *Feedback* is verbal or nonverbal response to an object, a message, behavior, or performance that often affects the receiver either positively or negatively.

Managers must go beyond simply hearing and listening to effectively understand others. The best way for one to progress toward effective listening is to make some conscious changes to become better. There are varying types of listening such as casual, attentive and empathetic, each increasing in level of concentration. *Casual listening* uses minimal attention, as with TV or radio. *Attentive listening* requires analysis of information, remembering content, and questioning the speaker; while in *empathetic listening*, there is full understanding of the speaker's views, values, attitudes, emotions, and feelings.

Knowing more about oneself may be a key not only to communication but also to performance in a range of life areas. Unless self-awareness is recognized, there is an incomplete understanding of this central part of the communication process. The mental process is categorized into the conscious and unconscious thinking. The Johari Window developed by Joseph Luft and Harrington Ingham is a matrix with four quadrants (the open, hidden, blind, and unknown self) that visualize the self-based on information known or not known to self and others that can be used to increase self-awareness. It also gives an insight into how people communicate in organizations. The *open* self represents all the information, behaviors, attitudes, feelings, desires, motivations, and ideas that an individual knows about him or herself, and those that others know. The *hidden* self consists of all that information someone knows of him or herself but is kept within them. The *blind* self represents all the things that others know about someone but of which the person is ignorant. Communication and interpersonal relations generally expand as the blind-self shrinks, and can only become smaller by listening to feedback about oneself. The *unknown* self represents things that are not known to the individual or to others. Sometimes merely forgotten items, or information repressed by the individual is found in this area. One will usually not learn the content of the unknown self, but it may reveal itself through dreams, hypnosis or sensory deprivation. According to Charles Beck, intrapersonal communication is internal, driven by the individual personality type. The growing recognition of the significance of this area of self-awareness provides a way to understand and reflect on the blind self and to reduce the hidden self. For understanding managerial communications with homogenous or diverse workforce, one has to recognize that intrapersonal awareness exists in everyone and that all people differ in the way they process and analyze their own processes.

Good listening is a key to success in any business environment. Listening effectively can increase income, improve company's profits, keep one aware of what is going on in the organization, make an individual more "promote-able," increase job satisfaction and improve the ability to solving problems. Poor listening is one of the most significant problems facing businesses today. Business relies on clear communication, when communication breaks down, costly mistakes are made. Organizations pay for mistakes caused by poor listening with lower profits, and consumers pay for the same mistakes with higher prices.

Listening Basics

Listening is a gift which does not cost anything; yet lack of it will. Listening is a skill that anyone can learn and develop. Listening is about caring and acknowledging the other person; so we should do it often and with sincere and honest intentions. Most people listen at about 25-30% of their capacity. So, we have a tendency to ignore, forget, distort or incorrectly interpret 75% of what we hear.

Today's business environment has an abundance of information that crosses one's ears and most of it is blocked by the subconscious mind because it adds little to no value to the current work process. This process, through the perceptual filters, conditions the mind to constantly block information that is not valuable at the present moment. The negative side of this is that we lose much valuable information because of the tendency to block things and not overload ourselves. Therefore, making an effort to clearly communicate is important in today's society, in personal events and in business settings.

Miscommunication can be very costly in both one's personal and professional lives. In general, an average person is likely to daydream about 50% of the time. If you wander at least once per minute, it is too much. You would need to force yourself to listen harder and concentrate by improving your listening skills. Not listening effectively can cause many costly mistakes and hurt feelings. For example, a dispatcher routed a fleet of drivers to deliver building material to the wrong state due to miscommunication. The dispatcher heard the city (Portland) but not the state (Maine). So, eight trucks full of building material went to Portland, Oregon which is about 3,000 miles off the coast. This mistake cost the company over $100,000 and perhaps created many disappointed customers who did not get the materials on time. Listening is about caring and motivating. People normally do their best when they know someone is listening (caring) or paying attention to them. This was proven in the Hawthorn studies where worker productivity went up when the amount of lighting was increased or decreased. In other words, employees appreciated the fact that they were being given attention and consultants talked with them about their views, thoughts, and work environment.

The tendency to speak and make our points might be one of the major causes of not listening effectively. Because of this tendency, we listen in different ways and use various levels of listening at different situations. The following are the five identified levels of listening which are discussed in most communication courses.

- *Ignoring.* Not paying any attention, sleeping, talking, etc. Not caring. You don't receive messages at this level. You don't concentrate on listening.
- *Pretending.* Giving the appearance of listening, occasional nod or a response. You give the appearance of listening. You give an occasional head nod or similar form of body language to make the sender think that you're listening, but you're really not.

- *Selecting.* Grasping certain key words here or there but not listening. You select parts of the message that you feel are important. You don't hear or you instantly lose other parts of the message.
- *Attending or active listening.* Listening intently, grasping the content and perhaps even repeating back what you heard; listening with ears for the facts. You're focusing on the message being communicated. You're listening for content and asking questions for clarification.
- *Empathic.* The highest level of listening. Listening with the eyes and the heart for feelings and emotions. It is seeing how the sender sees the situation. You're now seeking to understand the emotions and feelings of the sender, as well as understand the content of the message being communicated. This is the highest level of listening.

Studies show that the first three of the five levels of listening are the levels people most commonly use. It is at the fourth and fifth levels of listening where effective listening takes place. In a multicultural and diverse environment, empathic listening is required to ensure mutual understanding between two or more parties.

Autobiographical responses

When one communicates with others, often he or she tends to listen only enough to be able to respond. We often do not listen to understand or empathize. Since we listen in this way, the responses are likely to be "autobiographical." That is, our responses come out of our own experiences and perceptual filters. Stephen Covey (1989), author of *The Seven Habits of Highly Effective People*, grouped autobiographical responses into four categories: advise, probe, interpret, and evaluate. The acronym for these responses is "A PIE." We have a tendency to use these autobiographical responses when we are in conversation with others, causing a major barrier to effective communication.

Autobiographical responses are the statements or judgments that you make about others based on your experiences. Autobiographical responses aren't always bad, but they are inappropriate when you use them before you've reached understanding. We all tend to diagnose a problem before having enough information and this can lead to miscommunication. As an effective communicator, your goal should be to first understand the other person and then have the other person understand you. These autobiographical barriers are being discussed to help you recognize and eliminate them.

- *Advise*: Telling others what they should do based on our (biased) perspective. We advise when we make recommendations or suggestions based on our own past experiences.
- *Probe*: Asking questions to direct the conversation toward things that come from our frame of reference. We probe when we question the speaker to find similarities with our past experiences.
- *Interpret*: Explaining why they are acting the way they do based on our experiences. When we interpret we are explaining others' behaviors and actions based on our own past actions.
- *Evaluate*: Judging (agreeing or disagreeing with) the situation, which could be verbal, facial, or through body posture, based on one's opinion. We are evaluating when we judge by either agreeing or disagreeing based on our own values.

None of these autobiographical responses meet the needs of the person with whom we are trying to communicate. The one thing the four autobiographical responses have in common is the assumptions we make about others based on our own experiences, which can become a barrier to effective listening and overall communication. The main connection between multicultural communication competency and autobiographical responses is our "mental tapes or perceptual filters." If, in a multicultural conversation, we are using autobiographical responses, we may very well be operating on "automatic pilot." Of-course, as you know being on "automatic pilot," or responding based on past conditioning, is never effective when communicating with people and making decisions regarding others.

Listening without Judgment
Listening is an active process rather than a passive one. However, most often, individuals think about what they are going to say next instead of actually listening. Furthermore, instead of trying to understand, individuals are often conditioned to advice, probe, interpret, and

evaluate (APIE) what the other person is saying. The key to effective listening is to avoid pre-judging the other person or what he or she is saying, and consciously focus on understanding before trying to present one's own perspective.

At least half of all communication time is spent listening. Studies show that we listen more than we perform any other activity except breathing. Yet we often take listening for granted, never realizing that it is a skill that can be learned. Listening is:

- Receiving information through your ears (and eyes).
- Giving meaning to that information.
- Deciding what one thinks (or feels) about that information.
- Responding to what one hears and sees.

We listen at about 25% of our potential, which means we ignore, forget, distort, or misunderstand 75% of what we hear. Poor listening is a significant problem in business today because business relies on clear communication. When communication breaks down, costly mistakes occur. The good news is that you can always assess your listening skills and improve upon them. For example, to get a numerical score about your listening ability you can rate yourself on the listening behaviors using the Listening Scale Survey (LSS – located at the end of this chapter).

Listening requires paying attention. Hearing is non-selective and involuntary. However, when you choose to listen, it is on purpose. From the constant noise around us, we select what we want to listen to because the information is determined to be useful. This information moves from short-term memory to long-term memory. Short-term memory is a "holding pen" for incoming signals from the senses. In order to protect us from too much stimulation short-term memory has a limited capacity and is easily disrupted. For instance, a mail clerk would not likely retain much information from a technical discussion about data transport protocols because he or she would have no use for the message. The information would probably be held in short-term memory for 1 to 30 seconds and then dismissed. If the information we hear is not recognized and selected for processing, it is dismissed from short-term memory and not remembered. In order for information to move to long-term memory, one must *choose* to listen.

Paying attention means not interrupting others and not being driven by emotions. Words, issues, situations and/or personalities trigger people emotionally. When these issues trigger one's emotional "hot buttons," verbal messages become distorted, either positively or negatively. When issues are emotional they can become barriers to effective listening. When hot buttons are activated, one tends to tune out, distort, or prejudge these emotionally charged messages. This can cause one to interrupt the speaker. Both listeners and speakers have mental filters, which help or hinder the interpreting process of listening. These filters are in our brain's database, and they attach personal meaning to information.

Questions are a listener's most powerful tool. With the right questions, you can manage a conversation, clarify what you are hearing and elicit more information. Use open-ended questions to probe for more information. Open-ended questions encourage the speaker to explain, expand, describe, explore, or elaborate. Use open-ended questions when:

◊ The speaker is uncommunicative or reluctant.
◊ You need to bring out the other person's concerns, ideas, or feelings.
◊ You need to understand the big picture.
◊ You're not certain exactly what information you need, or you need to clarify some points.
◊ You're trying to build involvement, trust, or rapport.
◊ You want to promote self-discovery.

Watch someone who listens attentively. This individual probably makes eye contact and/or focuses on the other person while actively listening. Effective communicators listen with their eyes as well as their ears. They acknowledge the person by nodding and making attentive noises from time-to-time. When acknowledging what you hear and, as appropriate, make sure you:

◊ Express your point of view.
◊ Present your evidence without backing the other person into a corner.
◊ Explain why.
◊ Acknowledge other person's feelings.
◊ Try to see the other person's point of view.

◊   Agree where you can.

Managers, leaders, teammates, and employees can listen actively to their team members and colleagues by practicing the skills of empathic listening as emphasized by Dr. Carl Rogers and Dr. Stephen R. Covey. Dr. Covey and other experts, as previously mentioned, have discussed the five levels of listening which are ignoring, pretending, selective, active, and empathic listening. The best levels of listening are active and empathic listening as they can lead to learning, understanding, and higher levels of trust among people. One can use the active listening process to understand what is being said in a professional work environment. However, when emotions are involved, when the listener does not feel understood, and when the speaker is not clear about what is being said then it is best to use the empathic listening process.

Listening Empathically

Empathic listening has been at the forefront of communication research since the 1960's. It was first discussed by Carl Rogers. It has also been known as the Rogerian communication exercise. Dr. William James of Harvard University says, "The deepest need of every human being is to be understood." We often fail to take the steps necessary to really understand our family members, associates, peers, and customers. We have a tendency to resolve the situation before making an accurate identification of the problem. If you have a tendency to solve problems before knowing the problem or its cause, then you're not alone. Sometimes our cultures condition us to listen, not with the intent to understand, but with the intent to respond. Therefore, it is best to fully explore the empathic listening process and skills to help you reach a higher level of understanding so that you may respond effectively and appropriately when interacting with others.

Empathy means compassion, commiseration, understanding, and emotional identification. While listening empathically you simply reflect on the other person's feeling and sayings. *Reflect* means to think seriously about or contemplate something. *Empathic listening* is the process of listening to both the content and the feelings of a message. You reflect on the meaning and emotions of the message and then restate your understanding to the sender. The process of empathic listening gives you the opportunity to reach true understanding in communication. Empathic listening can be very effective in achieving mutual understanding among two or more parties. However, empathic listening is not a panacea for major problems or personality concerns. It is simply a process that can lead to better understanding of what is being communicated. There are many examples of empathic listening leads or phrases you may use when you are applying the process of reflective listening. Some of the listening leads can include the following:

- As I hear it, you feel as if...
- To me, it's as if you're saying you want...
- What it sounds like you're saying is, you need...
- If I'm hearing you correctly, you feel that...
- I'm not sure, but it seems as though you desire...

As you can see, empathic listening responses seek to understand the feelings and emotions of the sender along with the content meaning. Empathic listening process is especially useful when there are emotional topics being discussed.

Overall, *empathic listening* is the process of discovering the sender's perspective, thoughts, and feelings by encouraging the sender to self-disclose through active listening and/or empathy. Empathic listening involves listening with the eyes and heart for feelings and listening with the ears for facts, thoughts and views. Since performance discussions between colleagues, managers and employees can be emotional, it is best to master the skill of empathic listening. It is important that listeners are caring, gentle and understanding in such situations without losing focus of the performance issue. Effective listeners use the empathic listening skills which can be done by:

- Repeating the message.
- Summarizing the content of the message.
- Expressing or reflecting on the feelings of the message.
- Restating both the content and feelings of the message in your own words.
- Using good judgment with regard to determining which of the above steps are appropriate for each situation.

Summary

Human beings have communicated for thousands of years; yet miscommunications seem to happen despite so much experience with it. Most people agree that communication skills are extremely important, especially for a culturally diverse workforce and their effective management. The chapter stated that effective communication is the process of exchanging information in ways that ensure a mutual understanding of content and feelings; this includes being heard and understood. This chapter described the various levels of listening, barriers to effective listening, and detailed the skill of empathic listening for effective communication and negotiation with one's family members, friends, as well as one's colleagues in a diverse workforce.

Discussion Questions

1. What is effective communication? How is "effective communication" different from "communication"?
2. Can one effectively be listening, thinking and talking with someone at the same time? Discuss.
3. What is listening? What is active listening? How is listening different from hearing?
4. What are some common barriers to listening? How can one overcome such barriers in order to listening effectively?
5. What are autobiographical responses and how do they impact listening?
6. Discuss the various levels of listening and example of each as used by your friends, colleagues and family members.
7. What is empathic listening?
8. Try the skill of empathic listening with four friends and colleagues and document your results. Try this technique with people that you do not know and document the results.

Listening Scale Survey

You can rate yourself on the listening behaviors using the Listening Scale Survey (LSS) and the following guidelines:

        4= Almost always
        3= Most of the time
        2= Some of the time
        1= Almost never

Place a check mark in the appropriate box. Multiply the rating number at the top of the columns by the number of check marks in that rating area and record the results in the sub-total columns. Add the sub-totals and place the results in the area marked "Total Overall."

	When listening I do the following:	4	3	2	1
1.	I pay attention, even though the subject may bore me				
2.	I refrain from finishing the other person's sentences				
3.	I wait for the speaker to finish before evaluating the message				
4.	I maintain eye contact				
5.	I listen for feelings as well as subject matter				
6.	I show nonverbal responses to demonstrate I'm listening: nodding, smiling, leaning forward				
7.	I give brief verbal responses: "Uh-hum, M-m-m, Oh"				
8.	I stop myself from interrupting the one speaking to me				
9.	I seek to reduce or eliminate distractions				
10.	I ask questions only to clarify something said				
11.	I demonstrate I have an open mind and do not respond negatively to the other's ideas or feelings				
12.	I often paraphrase what I hear to make sure I have heard it correctly				
13.	I work to make myself really want to listen				
14.	I listen carefully to understand the main message				
15.	I maintain emotional control, no matter what is said				
	Sub-totals				
	Total Overall				

Now, after totaling the scores see next page for the results.

Listening Scale Survey Results

Now that you have determined your overall total from the Listening Scale Survey (LSS), you can use the following ranges of numbers to determine your listening score area:

50-60	Congratulations! You are an excellent listener. Keep listening intently with everyone.
40-49	Good going! You are a good listener, and you could be even better.
30-39	Keep working on it. Listening skills will help you solve problems. Practice the skills of active and empathic listening when you can.
15-29	You really should get serious about learning to listen. Take classes and learn active listening skills. Try to consciously focus on hearing others and what they are trying to communicate both verbally and non-verbally. Once you have mastered active listening techniques, then, focus on using empathic listening skills when emotions are involved, when you don't understand the speaker, and when the other person does not feel understood.

CHAPTER 15

Conflict Management

Effectively resolving social and interpersonal conflicts are an important and mission-critical aspect of a global leader's responsibilities. Effective leaders, administrators and managers are always focused on the achievement of organizational goals with a balance of concern for people and production. As such, besides resolving conflicts, effective managers are performance-focused and developmental in their leadership and management styles as they are first and foremost concerned about the well-being, development and success of their employees. Furthermore, global leaders and administrators need to understand conflict and their own conflict management styles which are discussed in this chapter.

Conflict Management

With so much diversity around the world in terms of culture and national agendas, there are bound to be national and international conflicts among people and various countries. Conflict is a reality of personal, professional and political life, which everyone faces at one time or another. Leaders, managers, and team members thus need to understand the causes and effects of conflicts and how to respond in the best interest of all members concerned. Conflict is often a characteristic of change. Any attempt to adjust the status quo in an organization can result in conflict. If effectively handled, conflict can be a healthy way of airing differences. However, constant conflict can be anxiety-inducing, debilitating, and destructive. Conflict occurs within and between individuals, groups, teams, organizations, and societies. An effective conflict resolution process includes recognition, awareness, and choice.

Individuals react differently to conflict. Some people seem to thrive on conflict while others abhor it; yet, still a few other individuals can remain unruffled by the most conflicting situations. Individuals also deal with conflict in different ways, some people attack, while others tend to defend. However, most people are consistent in their individual responses to conflict, tending to respond the same way over time, developing a behavior pattern.

Conflict often is assumed to be a contest, and it is not. Conflict is part of nature; neither positive nor negative, "it just is". People can choose whether to make conflict a contest, a game, which requires that some players become winners and some losers. Winning and losing are generally the goals of games, but not the goal of conflict management. Effective conflict management requires thinking "win-win" with the goals of jointly learning, growing, and cooperating. Conflict can be seen as the interference pattern of energies as seen in nature: "Nature uses conflict as its primary motivator for change, creating beautiful beaches, canyons, mountains, and pearls" (Crum, 1987, p. 49). It is not whether one has a conflict in his or her life, because everyone experiences it; rather it is what one does with the conflict that makes a positive or negative difference. People need to naturally move into a "you and me" mentality where they see the world as abundant and supportive in all aspects of their lives, from their health to their financial well-being. Nature sees conflict in a positive light, and uses it as a primary motivator for bringing about lasting changes. For human beings, the strength, the will, and the needed skills are available, so long as they are willing to let go of tension, fear, stereotypes, biases, and boundaries.

Conflict is the struggle that results when two or more individuals perceive a difference or incompatibility in their interests, values, or goals. Conflicts can arise from ambiguous roles and goals, stereotypes, biases, different procedures, distribution of resources, irreconcilable differences, perception of information and personalities, and the structures in place. In a diverse workplace, every interaction has a potential for conflict. Some conflict is good for team performance. Too much conflict causes team leaders to spend much time responding to it. *Conflict management* is the process of dealing with conflict in an effective manner. Positive conflict (conflict that is managed effectively) is great for team performance, and negative conflict can be very hurtful. Managers can manage individual conflict by:

⇒ Increasing awareness of the source of conflict.
⇒ Increasing diversity awareness and management skills.
⇒ Effectively communicating and listening to the different sides.
⇒ Practicing job rotation and temporary assignments.
⇒ Using permanent transfers and dismissals if needed.
⇒ Changing the team's structure.

Furthermore, during an interpersonal conflict with a team member or colleague, one can remain focused on facts, feelings, and future expectations, rather than attacking the other person. Managers must "stick to the facts" and have effective conflict management strategies. According to industry literature and best practices over the past few decades, the following are short descriptions of some of the most common conflict management strategies.

- *Avoidance*: Some people do not feel comfortable dealing with conflict situations so they simply ignore it.
- *Smoothing or accommodating*: Other individuals (managers or workers) offer platitudes to cover up conflict similar to what a mother might do with her two small children, saying in effect, "Don't fight with your brother; let's all watch television together."
- *Authoritarianism, winning, or competing*: With this style, the manager or worker simply dictates the answer to the conflict. In this case, the person is forcing his or her solution on others and wants to win at all costs.
- *Expansion of resources*: In the event conflict is about scarce resources, like a new position in the budget, it is sometimes possible and wise to expand resources, e.g., add an additional position to the budget so that both managers can have a new employee. However, this expanding of resources option may not always be an option.
- *Compromise*: In compromise, everyone wins something. There is no winner and no loser; of course, nobody is completely happy either.
- *Mutual problem solving or collaboration*: Teamwork is the best way for long-term conflict resolution; mutual problem-solving

methods requires all conflicting parties to hear each other out and work on a solution together.

Day-to-day challenges with employees, colleagues, and bosses serve as laboratories for one to develop conflict management skills. It prepares expatriates to serve as effective leaders, managers, and workers in the workplace. Conflict is best resolved within and by the team itself or by individuals causing the conflict. The best way to resolve conflict is to seek cooperation from all parties involved and to create a win-win solution for everyone through collaboration and mutual problem solving. This way you can meet your needs and theirs. There are conflicts that can be ignored or avoided, but others must be dealt with appropriately.

No matter how hard one works to build a productive team, the behavior of some team members or employees can cause breakdowns and block team progress while hindering everyone's performance. Team members, managers, and team leaders need to recognize such behaviors and learn how to resolve conflicts that arise when diverse personalities are dealing with complex performance challenges. Quickly and effectively resolving such conflicts can speed up the team's progress toward achieving its purpose (performance challenge). When dealing with day-to-day conflicts, misconducts, and disagreements, remember to use the 4-F model by emphasizing the facts, feelings, future expectations, and following up.

> *Facts*. Stick with the facts and describe the behavior that is creating the problem or conflict. Avoid attacking the other person. Avoid using "you" statements.
> *Feelings*. State the impact of the problem or conflict, your feelings, the feelings of team members, and how the problem makes the team suffer. Use "I" statements by mentioning how the above mentioned problem or fact impacts you or your employees and colleagues.
> *Future expectations*. Clearly describe future expectations, norms, and rules of conduct.
> *Following up*. Managers should follow up with the parties involved to make sure employees are meeting the expected standards as agreed. If they are, then the manager has an opportunity to reinforce this good behavior. Otherwise, the

manager will have another opportunity to start the process again (or take drastic actions as appropriate).

When conflicts exist, all team members must persist on behavior change until it is changed so the team can effectively proceed with its objective. In most organizations, it clearly becomes imperative for managers to be able to address and effectively resolve conflicts. Also, when confronted with an ethical conflict in a culturally diverse organization, it is important for a manager to be capable of recognizing the key factors in order to determine the most appropriate strategy. Often, managers can use the Socratic questioning process to get each party to think of other "sides" to the issue in order to eventually reach a mutually agreed-upon solution.

Sharing information with others is a fact of life, but sharing misinformation with others is also a reality. The spread of misinformation often can be the root to much conflict and ill feelings among employees. As such, it is necessary that educated individuals not spread misinformation about community members, managers, leaders, politicians, or one's colleagues in the workplace. The Triple Filter Test provides the wisdom of Socrates about why "grapevine" or certain messages should not be shared with others especially when the message has not been verified to see if it is true, important or even useful. Perhaps we can use this story to take a stand and hopefully make ourselves or others "stop" and think about "the spoken words" and their impact on the department or persons involved. People often wonder why some people have such great friends and manage to keep them. If one successfully applies the "Triple Filter Test" in one's conversations, the same could work for everyone. The following is the story behind the "Triple Filter Test" coming from Socrates.

In ancient Greece, Socrates was reputed to hold knowledge in high esteem. One day an acquaintance met the great philosopher and said, "Do you know what I just heard about your new friend?" "Hold on a minute," Socrates replied. Before telling me anything I'd like you to pass a little test. It's called the Triple Filter Test. "Triple filter?" said the acquaintance. "That's right," Socrates continued. "Before you talk to me about my friend, it might be a good idea to take a moment and filter what you're going to say. That's why I call it the Triple Filter Test."

1. *"The first filter is Truth.* Have you made absolutely sure that what you are about to tell me is true?" "No," the man said, "actually I just heard about it and..." "All right," said Socrates. "So you don't really know if it's true or not."

2. *"The second filter is the filter of Goodness.* Is what you are about to tell me about my friend something good?" "No, on the contrary..." "So," Socrates continued, "you want to tell me something bad about him, but you're not certain it's true. You may still pass the test though, because there's one more filter left."

3. *"The third one is the filter of Usefulness.* Is what you want to tell me about my friend going to be useful to me?" "No, not really."

"Well," concluded Socrates, "if what you want to tell me is neither true, nor good, nor even useful, why tell it to me at all?" This is why Socrates was a great philosopher and held in such high esteem. If we are able to protect our colleagues, employees, friends, and those we love in this manner, we cannot be influenced by outsiders in having bad notions about them. Rumors, which seem to flow often among people in a diverse work environment, should be stopped and corrected instead of being spread when they have no reality. Rumors can damage an individual or the morale in the organization. Socrates certainly understood the idea behind systems thinking paradigm and how one part can impact the whole person, the whole department or organization, the community, and possibly the society over time. So, always remember the "Triple Filter Test" by passing messages through the filters of *"truth,"* *"goodness,"* and *"usefulness."* It is a moral imperative to always make sure what is said is true, good, and useful before it is passed on to others. Such a questioning process can reduce misinformation and eliminate possible challenges before they become major conflicts.

People come into a conflict situation with some experience and assumptions based upon their conflicting situations. Some employees and managers who face a conflict tend to "fight" it, while others might choose the "flight" approach. For example, would you choose the fight or flight approach if you were to have a conflict with an employee, colleague, or boss? Oftentimes, people tend to fall somewhere in between the continuum of "fight" or "flight." Once one determines what his or her natural approach might be to a conflicting situation with others, then he or she can determine the advantages and disadvantages of this approach, his or her approach's probability of success in various conflicting situations, and the means of adapting different styles to be more successful.

Most people tend to have one of the five conflict resolution approaches in the continuum of being assertive (meeting one's own needs) to being supportive (meeting others' needs): avoiding, accommodating, competing, compromising, and collaborating. To determine what your dominant style is, complete the conflict resolution survey (provided at the end of this chapter) and circle your two dominant styles.

Managers are likely to have one or two dominant styles of resolving conflict. It is best to know one's natural tendencies and, if needed, improve upon them as desired. While in some cases "avoiding" might be an effective style for dealing with a conflict, other situations might require the use of collaborating or compromising in order to get things done with other team members. The situational variables should determine the best style. While situations do vary, a person should always keep his/her composure because objectivity and rational decision-making is critical for effective conflict resolution. Furthermore, effective conflict resolution process requires the use of excellent listening skills. While listening effectively, managers can use objective and open-ended questions to clarify further areas of interest for all parties involved.

The essence of effective conflict resolution is to work together without offending anyone or being offended. Consequently, one should resolve all differences in a professional manner. It is also beneficial to remember that differences and disagreements can lead to better alternatives, better solutions, new ways of viewing each case, and opportunities for more quality communication. In each obstacle, there can be hidden opportunities. One needs to stay calm, stay "all together" in the face of disagreements, hear each other's' differences and views, and then make sure one's views are heard by everyone on the team before agreeing on a final solution. In the case of performance-related conflict with employees, if the conflict resolution process does not resolve the situation, managers then can use a formal employee discipline strategy to correct the process.

Positive and Negative Conflict

One should remember that there is good conflict and there is bad conflict. In *positive conflict*, individuals of different views and personalities tend to show mutual respect for each other's' thoughts and feelings in order to develop a strong partnership and eventually synergistic results. However, in *negative conflict*, people view each other as adversaries and are focused on "winning"; thereby, in negative conflict, people attempt to protect themselves, even if such a defense comes at a high cost to others.

Conflict management skills and techniques enable managers and leaders to reduce or eliminate those barriers that prevent individuals or a population group from achieving the results desired in the department or in the economy. One can summarize that conflict is simply a byproduct of bringing about new developments, growth, innovation, and change toward a better work environment and culture. Just like change, conflict is inevitable. By understanding how to deal with conflict in a positive and performance-focused manner, and actually preventing small issues from becoming major conflicts, market-based leaders' behavior can serve as a model for others in the organization. Leaders and managers can proactively sense and reduce/eliminate conflict by being visionary, giving feedback, getting feedback, defining expectations, and reviewing performance regularly with their employees. The benefits of conflict management can be better relationships with one's employees and colleagues, increased self-respect, personal development and growth, increased efficiency and effectiveness, creative and innovative thinking in the department, and synergy or teamwork.

Overall, when it comes to day-to-day conflicts, managers have a choice to deal with the conflict, ignore the conflict, or leave the area or department that is causing the conflict. The best choice in many cases, according to experts, would be to proactively deal with the conflict in an effective manner.

Conflict Resolution Options and Techniques

In order to communicate effectively, managers must be cognizant of the different ways in which they can resolve conflicts. Conflict resolution builds stronger and more cohesive organizations and more rewarding relationships. The following are twelve steps for effective conflict resolution which often are offered by academicians and practitioners.

1. The win/win approach. The win/win approach is about changing the conflict from an adversarial attack and defense, to cooperation. It is a powerful shift of attitude that alters the course of communication. One person continually applying a joint problem solving approach can make the difference. Until we give it some thought, we usually are unaware of the way we argue. We often find ourselves with a knee-jerk reaction in difficult situations based on long established habits combined with the passing mood of the moment. When challenged we experience loneliness; we feel disconnected from those around us. While people argue over opposing solutions- "Do it my way! No, that is not good! Do it my way!" the conflict is a power struggle. What is needed is to change the agenda in the conversation. The objective should be "I want to win and I want you to win too." It is about thinking "win-win" as explained by Stephen R. Covey in his popular *Seven Habits of Highly Effective People* book, which was originally published in 1989.

2. Creative response. The creative response to conflict is about turning problems into possibilities. It is about consciously choosing to see what can be done, rather than existing with how terrible it all is. It is in affirming that you will choose to extract the best from the situation.

3. Empathy. It is deemed necessary to develop communication tools to build rapport. Use empathic listening to clarify understanding. Effective empathic listening takes place when a listener fully understands the speaker's views, values, attitudes, emotions, and feelings associated with the intended message.

4. Appropriate assertiveness. It is imperative that managers apply strategies that attack the problem, and not the person. The emphasis of appropriate assertiveness is being able to state your case without arousing the defenses of the other person. The most important factor is saying how it is for you rather than what they should or should not do. "The way I see it…" attached at the beginning of one's assertive statement, helps. A skilled "I" statement goes even further. When you want to state your point of view helpfully, the "I" statement formula can be useful. An "I" statement says how it is on my side, and how I see it.

5. *Cooperative power.* It is very important to eliminate the "power over" to build "power with" others. When faced with a situation that has the potential to create conflict, ask open questions to reframe resistance. Explore the difficulties and then re-direct discussion to focus on positive possibilities.

6. *Managing emotions.* Express fear, anger, hurt, and frustration wisely to effect change. Additionally, these messages should demonstrate sincerity and trustworthiness matching the intent of the communicators.

7. *Willingness to resolve.* It is important for managers to maintain a willingness to resolve. The more someone inflames, angers or upsets a person, the more one realizes the need to learn more about themselves. We must constantly look within ourselves to see whether or not we are projecting, or if there is anything that has interfered with our willingness to resolve. Projection is when we see our thoughts and feelings in the minds and behavior of others and not in ourselves.

8. *Mapping the conflict.* Sometimes issues are simplified when they are written down. A good idea is to define briefly the issue, the problem or conflict in neutral terms that everyone would agree on.

9. *Broadening perspectives.* Everyone should learn to respect and value differences. Just as we are unique and special, so are other people. We all have distinctive viewpoints that may be just as valid from where we stand. Each person's viewpoint makes a contribution to the whole and requires consideration and respect in order to form a complete solution. This wider view can open our eyes to many more possibilities.

10. *Mediation.* The third party mediator should endeavor to be *objective.* He or she should validate both sides, even if the moderator silently prefers one point of view or when only one party is present. Secondly, the mediator should be *supportive.* He or she should use caring language. Provide a non-threatening learning environment, where people will feel safe to disclose personal issues. Thirdly, the mediator should be *unbiased.* He or she should actively discourage judgments as to who was right and who was wrong. Ask questions such as: What happened? How did you feel? The mediator should endeavor to *encourage participation.* Encourage suggestions from participants. Do not give advice. If your suggestions are really needed, offer them as options not directives. *Strive for a win/win situation* - Turn opponents into problem-solving partners.

11. Designing of options. It is best to explore all possible options and perhaps break the problem into smaller parts. Furthermore, one should research the situation, gather more information, and establish the constraints involved. When exploring options, always consider the following questions:

◊   Is the option satisfying the win/win approach?
◊   Does the option meet many needs of all parties?
◊   Is it cost effective?
◊   Is it fair?
◊   Does it solve the problem?
◊   Can the problem be settled with only one option?

12. Negotiation. The emphasis is on the relationships among team members. The strategy involves a series of controlled negotiations between participants. One should remember that negotiations involve several principles:

◊   The emphasis should be on the problem, and not on the person.
◊   Focus on the needs, not on positions.
◊   Emphasize common ground.
◊   Be inventive about options.
◊   Make clear agreements.

One always must focus on the issue while maintaining the relationship and trying to resolve the issue. After clarification, members must decide which items they want most and form into pairs to negotiate, usually with a third party to help in the process. Finally, there should be a written role negotiation agreement. The outcome of the negotiation is written down and spells out the agreements and concessions, which each party finds satisfactory.

Kofi Annan's Lessons and Recommendations[5]

Prior to leaving office as the Secretary General of the United Nations at the end of 2006, in an article entitled *"United Nations Lessons Learned,"* Mr. Kofi A. Annan offered several universal principles that can be extremely useful for reflection and strategic planning toward the creation of equality, justice, peace, and fairness for all. The five lessons

---

[5] Speech by the Secretary-General Kofi A. Annan, Truman Library; December 11, 2006; retrieved on December 14, 2006 from the United Nation's Website.

(published by the Washington Post on December 11, 2006) are a brief reproduction of his original thoughts that were emailed to the author by colleagues; however, the original lessons can be retrieved from the United Nation's Website (http://www.un.org/). The following are a brief summary of Mr. Kofi Annan's lessons offered before he left office on December 31, 2006:

Nearly 50 years ago, when I arrived in Minnesota as a student fresh from Africa, I had much to learn--starting with the fact that there is nothing wimpish about wearing earmuffs when it is 15 degrees below zero. All my life since has been a learning experience. Now I want to pass on five lessons I have learned during 10 years as secretary general of the United Nations that I believe the community of nations needs to learn as it confronts the challenges of the 21st century.

1. In today's world we are all responsible for each other's security. Against such threats as nuclear proliferation, climate change, global pandemics or terrorists operating from safe havens in failed states, no nation can make itself secure by seeking supremacy over all others. Only by working to make each other secure can we hope to achieve lasting security for ourselves. This responsibility includes our shared responsibility to protect people from genocide, war crimes, ethnic cleansing and crimes against humanity. That was accepted by all nations at last year's U.N. summit. But when we look at the murder, rape and starvation still being inflicted on the people of Darfur, we realize that such doctrines remain pure rhetoric unless those with the power to intervene effectively--by exerting political, economic or, in the last resort, military muscle--are prepared to take the lead.

2. We are responsible for each other's welfare. Without a measure of solidarity, no society can be truly stable. It is not realistic to think that some people can go on deriving great benefits from globalization while billions of others are left in, or thrown into, abject poverty. We have to give all our fellow human beings at least a chance to share in our prosperity.

3. Both security and prosperity depend on respect for human rights and the rule of law. Throughout history, human life has been enriched by diversity, and different communities have learned from each other. But if our communities are to live in peace, we must stress also what unites us: our common humanity and the need for our human dignity and rights to be protected by law. Policies that genuinely favor development are more likely to be adopted if the people most in need of development can make their voices heard. States need to play by the rules toward each other, as well. No community suffers from too much rule of law; many suffer from too little-- and the international community is among them.

4. Governments must be accountable for their actions, in the international and domestic arenas. Every state owes some account to other states on which its actions have a decisive impact. As things stand, poor and weak states are easily held to account, because they need foreign aid. But large and powerful states, whose actions have the greatest impact on others, can be constrained only by their own people.

     5. States can hold each other accountable only through multilateral institutions. Those institutions must be organized in a fair and democratic way, giving the poor and the weak some influence over the actions of the rich and the strong. Developing countries should have a stronger voice in international financial institutions, whose decisions can mean life or death for their people. New permanent or long-term members should be added to the U.N. Security Council…No less important, all the U.N. Security Council members must accept the responsibility that comes with their privilege. The council is not a stage for acting out national interests; it is the management committee of our fledgling global security system.

     More than ever, Americans, like the rest of humanity, need a functioning global system. Experience has shown, time and again, that the system works poorly when the United States remains aloof, but it functions much better when there is farsighted U.S. leadership. That gives American leaders of today and tomorrow a great responsibility. The American people must see that they live up to it (Mr. Kofi Annan's, U.N. Secretary General Kofi A. Annan; December 2006).

Summary

Managers who are performance-focused and developmental in their management styles characteristically are usually concerned about the well-being and success of their employees. Effective managers attempt to avoid negative and dysfunctional conflict through effective leadership and interpersonal skills. Furthermore, these managers understand the realities of conflict in a diverse organization and adopt appropriate conflict management styles in order to develop an effective team in the department. This chapter offered suggestions and steps for effectively dealing with conflict in the work environment.

Discussion Questions

1. What is conflict? How can conflict become dysfunctional?
2. What are some common sources of conflict for cross-cultural managers and expatriates? Mention five.
3. Discuss two strategies that can be used for settling conflicts.
4. Can cultural differences be a source of conflict? If so, how? Discuss examples.
5. What are some benefits of conflict?
6. Mr. Kofi Annan's five lessons are important for all managers, leaders, politicians, economists, educators, and spiritual experts.

Which of the following are important in your profession and discuss the reasons for the important:

    a. *First*, we are all responsible for each other's security.

    b. *Second*, we can and must give everyone the chance to benefit from global prosperity.

    c. *Third*, both security and prosperity depend on human rights and the rule of law.

    d. *Fourth*, states must be accountable to each other, and to a broad range of non-state actors, in their international conduct.

    e. *Fifth*, we must be working together through a multilateral system, and by making the best possible use of the unique instrument, such as the United Nations.

7. The fourth recommendation from the U.N. Secretary General which states that "*Governments must be accountable for their actions, in the international and domestic arenas.*" "As things stand, poor and weak states are easily held to account, because they need foreign aid. But large and powerful states, whose actions have the greatest impact on others, can be constrained only by their own people." Name five nations that can be considered to be the "large and powerful states," and discuss what can they do to create a better world for all?

Conflict Resolution Survey Instrument

Effective leadership, management, and communication require an understanding of one's dominant conflict resolution style or one's natural tendencies. To understand your conflict resolution style, use the following scale to describe your typical behavior in conflict.

> 0 = I never behave this way
> 1 = I seldom behave this way
> 2 = I sometimes behave this way
> 3 = I often behave this way
> 4 = I very frequently behave this way

Review the following elements and give yourself a score of 0-5, as per the above scale, to determine your natural tendencies. Be honest and candid as you complete this survey.

___1. Insult the other person.
___2. Disregard the existence of a conflict.
___3. Passively comply with the other's demands.
___4. Seek a mutually beneficial solution.
___5. Seek a quick middle ground.
___6. Use threats to intimidate the other person.
___7. Postpone dealing with the issue.
___8. Sacrifice my own wishes for the sake of the other.
___9. Give information so the other can understand my feelings.
___10. Exchange concessions.
___11. Demand to have my way.
___12. Avoid communicating with the other person.
___13. Give in to the other person for the sake of harmony.
___14. Solicit information about the other's thoughts and feelings.
___15. Split the difference with the other person.
___16. Escalate the confrontation.
___17. Sidestep the area of disagreement.
___18. Protect my relationship with the other person rather than win the conflict.
___19. Explore alternative solutions to the problem.
___20. Bargain or trade with the other person.
___21. Punish the other person.
___22. Withdraw from the situation if it becomes threatening.
___23. Yield easily to the other's position.
___24. Attempt to negotiate so that neither person must compromise.
___25. Concede some points in order to win some other points.
___26. Lose my temper.
___27. Change the topic to avoid confrontation.
___28. Let the other person have his/her way.
___29. Cooperate to find areas of agreement.
___30. Compromise.

Conflict Resolution Style Survey Calculation Table:

To determine your Conflict Response Orientation (CRO), calculate your conflict scores by adding the values marked for the question items in each column. The higher you score the greater your perceived tendency or orientation to utilize that specific communication style (Adapted from Tuttle, Waveland Press, 1985). As can be seen from Figure 15.1, the ultimate goal is to have a cooperating conflict resolution style which can best happen through a collaboration orientation.

Competing	Avoiding	Accommodating	Collaborating	Compromising
1.	2.	3.	4.	5.
6.	7.	8.	9.	10.
11.	12.	13.	14.	15.
16.	17.	18.	19.	20.
21.	22.	23.	24.	25.
26.	27.	28.	29.	30.
Total =	Total =	Total =	Total =	Total =

Figure 15.1 – Conflict Management Styles

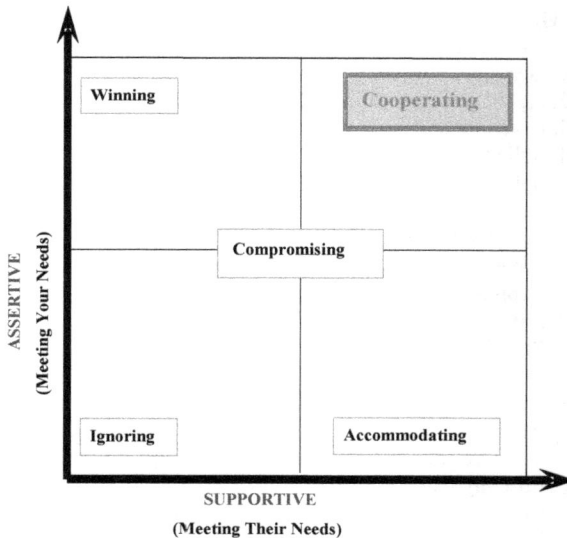

CHAPTER 16

Training and Development

One of the most challenging tasks for any company operating internationally is to effectively and efficiently work with expatriates. The statistics showing their efficiency are not encouraging. For example, the failure of U.S. expatriates (the percentage who return prematurely, without completing their assignment) is in the 20% – 40% range. Each failure could cost a firm a minimum of $250,000 to over $1,000,000 per expatriate and such costs can certainly be damaging to the bottom line profits. In Japan, the failure rate is less than 5% for their expatriates. One of the reasons for the difference is that Japanese expatriates receive far more cultural orientation training and language instruction than U.S. expatriates.

Besides exploring the importance of training and employee development programs, this chapter discusses the challenges faced by managers with regard to employee development and evaluation programs. It further discusses and reflects upon training techniques and processes.

Employee Development across Borders

The importance of having employees well trained within any business holds a large amount of weight. This element can vastly impact the success of a business, national or international. Without proper training by a company of their workforce, they are not putting an investment in the development of their employees. Within any business, employee retention is of great importance for the interests of the company. If employees feel as if they are an intricate part of the whole (company), they are liable to stay dedicated to their employer. Along with the employee retention, development of the individual's skills and status in the workforce ensures their tenure at the company and the satisfaction with their position.

Training is usually designed to improve employees' current work skills and behavior, while development opportunities usually aim to increase abilities. Types of training and development opportunities for an expatriate depends highly on the length of stay, category of assignment, location, and whether or not the expatriate is involved in a non-traditional setting. The most prominent of the tools used to prepare a candidate for going abroad is the level of pre-departure training needed, though on most occasions companies do not have the needed information or are limited in the data and information they can provide for an expatriate. The proper information may be handled with language training, submersion (or a visit to the foreign country), and cultural awareness.

A work environment of international business could use an expatriate position as an opportunity to develop the individual for a potential managerial or more senior position. The relationship building an expatriate must endure before they are successful in their host country would set them up for success on a national level. To ensure a candidate is appropriate for a possible managerial role an opportunity to hold a position abroad and mature within business on an international scale may be given. Once such an assignment has been completed that individual's worth may be heightened within the company. The importance of training and development of any employee, especially those of an expatriate, hold great weight not only for the employee to have progression within their career but allow for the company reputation to grow exponentially through their interactions and experience. Through relevant and timely employee training and development programs, the company is communicating that they value their employees.

Valuing Employees

Within any business, employee retention through effective employee development and training programs should be one main function of the human resource department. In international management, the focus of retaining the expatriate employee is even more prominent due to the high risk and cost related. For any employer, whether international or not, showing your staff the respect they deserve and gestures of affirmation toward their work is imperative in the development of the employee's dedication to the company. The manager has a responsibility; how do managers alter their own behaviors to encourage the employee in the correct manner? Appropriate attitudes and behaviors of the management team will deeply impact the attitude and response of the employee.

Every business has the desire to be successful, no matter the industry or country. The key for a true successful and profitable business is to have the right people within the workforce, be it managers, supervisors, or warehouse staffers–no business' failure should result from poor employee relations.

Within any business and/or company the employees are the backbone of a product or service. Without the employee there is no production. If employees are dissatisfied with their work they will not be as productive; the value of an employee cannot simply be what actions they perform. The employee must be valued for what they bring to the employer; if an employee is happy at work they will perform at or above employer's expectations. An employee's attitude and behavior depends on their interaction with either an active superior or an inactive/inattentive boss. The main differences are internal to the employee, yet those internal differences have a direct outcome on the physical actions and productivity of that employee.

In relation to an expatriate, managers and leaders must be aware of the feelings of their employee. Though it is an important part for all businesses, the expatriate not only costs the company more due to the nature of their work but they represent the entire company and country. Due to the expatriate's success holding such a vested interest for the company, managers should be following all necessary behaviors to ensure the expatriate is valued. The more the employee is valued for his or her work, the higher his/her productivity is likely to be on the job. The expatriate's failure may depend on several items including: spouse dissatisfaction, not adjusting to the culture, language difficulties, and varying management styles.

The expatriate needs managers who can listen to their requests and inquiries allowing for resolution. Again, an expatriate's success is dependent on their manager's ability to be clear in their purpose or project. Without a clear objective for the employee, the project may not come to fruition as scheduled and could cost the company an excessive amount of money. With the high rate of expatriate failure, the management role of affirmative comments and encouragement of the employees work would play an even more influential role on the expatriate's ability to feel connected to the project and company for which they represent. Without managers being actively engaged in the expatriate's success and feeling of significance within the company, the culture shock that may follow would be detrimental to all levels of the business. Conversely, if the employee is getting encouragement both from the host country and their main employer, they are more likely to succeed and go beyond the original expectations of their role in the company.

Provided an expatriate employee does feel accomplished and appreciated from their host country; what would be the possible outcomes of an expatriate not receiving the needed value from their main employer? One would surmise that if an employee were an expatriate, not feeling valued from their main employer, they may look to remain as an expatriate but with a new company as their host. The employee would not have the anxiety of relearning a culture; the expatriate could use this previous knowledge and adjustment as an advantage to lure the interest of a new company. If the employee's original employer did not attempt to encourage the expatriate, the employee's responsibility to that company would have dwindled, giving way for their need to look elsewhere for that affirmation of work and value. Experts encourage follow-up questions throughout an employee's tenure, and do not assume that workers understand your instructions. However, if an employee's word is the only way to judge their understanding, use open-ended questions to find out their satisfaction with the project and their status on their position.

To ensure an employee is feeling affirmed with their job (whether a national or an international position), encourage, listen, and asses the employee. If the employee, provided they are given the opportunity, approaches a manager with a desire, concern, or questions this is an opportunity for the employer to enhance the employee's dedication to the position and ensure the company a steadfast worker. An employee with a feeling of self-worth and accomplishment will stay working and continue to prosper with the company.

The Art and Science of Training

Employees usually want relevant and effective training that can help them do their jobs better so they can be prepared for future contribution opportunities to their respective fields. About 60 percent of trainees tend to report that the last training program was a good or great use of their time, and about 12 percent say that their most recent training session was a total waste of time. While most training programs are very valuable, professional designers and facilitators need to continually make sure all of their sessions are productive and audience-centered.

Training is a necessary activity in most organizations that deal with more than a few employees, new technology or knowledge each and every day. The term "training" is synonymous with teaching, educating, guiding, coaching, preparing, developing, instructing, and other such words that deal with knowledge creation, acquisition, and transfer. Training can often deal with the transfer, guiding, development, coaching, and creation of certain technical skills to new or existing employees. Training can be from a father to son, from teacher to a student, from a colleague to another colleague, from an expert to an apprentice, from a trainer to a trainee, or from a manager to an employee. Training has been part of society since the beginning of time and now it is a formal part of most organizations. Training is both an art and a science as it requires knowledge, intuition, and skill. In the workplace, training often refers to activities which are strategically designed for the acquisition of knowledge and skills that are needed for immediate use and application. While the term "*training*" is associated with skills that are used for short-term application, the term "*development*" usually implies the acquisition of qualities and attributes that help an employee become more competent in the long-term. It is important for trainers and managers to determine both the short and long term learning needs of their employees. As it has been said, if one does not know where he or she is going, then any road will be fine; however, if one knows where to go, then he or she is likely to get their faster and more efficiently. Furthermore, trainers should assess the trainee's readiness and trainability level.

While training is an important and often a mission-critical activity, many firms and senior leaders tend to think of it as a cost center, especially when they are not doing well compared to their competitors. Such thinking and paradigms are not effective conditions for innovation and creativity. Innovation in training requires time for creativity and experimentation which cannot be done when trainers are not certain whether they will have a job in the coming months or years. Ironically, these are the times when some firms reduce the training department's budget when in fact they should be increasing their investment on their people's development. When the times are tough, organizational leaders and trainers can clearly identify the benefits of training and demonstrate its return on investment. Trainers can demonstrate the value of training and learning within the organization by measuring hierarchical progress of employees, enhancement of morale, satisfied employees and customers, effective management, higher sales and profits, reduction of employee and customer complaints, and other tangible and intangible results. Furthermore, they should make sure that the training objectives are fully aligned with the company's strategic goals.

Companies should be investing in the development of their employees if they are to keep up with the competition in today's global and diverse environment of business. The best way to capture new sales, new markets, and higher profits is often through continuous innovation and creativity in delivering superior value to one's employees, the end-users and customers. The best way to achieve such superior results in today's competitive work environment is to invest an appropriate amount of a company's budget in employee training and development. Companies need to be innovative and keep up with their competitors by training their employees and developing their employee's minds, positively impacting their feelings, and making their behaviors more service-oriented. In other words, companies need to impact their employees' heads, hearts and habits if they are to remain innovative, productive and competitive in the twenty-first century's work environment. Companies that don't continually invest in employee training, creativity and development practices can suffer in the long-term. Studies have shown that creativity and innovation programs can help foster a culture of risk-taking, collaboration, out-of-the-box thinking, team synergy, and teamwork. Leaders must understand that innovation through an empowered and creative workforce is essential for a company's survival and long-term success in a competitive industry.

While training can be conducted in many formats and delivery modalities, employees can receive instruction and training without having to leave their offices. The virtual online classrooms have made learning and training easier both for trainers and trainees. Online training that is geared toward the needs of the audience can reduce costs since there is often no travel expense, buying of books, printing of workbooks, or ever having to leave the office at a specific time. Virtual training can take place asynchronously at one's own free time, at one's own preferred pace, and it can be conducted at the office, library or home. American firms from the United States tend to spend about $40 to $50 billion each year on training; furthermore, it is estimated that about 70% of the learning in the workplace is acquired through informal means. Many of the large firms offer about 140 hours of training for their employees each year. The training comes both in formal and informal modalities through on-ground and virtual platforms. While about 60% to 70% of training is still conducted using regular or traditional modalities, more and more organizations are using the electronic media to conduct much of their training through web-based instruction, computer-based training, CD-ROMs, virtual classrooms, and videos. One of the most impressive aspects of virtual or online training is that people learn at their own pace and time. Some employees learn faster than others and such innovative training techniques can make allowance for individualized learning preferences. Just like online academic classes, web-based training sessions can involve interactive activities with the trainer or instructor using virtual chatrooms, voice café, and teleconferencing. So, online or virtual training can be in real time and collaborative as needed according to the complexity of the material and the readiness of the trainees.

Some online software programs for virtual training can allow trainers to provide real-time audio instruction to the trainees. The trainers can be connected to the trainees' computers via intranet or the world-wide-web. In a real time virtual training scenario, trainers can point to or call on a trainee using the computer as do faculty members who hold synchronized chat sessions with their classes in the academic environment. The trainers can privately communicate to a trainee while the virtual session is being conducted or make the interaction public so others can benefit from what is being said or communicated. Most virtual training programs are set up to support various diverse teaching tools such as blackboard, e-university, WebCT, whiteboard, a training resource, proctored or real-time quizzes, Microsoft Word or PowerPoint applications, and HTML files. Since there are many tools and options for various training sessions, facilitators should be careful in choosing the right platforms and software for their needs. Selecting the right virtual training option depends on the training activity and objectives as well as the skill level of the audience. Furthermore, each trainee's readiness level and competency with the software must also be considered. Most updates, policy changes, and dissemination of new information can easily be completed through virtual collaboration software. However, for training new employees or passing on complex information to existing employees, trainers should use a software program that offers interactive collaboration opportunities between the facilitator and learner. Trainers should also be aware that some skills such as driving a car, operating on a patient, running a new machine to manufacture products, and other such complex devices that need hand-on experience cannot be mastered through virtual platforms. However, most knowledge-based and routine training sessions can successfully be completed using web-based applications and modalities.

Training Techniques

The traditional rule of thumb for training people has been a five step process, which is: tell them (trainees or learners) what needs to be done, show them how it needs to be done, let them tell you how the job should be done, let them show you how they are doing the job, and collaboratively set goals for further development and/or the next session's objectives as needed. While the traditional five step process seems easy, it can be very complex as the "telling" and "showing" can be conducted in many different varieties and modalities. Whatever modality trainers use to transfer knowledge or skill to learners, they should use a formal training process to document the process for consistency and learning accumulation. An effective training model provides one process that trainers can adapt for their usage. The identification of the training needs and objective is the initial starting point, and learning from the process through formal evaluation of the results for continuous improvement purposes is often the last step.

Regardless of the modality used for training, professionals should become aware of and involve different teaching techniques and facilitation methods to enhance the learning process for their adult audience. In other words, trainers should use as many mediums and approaches as possible to impact the thoughts (head), feelings (heart), and behaviors (habits) of their learners.

In an effort to make training more effective and satisfying, educators should evaluate the learning strategies that they incorporate into the programs and activities that they develop. If educators understand how the brain works and the way people learn, they can develop activities that will engage the learner and help them to learn better. The analysis and design of a course are crucial, but if the intended learning is to actually take place, the learning experience has to address multiple intelligences and different learning styles. The goal is to meet associates' training needs in the most effective way applying the most current brain research.

Experts recommend teaching in such a way that make learners reflect and think. In other words, it is best to get their head (thoughts and knowledge), heart (feelings) and habits (behaviors) involved in the training process. Research suggests that feelings are critical to the learning process in many ways. Feelings help determine:

- If a learner wants to learn a subject,
- How one feels about a subject,
- Whether one wants to learn about a subject,
- If one believes whether the information is true,
- Whether one is able to apply the information to his or her daily activities, and
- How long one remembers the information.

Learners can understand a topic without having feelings about it, but it may not mean as much to them until an emotion is attached to it. It simply is not real to the brain until one feels it is real. Learning without feelings is incomplete as it may not last for long nor be applied into the workplace. Perhaps the brain is analogous to a box packed with emotions. So, the question for a trainer becomes, "How can one integrate emotions more productively into the learning process?"

Regardless of the current techniques used by trainers to make their sessions more innovative and more effective, it is always best to understand and become aware of new strategies and terminologies applied in facilitation activities. Some of the more unfamiliar terms and techniques for learning activities with new trainers are as follows (as presented by facilitators at Publix based on the work of experts such as Jenson, 1997).

- *Active imagination* is using one's mind to discover pictures, shapes and designs. It can also create visual relationships and intuitive connections which transform apparent chaos and confusion into a place of creativity and imagination.
- A *classifying matrix* is a way of classifying things on a chart with certain categories across the top and others down the side of the chart; items in the chart must meet the criteria of both the top and side category.
- A *cognitive organizer* is a visual aid that helps learners order and patterns their thinking in ways that are both logical and that promote higher order reasoning.
- *Cross laterals* are body movements that involve the right side of the body interacting with the left side of the body. *Cross laterals* force the brain to talk to itself and use both hemispheres. The purpose is to activate the brain through movement. For example, touching hands to opposite knees is a *cross lateral* movement.
- *Each one teach one* is an interactive group strategy in which each person in a group learns something and then teaches it to the others in the group. This is similar to a three-person teaching process where each person takes turn teaching his or her learning to the other two group members.
- *Empathy practices* develop sensitivity to another person's perspective and feelings. We work on ourselves and then transfer this skill to real situations with other people.
- *Forced relationships* are finding connections between things that normally would have no relationship. However, when forced together, they make perfect sense. For example, how is a radio like an apple?
- *Guided imagery* is a thinking process that activates one's imagination and capacity to pretend. The facilitator *guides* the imagery.
- A *human graph* is a thinking strategy that asks people to physically stand along a spectrum that indicates how they feel

or think about an issue. Privilege walk exercise, which is often conducted in diversity training workshops, is one example.

- *KWL (*what do you *know,* what do you *want* to know, what have you *learned) goal setting* is a graphic organizer that helps one assess prior knowledge and current questions for a learning task, and then to assess what was actually learned after the task is completed.

- The literal meaning of *metacognition* is "thinking about thinking"; the ability to step back from a situation in which you are involved and watch yourself.

- *Mindfulness* is the ability to observe your thoughts, feelings, actions, and sensations in a detached, objective way without getting caught up in emotions, opinions, intellectual ideas or theories, and immediate reactions.

- *Multi-tracking* is any physical exercise that involves performing several different actions simultaneously (i.e., rubbing the stomach and patting the top of the head while jogging in place).

- A *syllogism* is an argument or form of reasoning in which two statements or premises are made and a logical conclusion drawn from them. For example, all mammals are warm-blooded; whales are mammals; therefore whales are warm-blooded.

- *Turn to your partner and...* is an interactive strategy in which two people who are seated next to each other discuss and/or process information, share feelings and thoughts, and explore ideas.

Summary

Managers must focus on the management of human resources on a global basis. An organization's strategy on globalization strongly affects the approach it takes to human resource management. Both employers and employees must be educated about the importance of training. The learning styles, job training and productivity, and the commitment of employers to job training are crucial to any efforts to shape the development of effective workforce. The business leaders must build up a training policy with the entire human resources asset of the organization that will both encourage managers to implement training programs and enhance and improve the skills of all employees.

Training brings a change and managers often complain that people resist change. Firms also find that as vital skills and competencies within the workplace have become harder, it is necessary to tackle fundamental skills deficit through more comprehensive training, often before job-specific skills training can be successfully given. Effective managers and professionals work strategically to make sure all their employees are as successful as they would like to be based upon each employee's qualifications, goals, abilities, and competencies. This is the essence of employee development and effective cross-cultural management practices.

Training can give you the skills you need to complete any task or job. However, you need to regularly inspire yourself through visionary reflections and motivational readings. It has been said that time decides who you meet in life, your heart determines who you want in your life, and your behavior influences who stays in your life. I hope that as a manager you always get there at the right time, make the right decisions by listening to your compassionately kind heart, and consistently behave in such a way that you attract the best minds as your colleagues and friends.

Discussion Questions

1. What is training? Why is there a need for cross-cultural training?
2. Should training programs vary when one is dealing with people of a high context culture versus when one is working with people of a low context culture? Discuss and provide your reasons.
3. What challenges do expatriate employees face when they go to a new foreign culture?
4. What are some common developmental plans and strategies that firms can use to develop their employees?
5. What are some best practices that you have seen or observed in cross-cultural training in today's modern and multinational organizations? You may speak with managers of multinational firms or check out their training programs through their websites or the consultant's offerings.

CHAPTER 17

CASES

Management related cases can serve as laboratories for the application of theoretical concepts and long-term retention. The following pages provide a number of diverse cases, dilemmas and scenarios for individual and group discussion purposes. Read each case and answer the questions factually based on your understanding of the concepts and based on your further research on each topic. You can look at relevant textbooks, articles and websites for the definition of the terms and understanding of the concepts.

Always support your thoughts and answers with recently published articles and examples from the workplace. In your analysis and discussions with colleagues (face-to-face and online), please use constructive criticism for reflective thinking and development purposes. Constructive criticism includes a balance of analysis and feedback. Critical thinking and constructive criticism can help identify relevant issues to focus on during team discussions. One must use logic, patience and objective data to support one's point of view. Unfortunately, due to the overuse of poorly written negative and nagging comments, some people can easily become defensive even when constructive criticism is given in a spirit of good will. Keep in mind that constructive criticism is more likely to be accepted if the comments are objective and focused on the work or agenda rather than a person's personality or background. That is, attacking personality issues and cultural traditions must be avoided in order for effective collaborations to take place among diverse teams.

Culturally sensitive individuals can adopt a passive, nonviolent attitude if they view a situation as personal, pervasive, or permanent in order to effectively collaborate with others on the team or group. Other individuals may adopt an aggressive response, but such aggression must be professional, objective and to the point. One must keep in mind that constructive criticism can be easily misinterpreted and aggressive exchanges often spiral out of control, resulting in "flaming" responses. Effective interpersonal communication skills can be helpful to assess a responder's frame of mind or paradigm. During initial exchanges or when encountering defensive individuals, effective criticism calls for softer language and inclusion of positive comments. It is best to remember that when a speaker strongly identifies with contentious areas (such as politics or religion), non-offensive criticism can become challenging. So, be careful in your discussions and use constructive criticism to get your points across to diverse team members and colleagues.

For a standardized and formal process, unless suggested otherwise, you can use the following suggestions for analyzing each case:

1. Review and thoroughly read the case and several other recently published articles related to this topic. Provide a brief summary of the case (or topic). Discuss the dilemma, the challenge or problems that are apparent.
2. Next, clearly state one main Problem or Opportunity Statement facing you in this case. Remember that the Problem or Opportunity Statement must be in the case or in its questions.
3. Provide at least one good alternative to solve the problem, enhance performance (capitalize on the opportunity) or enhance the work environment. Justify your alternative.
4. Offer an implementation plan and relevant steps for the stated alternative (preferably using a table or Gantt chart).
5. Provide an overall summary and discuss what employees, managers, and firms can learn from the lessons offered in this case.

Overall, the analysis can be in an academic format. If relevant, you can include data, tables, figures, models, and graphs as such visuals make the material easier to read and more interesting. Make sure to label your visuals appropriately. Make sure to provide full references at the end of your analysis.

Case 1: Tour Planning to Vinh Long

Kim Dinh Le has a small tourism company in Ho Chi Minh City (aka: Saigon) and often takes tourists to Vinh Long so they can see the beautiful gardens around the An Binh and Binh Hoa Phuoc Islands which emerge from the Tien River that is located opposite of the Vinh Long town. Dr. Lam wants his tourism students from Thailand, Germany and the United States to see how Vietnamese farmers manage their livestock in Vinh Long. As such, Dr. Lam approaches Kim Dinh Le to plan a tour for 50 graduate students to Vinh Long for two days.

While all of the students speak and understand English, over fifty percent of these students' dominant languages are Thai and German. Kim Dinh Le's job is to plan the tour for these students and provide Dr. Lam with a reasonable agenda and price which is inclusive of the tour, meals, and activities for the entire trip. Dr. Lam will review the plan and make a decision on whether to hire Kim Dinh Le or one of her competitors based on the overall value that they promise to deliver for this tour.

Discussion Questions:
1. What are some considerations in planning this tour? How do you plan for this opportunity?
2. What language should the tour guide speak with these students?
3. What activities should be included in this tour to make sure the students receive the most value for their trip?
4. Should the tour be priced high, in the middle range, or low compared to the competitors?

Case 2: Cross-Cultural Blunders

A cross-cultural blunder is basically any unintentional decision that negatively affects the foreign operations of a firm along with the value of its brand. The negative impact can be a loss of revenues, loss of reputation, or simply a loss of brand image. While the word blunder naturally carries a negative connotation, cross-cultural blunders in business have, in some cases, positively surprised companies with increased sales; however, most blunders have resulted in loss of money, reputation and sometimes irreparable damage to business relationships. Such negative blunders in a cross-cultural work environment are usually attributable to their lack of knowledge in cultural differences. Every now and then, the positive side of a blunder could be due to the fact that the blunder leads to yet another cornerstone of a successful business, namely better or free marketing and exposure.

There are many examples of cross-cultural blunders. The following are some examples:

1. A Japanese tourist agency entered the U.S. market under a misinterpreted name. When their company first entered the English speaking markets, the agencies began to receive requests for unusual sex tours. It was later discovered that the reason for these requests was due to the name of the company which was *"Kinki Nippon Tourist Company."*
2. A company by the name of ESSO found that its name pronounced phonetically meant, "stalled car" in Japanese.
3. A new Japanese manager in an American company was asked to give critical feedback to a subordinate during a performance evaluation. They were unaware of the fact that Japanese use high context language and are uncomfortable giving direct feedback. It took the manager five tries before he could be direct enough to discuss the poor performance so as to effectively convey what he was saying to the American.
4. The statement "As smooth as a baby's bottom" was translated into Japanese as: "As smooth as a baby's ass."
5. Proctor & Gamble blundered in Japan trying to market Camay Soap. Their marketing campaign featured a woman bathing and her husband entering the bathroom, touching her approvingly. Such ads are often considered inappropriate by the Japanese.

As can be seen from these cross-cultural blunders, the selection and training of expatriates is highly critical to the success of communication in an international venture and expansions. According to experts, an effective expatriate manager must possess special abilities and traits if he or she is to avoid blundering. Among the most important characteristics are:

1. An ability to get along well with people
2. An awareness of cultural differences
3. Open-mindedness to respect others' values
4. Tolerance of foreign cultures
5. Adaptability to new cultures, ideas and challenges
6. An ability to adjust quickly to new conditions
7. An interest in facts, not blind assumptions

8. Previous business experience, specifically with foreign cultures
9. An ability to learn foreign languages.

Of course, effective cross-cultural training should take place before and during the expatriate assignment, and training serves general functions of preparing the expatriate to both work in the local culture and live in the local culture. To ensure success, training should be given to the manager, spouse and other dependents.

Discussion Questions:

1. What are some examples of cultural blunders that you have seen or heard of in the recent years? Discuss the situation.
2. Cross-cultural blunders are not limited to the American and Japanese cultures. What are some other examples of such mistakes and miscommunications in other countries?
3. How can firms avoid cross cultural blunders?

Case 3: Transliteration of Coca-Cola in China

In 1928, Coca-Cola, the leading soft drink manufacturer in the world, set its eyes on the potential untapped market of the Chinese population; it was composed of roughly five-hundred million people plus the large foreign community living in China. This seemed at first a tough task since the Chinese had been accustomed to drinking their own beverage of choice, green tea. Moreover, the large foreign population had already set their social customs based on the British style. Nevertheless, Coca-Cola managers set on their mission of trying to convince the masses that the soft drink was indeed delicious and refreshing.

It was obvious that if Coca-Cola wanted to succeed in its campaign, the trademark had to be transliterated into the Chinese language in order to reach all sectors of the market. This presented a huge inconvenience, since both written and spoken Chinese are completely alien to any other western language. On top of that a need arises for selecting one of the different tongues spoken in China. To find the nearest phonetic equivalent, a single separate Chinese character was required for each of the four syllables. Out of the nearly 40,000 characters there are only about 200 that are pronounced with the usual sounds needed and many had to be avoided because of their meaning.

After doing the research for the suitable characters, the marketers in charge of the ad campaign adopted a couple of the characters' groups. One of these sounded like "Coca-Cola" when pronounced, but the meaning of the characters came out something like "female horse fastened with wax." Another of the ingenious groups meant, "bite the wax pole". After a disastrous advertising beginning and securing their name into history's biggest marketing blunders list, Coca-Cola finally recognized the mistake and went on to fix it. The company chose to translate their name into Mandarin because it is a dialect spoken by the great majority in the China mainland. The closest trademark translation was something like "to permit mouth to rejoice" or "something palatable from which one derives pleasure."

Incidentally, Coca-Cola learned that Chinese has to be interpreted into English rather than translated. This embarrassment could have been saved, according to experts, if the company's executives in charge of the market penetration would have been concerned with the meaning of the Chinese characters instead of just the phonetic equivalent of "Coca-Cola." Furthermore, this marketing blunder teaches that nobody is exempt of making cultural indiscretions in the international business arena and that care must be taken when dealing with a foreign culture.

Discussion Questions:
1. What are some examples of translation mistakes that you have seen or heard of in the recent years? Discuss the situation.
2. What can multinational firms do to make sure they avoid such blunders in foreign cultures?
3. What recommendations you have for effective translations of ads and company slogans in the different languages? Discuss best practices.

Case 4: Religious Minority and Recruitment

Religious influence tends to be a strong driver of behavior for many believers. Every country has its own majority and minority groups who are often very diverse in terms of their values and beliefs. These values and beliefs are usually inculcated into individuals and groups during their socialization years as young children and teenagers. One example of a minority group within the Vietnamese culture is the Chan ethnic group. While the Vietnamese religious beliefs are influenced by the combined values of traditional religions forming the Tam Giao (Buddhism, Confucianism and Taosim) as well as Islam and Catholicism, the Chan members are socialized in Islamic traditions. The population of Muslims in Vietnam is growing steadily and it is estimated to be over 100,000 individuals. Yet, the Muslim community is still a minority group in Vietnam where the population is close to one hundred million people.

An Arab company wants to invest 400 million dollars in East Asia, perhaps in Vietnam, but wants to hire mostly local Muslim employees so they can easily interact with them due to the commonality of values. They will need to hire around 400 people during the first year of operation and some of these employees will have to travel across borders in the region. The Arab firm has looked at Ho Chi Minh City as one of the possible locations; other locations being looked at include Penang of Malaysia, Chaing Mai of Thailand, and anywhere in Cambodia as the labor costs seem to be very low. You are working for the import and export authority of Vietnam and your job is to attract more foreign investors to the country.

Discussion Questions:
1. Why should this Arab firm come to Vietnam? What can you do to encourage this firm to invest in your country?
2. How do you negotiate with this company to make sure they bring their business to Vietnam?
3. How do you organize your team and meetings to make sure everything goes according to the plan of making sure they invest in Ho Chi Minh City? Discuss various tasks associated with the organizing function of management for this opportunity.

Case 5: Thai[6] Airways: Governance in the Eyes of an Investor?

Thai Airways International Public Company Limited (THAI) was formed as a state run company with overseas flights inauguration and intercontinental services in 1971. Nowadays, THAI flies to 71 destinations in 35 countries by using a fleet of 91 aircraft, and is member of the "Star Alliance". THAI has operated under the vision "The First Choice Carrier with Touches of Thai".

On 18th June, 2009, Piyasvasti Amranand has been appointed as Chief Executive of Thai Airways International Pcl. At that time, THAI had been facing a deficit situation. Therefore, Piyasvasti had to modernize the fleet and cost cuts in 2009. It helped THAI rebound from its largest ever loss the year before to a record profit in 2010. Next year, Thai Airways International has been ranked by Skytrax as "The top five airlines in the world". Piyasvasti had brought THAI back from a loss of more than 20 billion baht to profits in two years and managed its costs including those of fuel toward a targeted profit of 6 billion baht this year. Also, THAI fuel forward hedging strategy that resulted in income of 909 million baht in the first quarter and 430 million baht in one month. Moreover, the passenger numbers rose by 14% last month in what is in fact the low season.

THAI

Spirit

Towards Professional Excellence

Teamwork
Trust
Happiness
Hospitality
Awakening
Accountability
Inspiration
Integrity

Beside the financial figure, THAI's president also pushes very hard on corporate governance and building a THAI Spirit culture that stand for Team & Trust, Happiness & Hospitality, Awakening & Accountability, Inspiration & Integrity at least through his statement that "My success in not making the company good profit or buying a new fleet but my success while I am working here is to build a new culture for THAI, this my most important achievement"

He emphasized the important soft side of the organization through placing new core values "Since our values should meet passenger expectations, we've incorporated new core values representing who we are and what we have to be." Said Dr. Piyasvasti. He said these values can also be remembered easily as they too start with THAI—trust is important as the airline is in a Hospitality business, while Accountability and Integrity demonstrate the mindset of not only employee, but also those at the top, the management and the board of director.

But on 21st May 2012, his contract was terminated after three years by THAI's board. Ampon Kittiampon, THAI chairman, told a press conference that although Piyasvasti passed his performance evaluation, he had communication problems with the board, and the company needs a new executive who can realize personnel development and marketing plans.

How can an outcome be good like this if he had problems in communication with the board? Because of quibble over answer, some source assumed it was also possible that his firing resulted from his investigations in THAI, from his punishment of corrupt THAI staff who might have sought help from some powerful figures, and

---

[6] Contributed by Jatuporn Sungkhawan, Southeast Bangkok College, Bangkok, Thailand.

from the political interference. Piyasvasti's wife, Anik Amranand, takes a position of the Board of Directors of the Democrat Party and has been an Abhisit adviser (Abhisit use to be the Prime Minister). However the government said it's not political interference because most of the board was appointed by the last government.

According to THAI's ethics "Treat all clients and business associates fairly and honestly and protect the interests of all our customers, and be politically impartial for the sake of the nation and society." Moreover, THAI is a "State enterprise" and also a "Public company." Therefore, THAI will have to clarify to the government who is a largest shareholder motivated by politics as well as to Thai people who are part of their National carrier. Otherwise it will be like Piyasvasti's word "you better pity country than me".

Questions for Reflection:
1. Do you agree or disagree with this termination decision? What do you do differently if you do not agree with this decision?
2. What do you think about good governance at Thai Airways?
3. Can politics be avoided in the workplace?
4. What are the pros and cons of politics in the workplace?

Case 6: Global Management Orientations and Strategies

Global managers and leaders know that there are different ways that most international professionals lead their operations. As such, an understanding of ethnocentric, polycentric, regiocentric and geocentric management orientations are a necessity for global management. These strategies can be seen as follows:

- *Ethnocentric management* is where the home country management style is imposed on the host country. The assumption is that what works at home should also work overseas.
- In *polycentric management*, the foreign market is "too hard to understand," so host-country managers are relatively free to manage their own way.
- *Regiocentric management* is the style most parent organization use when they feel that the regional insiders best coordinate operations within the region.
- *Geocentric management* is a highly interdependent system that speaks in terms of the global village. The focus is at once both worldwide and on local objectives.

Discussion Questions:
1. Which management orientation best matches a new company entering a new country?
2. What are the advantages and disadvantages of each management orientation for hiring staff?
3. Can a company be ethnocentric and polycentric at the same time? Explain with a specific example.
4. Which style of global management orientation best matches the concept of an inclusive workplace?

Case 7: High and Low Context Cultures

According to anthropologists and experts on culture, a *high context* culture is one in which much of the information in communication is in the context or in the person rather than explicitly coded in the verbal messages. On the other side, a *low context* culture is one that derives much information from the words of a message and less information from nonverbal and environmental cues. High context cultures have a greater amount of shared knowledge. Low context cultures deliver messages which are highly explicit, assuming much less previous knowledge. These differences in communication styles can lead to major misunderstandings.

According to previous studies and research, common characteristics of high context cultures:

- Less verbally explicit communication, less written/formal information.
- More internalized understandings of what is communicated.
- Multiple cross-cutting ties and intersections with others.
- Long-term relationships.
- Strong boundaries- who is accepted as belonging versus who is considered an outsider.
- Knowledge is situational, relational.
- Decisions and activities focus around personal face to face relationships, often around a central person who have authority.

And, common characteristics of low context cultures:

- Rule oriented, people play by external rules.
- More knowledge is codified, public, external, and accessible.
- Sequencing, separation--of time, of space, of activities, of relationships.
- More interpersonal connections of shorter duration.
- Knowledge is more often transferable.
- Task-centered. Decisions and activities focus around what needs to be done, division of responsibilities.

High context cultures can be difficult to enter if you are an outsider (because you don't carry the context information internally, and because you can't instantly create close relationships). Low context cultures are relatively easy to enter if you are an outsider (because the environment contains much of the information you need to participate, you can form relationships fairly soon, and the important thing is accomplishing a task rather than feeling your way into a relationship). Every culture and every situation has its high and low aspects. Most cultures are somewhere in between in the continuum of high and low contexts. Often one situation will contain an inner high context core and an outer low context ring for those who are less involved.

Discussion Questions:

1. What are some typical cultures or countries that might fall as example of low context cultures? Why are these nations considered to be low context cultures?

2. What are some typical cultures or countries that might fall as examples of high context cultures? Why are these nations considered to be high context cultures?

3. What are some of the advantages of a manager from a high context culture going to a high context culture?

4. What are some of the disadvantages of a manager from a high context culture going to a low context culture?

5. What are some things that a manager should be aware of if he or she is going from a low context culture to a high context culture? Discuss specific examples.

Case 8: Time Orientations and Culture

Culture tends to reinforce the information or misinformation that we learned in our earlier influences. We form what we can call a "cultural filter or lens," in our heads, that all information tends to pass through. What the information is actually passing through is an accumulation of all stereotypes and prejudices; in other words, the information gets filtered through our preconceived notions. We tend to make assumptions based on these preconceived notions and then act on them as if they were fact. This is a part of what is known as being ethnocentric. That is, a belief that "our" culture is the right one and anything different is suspect. *Ethnocentricity*, as discussed before, is a trait that is especially true of members of dominant cultures. The assumptions we make are influenced by the culture we were brought up in.

Sometimes our behavior is influenced by our culture. Understanding culture can help us to keep it from being a source of conflict when we encounter people who see the world differently than ourselves. Every culture is unique and has many elements that must be considered when learning about them. Understanding culture and its importance in shaping what we believe can help us to recognize when cultural differences are the cause of our conflict.

Culture tend to explain that there are differences in time systems around the globe. As explained in the book, two major systems are monochromic and polychronic time orientations. *Monochronic time* means paying attention to and doing only one thing at a time; *polychronic time* orientation means being involved with many things at once. In monochronic cultures, time is experienced and used in a linear way. Monochronic time is perceived as being almost tangible: people talk about it as though it were money, as something that can be "spent," "saved," "wasted," and "lost." Because monochronic time concentrates on one thing at a time, people who are governed by it don't like to be interrupted. Monochronic time seals people off from one another and, as a result, intensify some relationships while shortchanging others. Time becomes a room which some people are allowed to enter, while others are excluded. Monochronic time dominates most business in much of the western world. Polychronic time is characterized by the simultaneous occurrence of many things and by a great involvement with people. There is more emphasis on completing human transactions than on holding to schedules. Proper understanding of the difference between the monochronic and polychronic time systems will be helpful in dealing with the time-flexible Mediterranean peoples. In monochronic time cultures, the emphasis is on the compartmentalization of functions and people. In polychronic Mediterranean cultures, business offices often have large reception areas where people can wait. Polychronic people feel that private space disrupts the flow of information by shutting people off from one another. In polychronic systems, appointments mean very little and may be shifted around even at the last minute to accommodate someone more important in an individual's hierarchy of family, friends, or associates. Some polychronic people (such as most Asians, Latin Americans and Arabs) give precedence to their large circle of family members over any business obligation.

Discussion Questions:
1. How does culture influence a person's values in regard to time, jobs and life obligations?
2. What is a monochronic time orientation? Discuss examples of monochronic cultures.
3. What is a polychronic time orientation? Discuss examples of polychronic cultures.
4. What is ethnocentricity and how does not link to people's time orientation and expectations from others? Discuss.

Case 9: The ASEAN Trade Agreement and Vietnam[7]

The Socialist Republic of Vietnam is one of the ten members of the Association of Southeast Asian Nations (ASEAN). Vietnam has a population of nearly 100 million people, of which almost 70% are in the age range of 15-64 years. There are 58 provinces and 5 municipalities (major cities) including Ho Chi Minh City and Can Tho in the South, Hanoi (the capital), Hai Phong in the North, and Da Nang in the Central. Vietnamese is the official language while English is increasingly referred to as second language. Other commonly spoken languages include French, Chinese, Khmer, and mountain area languages (Mon-Khmer and Malayo-Polynesian).

Vietnam today is a developing country that has been one of the fastest growing and the most promising economies in Asia over the past decade with an average annual GDP growth of 7.6% between 2000 and 2009. As a part of the global economy, however, Vietnam economy has been negatively impacted by the global recession, which has reduced its GDP growth rate to less than the 7% per annum average between 2009 and 2011. The International Monetary Fund had projected around a 5% GDP growth in 2013 for Vietnam.

Since its adoption of an economic reform called "Doi Moi", or renovation, a shift from a centrally planned economy with a high level of state ownership and frequent government interference to a market economy in 1986, Vietnam has opened up its economy to the world, and attracted a large volume of foreign investment. The business environment has been improved significantly as the result of the government commitment to the global integration. With this economic reform and global integration, many have seen a significantly positive change in Vietnam: steady economic growth, reduced poverty and more prosperity over the past decade.

---

[7] Contributed by Lam D. Nguyen, Bloomsburg University of Pennsylvania.

Since its formal normalization of diplomatic relations with the United States in 1995, followed by the U.S.-Vietnam bilateral trade agreement (BTA) in 2001, Vietnamese government has achieved several key economic policy goals and attracted many domestic and foreign investors with its large, skilled and low cost workforce. Trade between Vietnam and the U.S. has grown tremendously. The total trade volume in 1995 was $451.30 million and in 2011, the trade volume reached $21,796.20 million.

Vietnam's economic development reached another milestone when it joined the World Trade Organization in January 2007. Vietnam becomes a strategic partner and plays an important role in South East Asian region as well as in the world economy. Facing the global recession, Vietnamese authorities continue their commitment to international integration and an open market economy. At the beginning of 2012, Vietnam had planned a major restructuring of public investment, state-owned enterprises and the banking sector in order to maintain and sustain its macroeconomic stability and strengthen its economic growth. IMF has projected a good growth prospect in Vietnam as a result of tightened macroeconomic policies, rapidly declined inflation, increased confidence in the Vietnamese Dong, and recovered international reserves.

Discussion Questions:
1. Are Vietnamese people living in a collectivistic or individualistic society?
2. Is Vietnam a high context or low context culture?
3. Discuss Geert Hofstede's cultural dimensions as they relate to the Vietnamese culture.
4. If Vietnam is to receive maximum benefit from the ASEAN trade agreement, what specific things should public and private sector managers be doing to attract more foreign investment?
5. How does Vietnam rank on ethics and corruption perception index compared to other ASEAN countries? Is this ranking a positive factor or a deterrent for international investors? Discuss.
6. What can Vietnamese leaders do to further enhance the business reputation of the country to attract more foreign direct investments? Provide specific suggestions.

Case 10: Unwanted Publicity: Gau Do Instant Noodle[8]

It seems it all started when one person posted an online article on how he felt about a 30-second TV commercial of Gau Do (pronounced "gau door", Vietnamese for Red Bear), an instant noodle brand of Vietnam's Asia Foods Corp. The ubiquitous TV commercial was the cornerstone of the "love & care connection" campaign, which earned the company recognition "A Business for Community", to promote the Gau Do brand. That person indicated that he was sincerely moved by the image of helpless sick boy named Tuan, his innocent smile featured in the commercial and thanked the efforts made by the brand to contribute to a charitable fund in support of severely-ill children without financial means.

---

[8] Contributed by Ricky Hieu Nguyen, RMIT University – Vietnam.

Big Message – Not So Big Contribution:

However, the main message of the article was his disappointment of the negligible amount the company was contributing. The company promised to set aside for charity an amount of 10 Vietnamese Dongs for every pack of Gau Do instant noodle sold (US\$1 = 21,000 Vietnamese Dongs). The selling price of one pack of Gau Do was about 3,500 Dongs (US 17 cents). He argued that in order to contribute a tiny amount of 10,000 Dongs (less than 50 US cents) for the fund, he would have to consume one pack of Gau Do instant noodle every day for the entire 3 years. And for that the motive of the campaign was questionable.

The TV advertisement of Gau Do:

The TV commercial showed a child cancer patient, Tuan, meeting other patients, nurses and doctors in a hospital, saying goodbye to them with his big happy smile as he was leaving the hospital on that day. It looked like he was discharged from the hospital after a successful treatment. It was not. The scene showed Tuan's parents, who walked slowly in despair after Tuan as they left the hospital, tears in the mother's eyes. They were forced to leave the hospital because they had no money to continue treatment for him. The advertisement then started showing Gau Do instant noodle and stated that by buying one more pack of Gau Do instant noodle, there was one more chance for children like Tuan. The advertisement displayed a supermarket shelf full of Gau Do instant noodle and a sticker that read *"buy 1 pack you contribute 10 Dongs."*

One person's comments quickly started one of the epic battles in online media in Vietnam, generating thousands and thousands of comments in online forums and websites. Supporters for the campaign claimed that it would not matter 10 Dongs or 10 billion Dongs being contributed, the company was doing real charity while many other companies were doing nothing, especially a low profit margin business such as instant noodle. And by attacking the company's campaign, those who object were putting the charitable efforts by Gau Do brand in jeopardy.

But supporters of the brand's campaign were quickly outnumbered. Those who objected the advertisement soon exposed much information against Gau Do. The major one was that Tuan, whose frail body and bald head as result of the chemotherapy shown convincingly in the commercial, was not a real cancer patient but a talented actor hired by the brand. The revelation drew massive wave of negative comments indicating how outraged viewers felt about it. They felt betrayed and stated that the brand represented deceit, using false compassion for commercial gains.

In response to criticism, Gau Do brand announced that they had to hire an actor because filming was not good for real patients, and the decision was purely based on humanitarian reasons. But the damage has been done. After the first wave, many articles posted on online media revealed actual child patients receiving support from the fund were not adequately looked after. One child had to pay part of the treatment although they were supposedly fully paid for by the charitable funds. The other really sick child in hospital received only 35 meal coupons worth a little more than US\$ 1 each.

Another article reported that the company was giving expired Gau Do instant noodle to children with cancer, on which the company promptly blamed their distributors and employees for their mistakes.

Many experts in marketing and advertising industry also discussed the case; many of them were not quite in favor of the campaign by Gau Do. Someone even quoted the law saying the advertisement of Gau Do should not have been allowed. Others stated that the posters showing Tuan make them lose their appetite when eating instant noodle, a very popular food in Vietnam.

Criticism also came from Secretary of the Vietnam Consumer Protection Association. He stated the brand was taking advantage of consumers by exploiting situations of cancer-stricken children; the TV commercial was misleading among other negative comments.

Many people questioned how much money had been spent on the campaign, given the frequency of the commercial being aired in expensive primetime TV spots, thousands of large-sized banners and posters on the streets and buses in major cities in Vietnam. The company refused to answer such questions citing business confidentiality. The airtime fee was later disclosed by one National TV station that Gau Do had to pay as high as US$1,500 for a single 30-second spot.

The attack was not ending. When Asia Foods Corp. launched another brand of instant noodle – Gau Yeu (Lovely Bear) for children emphasizing the 'absolute safety' for young consumers, an article from a magazine showed evidence that the advertisement was misleading and the noodle was in fact harmful, accusing the company of malpractice.

The company went into damage control, while refusing any wrongdoing, they stated they would not use actors and would only film actual patients in their future advertisements. They also made known how much money they have raised from the campaign, how many families of sick kids were benefited from the fund. They even stated they would be willing to ask KPMG, an audit firm, to audit how many packs of Gau Do instant noodle have been sold and how the fund would be managed. And as one of the final efforts to deal with the crisis, they suspected foul play, claiming that their campaign could be sabotaged by competitors and they would ask the authority to conduct an investigation.

At the time of writing this case in 2012-2013, the campaign was still on but it is very quiet. No image of Tuan is being used and it seems the main activity is the campaign's website (http://www.gaudoganketyeuthuong.com.vn/) showing how many cases of sick children receiving support from the fund and how much money they have raised so far through selling instant noodles.

One marketing specialist finally stated that if the company had contributed in the range of 50 Dongs to 100 Dongs for each pack sold and managed the affair a bit more carefully they would probably have not received such a negative backlash.

Discussion Questions:

1. As a consultant of the Gau Do brand, explain what you think are the main issues in the case?
2. Do you agree or disagree with the campaign by Gau Do?
3. As a brand manager of Gau Do, what would you do differently?

4. Do you agree with the comment from the marketing specialist in the last paragraph?
5. Do you think consumers would react differently in your country, given the cultural differences?
6. Should actors be used in such ads? What are the ethical issues for consideration? Discuss.

Case 11: Words and Slogans in Different Cultures

Sometimes, words that mean one thing in one language or culture, can mean something totally different in a new culture. The same is true of slogans and value propositions that companies use to communicate their brand or to build loyalty with a specific product. Earlier in 2006, it was reported that the Former Secretary of State, Madeleine Albright, used the word "cojones" to lambaste Fidel Castro. Miriam reports that Americans use this term colloquially to describe someone who is gutsy and one who speaks his/her mind regardless of the consequences. Miriam goes on to state that "Cojones is a Spanish word that means, literally, testicles. In the U.S., however, it's a sort of catch-all term for daring. That's approximately what Volkswagen was going for in a blunt black-and-white billboard featuring its GTI 2006 model accompanied by two words in big, bold letters – 'Turbo-Cojones.'" However, Volkswagon AG is getting flak for using it in billboards to advertise a sporty model to prospective Hispanic customers in the U.S.

Volkswagen took the billboards down in three cities after they quickly generated a firestorm in Cuban-dominated Miami. In the English language, Turbo-Balls do not sound so offensive, but in the Spanish-speaking community, it is offensive and it has a vulgar connotation. Volkswagen is not the first advertiser to discover that words that are amusing in one culture can be inappropriate in another. A few Asian countries have banned Australia's latest tourist slogan, "Where the Bloody Hell Are You?" Some of the ads that were found inappropriate have been replaced with other billboards that play on Spanglish, or Spanish-English blends such "Here Today. Gone Tamale," or "Kick a Little Gracias."

Real learning of the language (such as the cultural norms, nuances, accents, and implied meaning that accompany phrases) takes place when one is living in a culture for many years. Just think about how complex the English language is to many of us who were not born speaking it. English, as far as we know, is the most widely used language in the history of the planet. One, or more, in every six human beings (over one billion) is able to speak it. More than half of the world's books, and three quarters of international mail are supposedly written in English. It has been said that of all languages which exist in the world today, English has the largest vocabulary – perhaps as many as two million words – and one of the noblest bodies of literature. Nonetheless, it has been said that English is a complex, yet crazy language as the following examples which have been gleaned from the sayings and writings of many creative individuals (colleagues, writers, teachers, trainers, and friends). For example, it was a hard lesson to learn that there is no egg in eggplant, neither pine nor apple in pineapple, and no ham in hamburger. Bathrooms are referred to as "John" by some Americans and as "Box" by some of the British while others call it "lady's room," "powder room," "little boy's room," "washroom," or even "restrooms." Why is it that one can tell a baker that his bread is tasty but can't really tell him that his "buns" are to die for? How is it that the word "read" can be used with the same spelling for both the present and past tense? In what other language do people drive on a parkway and park in the driveway? Fly on a runway and run on a highway? Recite at a play and play at a recital? Ship by truck and send cargo by ship? Have noses that run and feet that smell? How can a slim chance and a fat chance be the same, while a wise man and a wise guy are opposites? How can overlook and oversee be opposites, while quite a lot and quite a few are alike? How can the weather be hot as hell one day and cold as hell the next?

While the use of the same words in different cultures can confuse one, there are also many stereotypes and biases attached to the daily interactions. A colleague at a diversity workshop in Washington D.C. once said the he is often picked first for basketball teams due to his height advantage and ability to "steal," "shoot" and "run." Of course, he said, as an African-American male people often assume that I am good at "stealing," "shooting" and "running" simply because of the color of my skin. The reality is that the best basketball players are great at "stealing" the ball, "shooting" the ball to the basket, and "running" the ball up the court, and these skills are the result of hard work, practice and talent (and not necessarily a person's ethnicity, gender or skin color). The same thing is true for higher education; the best students will eventually become known for their talent, hard work and practice by reading, writing and teaching a specific topic that is their area of passion. Overall, one must remember that the improper use of language and words often convey stereotypes which can lead to confusion and miscommunication, this is especially true when one is working in a global environment.

Discussion Questions:

1. What are some confusing words in the English language?
2. Can some of the words in the English language mean something totally different in other cultures or languages? Discuss.
3. What causes miscommunication between a company and its customers and suppliers? Discuss.
4. What are some other blunders that companies have made over the past fifty years when it comes to translations and usage of words or terms in another culture?
5. What can firms to do avoid miscommunication with their diverse clients, customers, and communities?

Case 12: Healthy Employees[9] – Employer "Carrots and Sticks"

Employers want lower health insurance costs and more productive employees; and one way to achieve these goals is to have more healthy employees. The question, and one with legal, ethical, and practical ramifications, is how to attain these objectives. Should the employer take a "carrots" or a "stick" approach? Should employees who adopt healthy lifestyles be rewarded? Or should employees who choose to lead unhealthy lifestyles by penalized by the employer? The *Miami Herald* cited the

---

[9] Contributed by Frank J. Cavico, Nova Southeastern University.

"carrots" example of Baptist Health South Florida, which the paper stated was a leader in encouraging its 13,000 employees to lead more healthy lifestyles. For example, the hospital offers benefits such as free 24/7 gyms at work and discounted low-fat meals in its cafeteria. So, Baptist Health has chosen the "carrot," said the *Miami Herald*, as opposed to the "stick," in order to promote employee wellness and to decrease rapidly increasing healthcare costs. Another "carrot" approach used by employers is to reward employees who are effectively dealing with chronic problems. For example, employers can reduce premiums for overweight employees who regularly exercise in a gym or who meet certain weight loss goals. However, the paper related that Baptist and other "carrot" approach employers may now believe that the "carrot" is not enough since healthcare costs have continued to rise. Consequently, some companies are not taking a "stick" penalty approach to motivate employees to be more healthy people. One typical "stick" approach is to require that employees with unhealthy lifestyles and habits to pay more for insurance. The paper reported on a survey on a survey of 600 major companies by a national consulting firm that found that 33% were planning in 2012 or later to reward or penalize employees based on targets for such issues as weight or cholesterol levels.

The *Miami Herald* noted that employers are concerned about a rising obesity level for employees and the growing number of diabetic employees, and thus about rapidly increasing health care costs. The newspaper reported on another survey in Florida by a consulting group of 100 Florida employers which disclosed that their health care costs had risen 5.7% in 2011. Another survey reported in the paper revealed that the major health care challenge for employers in obtaining affordable health care is the poor health habits of their employees. The *Miami Herald* reported on another survey from the Center of Disease Control and Prevention that estimated that the average smoking employee costs to an employer equals $1600 in additional medical expenditures and $1760 in lost productivity each year. Wal-Mart has begun to charge employees who smoke up to $2000 a year in what they estimate to be the increased health care costs. Safeway, as reported in the *Miami Herald*, has more of a "carrot" approach. The company will reduce yearly health care insurance premiums for about $1000 for an employee and the employee's spouse or partner for an additional $1000 if the employee does not smoke and meets certain standards for weight, blood pressure, blood sugar, and cholesterol. Ryder Company has commenced a new wellness initiative, where the company offers diabetic counseling, nutrition advice, and exercise and weight loss classes, and rewards employees up to $300 for participating in the program.

One potential legal problem for an employer when it comes to weight provisions and height and weight indexes is that some employees may contend that their weight is based on a medical condition or genetics, and in the latter case tied to racial or ethnic background, and thus the employee is protected by federal discrimination law, such as the Americans with Disabilities Act and the Civil Rights Act. Moreover, all these health issues must be kept very confidential so as not to trigger lawsuits based on the common law tort of invasion of privacy.

Accordingly, most employers, says the *Miami Herald*, prefer the "carrot" approach because it does not alienate employees. Yet, if the "carrot" approach does not work, and employees cannot or will not take care of themselves, and consequently employers continue to see health care costs rise, employers may consider penalizing unhealthy employees.

A prime health target is to cut down on smoking by employees. Baptist Health gives its non-smokers a "carrot," that is, a $30 reduction in premium payments per each bi-weekly pay period. Florida Power and Light offers a $5 bi-weekly reduction for non-smokers. However, the University of Miami uses a "stick," that is, the university adds a $50 monthly fee onto health premiums for smokers. All these employers rely on employees to voluntarily and honestly answer all health care questions. All employers also provide free smoking cessation programs.

Despite the good goals of these wellness programs, there are ethical issues that arise. For example, a health policy professor at the University of Miami, as reported in the paper, stated that employers using the "stick" produced some negative implications, such as being invasive and paternalistic. Also the professor said that there are ethical concerns if the employee is a single mother who is pressed for time and thus who cannot go to employer gym classes to lower her premiums.

Bibliography: Dorschner, John, *"Employers weigh penalties and rewards,"* The *Miami Herald*, December 3, 2011, pp. 1C, 4C.

Questions for Discussion:

1. What are some of the legal issues involved in the effort by employers to have more healthy employees; and how should these legal issues be resolved?
2. What should be the ethically egoistic approach for employers to take to have more healthy employees and thus reduced health care costs? Why?
3. Is it moral pursuant to Utilitarian ethics for employers to "force" their employees to be healthy? Why or why not?
4. Is it moral pursuant to Kantian ethics for employers to "force" their employees to be healthy? Why or why not?

Case 13: Establishing and Managing a Virtual University

The Virtual University of Pakistan, which is one of the first universities around the world that is based on modern communication technologies,[10] was established by the Pakistani government as a public sector, not-for-profit institution with a mission "to provide extremely affordable world class education to aspiring students all over the country." As part of its education process, VUP uses free-to-air satellite television broadcasts and the Internet, which allows students to follow its rigorous course and programs regardless of their ability to attend face-to-face sessions or their physical locations. This process alleviates the lack of capacity in the existing universities while simultaneously tackling the shortage of qualified professors in each field of study. By identifying the best professors within the country or outside of the country in various subjects, regardless of their institutional affiliations, and requesting them to develop and deliver hand-crafted courses, VUP aims at providing the very best courses to

---

[10] Interview with Dr. Naveed A. Malik, Rector of VUP. Coauthored with Talat Afza, COMSATS Institute of Technology. These contents are also available online at: http://www.vu.edu.pk/

students around the country. VUP's degrees are recognized and accepted all over Pakistan as well as overseas. VUP opened its virtual doors in 2002 and in a short span of time its outreach has reached throughout the country serving over 100,000 students. Furthermore, VUP is associated with more than a hundred institutions providing infrastructure support to students across the country at a fraction of the cost of traditional educational organizations.

VUP delivers education through a thoughtful combination of broadcast television and the Internet. VUP courses are designed and delivered by knowledgeable and published experts in the field. For each course's topics, professionally developed lectures are recorded at the school's studio environment and they are accompanied by relevant slides, video clips and other materials for broadcast to students. Besides being broadcasted over the television networks, course lectures are also made available in the form of multimedia CDs which are sent to registered students. These course lectures are also be made available as streaming media from the Virtual University's servers to their students.

The multiple formats allow flexibility for students who may view the lectures at a time of their choosing. In addition, comprehensive reading materials, lecture notes and other help learning tools in the form of web-enabled content are provided through a comprehensive Learning Management System (LMS) hosted on the VUP Web Servers that accessible over the Internet at any time. The LMS also provides an e-mail facility to each and every student as well as asynchronous discussion boards for interaction within the VUP community. An important feature of the LMS is a Question/Answer board where VUP faculty provides answers to questions posed by students on the subject matter covered in the lectures. The question/answer board, moderated to enhance learning, provides separate sessions for each lecture of the course. In addition, read-only access is made available to previous question/answer sessions and this constitutes an extremely useful study resource for students. VUP faculty monitors this board on a continuous basis and answers to student questions are provided regularly within a short space of time. Assignments are submitted through the LMS and graded within a short span of time so students can receive feedback as quickly as possible.

Pop-quizzes and practice tests are also conducted through the LMS. Examinations are conducted in a formal proctored environment at exam centers throughout the country. The formal examination atmosphere assists in critical quality assurance of the student assessment system. Such comprehensive learning programs and detailed focus on learning has enabled VUP's enormous success in less than a decade.

One critical point is that VUP provides an identical education to all its students regardless of their geographical location. A student can live at home to help his/he parents and work on a full-time basis, and still complete his or her educational degree in a realistic time-frame. All Virtual University students, regardless of whether they live in large cities or small towns or even remote areas are taught by the same professors, receive the same study materials and master the same course competencies. All these proctored examinations are identical throughout the country. This process ensures that every graduate has the same credentials and qualifications upon obtaining his/her degree. Graduates of VUP have gone on to be accepted at masters and doctoral programs throughout the world. Many of these graduates are working in great professional jobs in Pakistan or other countries across the globe. VUP is a great success story of human intellect combined with modern technology to make learning more flexible and affordable by the general population.

Questions for Discussion:
1. Are virtual universities becoming the norm for learning and education? Discuss.
2. What are some challenges that virtual universities face as they try to education students in the same competencies as traditional universities?
3. What challenges do the administrators face as they start virtual programs?
4. What skills are used to manage such a program? How are virtual and distance education programs managed?

Case 14: Employee Turnover [11]

Employee turnover is a problem faced by all organizations, including healthcare firms in Thailand. As such, organizational managers and leaders must be cognizant to not lose qualified and experienced employees.

High employee turnover rates have been associated with decreased customer satisfaction, productivity, future revenue growth and profitability. Recruiting new staffs is an expensive process and causes problems in the work process, especially in sales-based organizations. Employee turnover can be detrimental from a managerial perspective. Retaining the top performers is one of the company's competitive advantage necessities. Staff retention should therefore be considered a top priority for companies. Research shows that a large percent of the employees who resigned made the decision to change because of poor management, namely leadership styles. For many salespeople, remuneration package may just be a temporarily motivator. Ultimately, however, they will need to have a greater sense of job fulfillment to remain committed to the organization. In many cases, leadership styles whether transformational or transactional can fulfill this need. Transformational leadership is seen as an organizational force that can transform the unfulfilled and non-committed employee to a productive employee who works at optimal capability and organizational loyalty.

Questions for Discussion:
1. Why do employees leave their companies? List the top five reasons for companies in your city or country?
2. Why should organizational managers and leaders work on developing their employees' potential? How can they actually do this…by giving educational and training activities or others? Discuss.
3. What can managers do to improve subordinates' productivity and job satisfaction?
4. List some of the costs associated with employee turnover.

---

[11] Contributed by Somsak Kaveetriphop, Ramkhamhaeng University, Institute of International Studies.

Case 15: The Move toward Green Management[12]

In the past, industrialists, innovators and entrepreneurs have created many products without fully knowing their long-term impact on people or society. Nowadays, people are expected to responsibly use modern technology to create value for people around the globe without causing undue negative externalities such as air pollution. After major disasters caused by atmospheric problems and pollution, many professionals have changed their way of thinking in an attempt to save the world by taking part in "green management" and conducting business in the green way using the 5Rs (reduce, reuse, recycle, renew, and respect) to manage the organization.

Green management is for those organizations that want to attract and retain a great human resources group while improving their environment. These 21st century organizations focus on the economic, social, agricultural, business ethics, and social responsibility to add value to society using their human resources asset. Many companies strive to grow and increase their profits. These companies have tried to create a competitive advantage by becoming environmentally responsible. Nowadays, companies try to go green with everything in the company's value chain from their ground level manufacturing to their top management.
Green management is the way of being environmentally friendly for organization.

Questions for Discussion:
1. Why should companies be focused on environmentally friendly work procedures?
2. List two companies that are considered to be socially responsible regarding green management?
3. How do green management initiatives lead to sustainability in the society? Discuss.

Case 16: Criticizing Your Employer on Facebook[13]

The *Wall Street Journal* in December of 2011 reported on a growing legal employment controversy involving social media. The controversy arises when employees are discharged or disciplined for criticizing their employers on social networking sites, such as Facebook and Twitter. Employers believe they have the legal right to fire employees who criticize them or who post rude, insulting, or hostile comments. However, sanctioned employees have sought legal protection under federal law, specifically the National Labor Relations Act (NLRA) of 1935. The law gives private sector employees (but not supervisors or managers as they are not protected "employees") the right to complain about pay, safety, and other working conditions; however, as emphasized by the *Wall Street Journal*, the law does not protect "simple griping." The paper noted that in 2011 about 100 employers, including Wal-Mart Stores, a BMW dealership, and a saloon, have been accused by employees of improper social media policies and practices regarding employees. It is to the National Labor Relations Board (NLRB), the federal agency that enforces the NLRA, to determine if the employees' complaints have merit. In one case reported in

---

[12] Contributed by Nisarat Aimkij, Ramkhamhaeng University, Institute of International Studies.
[13] Contributed by Frank J. Cavico, Nova Southeastern University.

the Wall Street Journal, a paramedic, employed by American Medical Response of Connecticut, was terminated after calling her supervisor a "scumbag" on Facebook on her home computer. She was unhappy because her supervisor had questioned her regarding a customer complaint. In that case, the NLRB decided that her discharge was illegal because the discussions were made during an online discussion among employees about supervisory action. The agency reasoned that the employee comment was part of the online discussion and thus "protected concerted activity" pursuant to the NLRA. The fact that the employee's comment was motivated by the supervisor unlawfully denying union representation to the employee regarding the customer's complaint was an important factor in the determination. The company said that the employee was fired because she violated company protocols and procedures. The case was eventually settled before it was appealed to an NLRB administrative law judge. As part of the settlement, the company agreed to revise its Internet posting policy so that it would not violate employees' rights.

According to the NLRB's latest data, in May of 2011, the agency had received 113 complaints related to social media. As noted in the preceding dispute, the key legal issue is whether the employees' online postings rise to the level of "protected concerted activity." Pursuant to the NLRA, also called the Wagner Act, employees are protected when discussing work conditions on behalf of themselves or other workers. Discussing with other workers on how to improve workplace conditions is also protected. Thus, the critical factor in the legal analysis is whether the employee activity is "group activity" as opposed to mere complaining, which is not protected. However, the line between group activity and complaining is not clear; and furthermore, as noted in the *Wall Street Journal*, the NLRB has not yet provided any specific guidance. For example, if an employee posts a message to a group of employees and no one responds, is the activity protected "group activity." Human resource managers emphasize that online postings by employees could damage a company's reputation; and thus they underscore that the federal agency has to provide some clear guidance. Yet the *Wall Street Journal* reported on some cases that seemed "clear." In one, a warehouse employee at Frito-Lay on writing of Facebook that he was a "hair away from setting it off in that b___," apparently referring to the warehouse where he worked. He made the comment after a supervisor said the employee would lose attendance points if he left work early because he felt unwell. An HR manager later told the employee that the comment sounded like he was going to shoot everyone at the warehouse. The employee said that he was just 'venting" and that "setting it off" meant swearing at someone of "walking-off" the job. The NLRB concluded that the employee's comments were not protected. In a Wal-Mart case, the NLRB determined that an employee's comments were not protected when the employee called an assistant manager a derogatory name during a series of Facebook posts and was consequently reprimanded. The company spokesperson said that the employee's comment was "inappropriate" regardless of where it occurred, and that the comment had a negative impact on the workplace environment. Threats, physical or verbal, thus are not protected activities. Moreover, merely complaining or "griping" solely on behalf of oneself, and with no evidence of group interaction or intent for group action, is also not protected. Name-calling most likely is not protected activity too; but the NLRB said that name-calling cases depend on the facts.

One important question that is still not resolved is whether employee negative comments made from work computers are protected. One point is clear and that is an employer cannot have a policy that restricts employees from discussing working conditions online.

Bibliography: Trottman, Melanie, "Workers Claim Right to Rant on Facebook," *The Wall Street Journal,* December 2, 2011, p.p. B1-2.

Questions for Discussion:
1. What are some of the key legal issues that arise when employees' criticize their employers on social media; and how should these legal issues be resolved. Specifically, where do you think the line should be drawn between protected group activity and mere complaining? Why?
2. How should an ethically egoistic employer approach the subject of employees discussing work online? Why?
3. What would be a moral employer policy regarding social media pursuant to Utilitarian and Kantian ethics? Why?

Case 17: Sharing Knowledge[14]

Today, knowledge is regarded as the most important strategic asset for organizational effectiveness and competitiveness. Effective knowledge management not only brings about many organizational benefits, such as improved contingency response, innovation capabilities, rapid commercialization for new products, response to market changes, etc., but also ensures long-term survival or sustainability. That is why most organizations attempt to implement effective knowledge management (KM) strategies. While managers recognize the importance of knowledge sharing amongst their employees and are eager to introduce the KM paradigm in their organizations, many of them still lack sufficient knowledge about the determinants of the individual's knowledge sharing behavior, which is why many past attempts have been unsuccessful.

Of course, it should be noted that KM is not a new concept. Forward thinking organizations have been implementing KM for years. However, many past attempts often resulted in failure because organizations continually overlooked motivational drivers that encourage and/or discourage individuals' involvement. The identification and recognition of knowledge sharing barriers plays a crucial role in the success of a KM strategy. Particularly, since knowledge resides within individuals, the movement of knowledge across individual and organizational boundaries, into and from repositories, and into organizational routines and practices is ultimately dependent on employees' knowledge sharing behaviors. For this reason, it is imperative that organizations become more attentive in finding ways to encourage their employees to share knowledge.

In recent years, many KM initiatives in many countries have been disappointing. This is because many organizations are inconsiderate of motivational drivers conducive to individuals' knowledge sharing behaviors. Given that the key

---

[14] Contributed by Tanin Kaweevisultrakul, Ramkhamhaeng University, Institute of International Studies.

success factor to managing knowledge is being perceived as largely dependent on individuals' connections within the organization, KM implementation requires changes in an organization's culture especially employees' involvement and participation. One of the core necessities for knowledge creation, transfer, and sharing is that employees contribute their knowledge or expertise to the organization. Therefore, human issues must be considered a key factor. Accordingly to the theory of reasoned action (TRA), it can be expected that individuals will share knowledge if they hold positive attitude toward knowledge sharing. Thus, it is consequential that organizations recognize what factors encourage employees' knowledge sharing behaviors.

Questions for Discussion:
1. What is knowledge sharing and why is it important in today's workplace?
2. What is knowledge management? How are firms managing the knowledge which may exist among their diverse employees across different departments, cities and countries?
3. What are some challenges regarding knowledge management and knowledge sharing?

Case 18: Bribery and the Salesperson[15]

John Benson, an American citizen, and a key salesperson for the American Machinery Company, is very worried. His company is in dire financial condition, as it is deeply in debt and financially over-extended. The company has staked its future in successfully penetrating foreign markets. The president of the company has been assiduously tying to interest the government of a rapidly developing foreign country to make a major purchase. This contract, if agreed to, will not only be a very large one which will save the company, but it will also open the door to even bigger sales by the company to the foreign government in the future. John has been given the critical role of being in charge of the negotiations and securing the contract. If John is successfully, not only will the company be saved but John will return as the "hero" to a certain promotion and big raise. However, if the American Machinery Company does not make this sale, or get some other very big orders soon, it at the least will have to close a material part of its operations, which would cause massive lay-offs and also be disastrous for local communities adversely affected. The company had been regarded, and rightfully so, as a very socially responsible company in these communities as it was involved in civic and charitable affairs. Now, it all that "good" may be gone as the company may go bankrupt without the contract.

John had been convinced that the deal would go through until he speaks with the high level government official in charge of negotiating the contract. The official tells John that his company's bid is looked upon very favorably by the foreign government regarding price, quality, and service, and in fact American Machinery's bid is the lowest bid. Moreover, the foreign government is aware that John's company is known to act in a socially responsible manner in the communities where it does business. However, much to John's surprise, the foreign government officials

---

[15] Contributed by Frank J. Cavico, Nova Southeastern University.

says that in order to finalize the contract it will be necessary for the company to pay the official a $100,000 "commission fee." Furthermore, the official says that if the company does not pay the commission, the official regrets that the contract will go to the next highest bidder. Yet the official assures John that the payment of the "commission fee" is proper locally in the host country.

John well knows that this contract is absolutely critical to the well-being of the company and its stakeholders, including, and especially, himself. He also believes that the host country and government and its people will get a very good and fair deal from his company by buying their equipment. John also knows that the amount of $100,100 is really a trivial sum when compared to the contract amount and expected profits as well as the potential future profits represented by getting a foothold in the host country. Moreover, John is award that these types of payments are common and accepted practices in many countries; but he has always felt that they were wrong; he has never used them to secure a deal; and he is also keenly cognizant of the fact that there may be serious legal ramifications under the host country law and the U.S. Foreign Corrupt Practices Act by making such a payment. So, what is John to do?

Questions for Discussion
1. Is this proposed payment an illegal bribe pursuant to the Foreign Corrupt Practices Act? Why or why not?
2. Is this a moral bribe pursuant to ethical egoism, ethical relativism, Utilitarianism, and Kantian ethics? Why or why not?
3. How should the host country seek to prevent this type of corruption?
4. Assuming the company secures the contract, what should it be doing in the host country to be a "socially responsible" organization?

Case 19: The Benefits and Costs of Free Trade[16]

Since 1980, the orthodox recipe for economic growth has been the reduction of barriers to the free flow of commerce and capital. International institutions such as the International Monetary Fund (IMF) and the World Bank have contended that the free market approach to development will create faster levels of economic growth and alleviate poverty. The integration of markets has been largely achieved through regional free trade agreements and unilateral liberalization. It has also been facilitated by deregulation, the shrinking costs of communications and transportation and the IT revolution.

Some developing countries benefited from trade liberalization. China's ratio of trade to GDP doubled. Brazil, Mexico and other middle-income countries registered large increases in their volume of trade. They managed to export a range of manufactured goods often as part of global production networks. In China, the number of poor people (earning less than $0.70 a day) went down from 250 million (1978) to 34 million in 1999. Similarly in India, the number went down from 330 million in 1977 to 259 million in 1999.

In the case of many other nations, however, the laissez-faire approach appears to have worsened growth rates and income distribution. In 1980, for example,

---

[16] Contributed by Belay Seyoum, Nova Southeastern University.

the medium income in the richest 10 percent of countries was 77 times greater than in the poorest 10 percent. By 1999, this gap had grown to 122 times. Many studies have shown that trade liberalization in Latin America, for example, led to widening wage gaps, falling real wages for unskilled workers, and rising unemployment. In many countries, trade liberalization, deregulated markets have induced rapid structural changes often leading to declining wages, working conditions and living standards. The challenge today is to make trade liberalization work for the poor. This requires a wide-ranging reform in national institutions and policies.

Discussion Questions:
1. How can trade liberalization be made to work for the poor?
2. What can world leaders do to reduce poverty?
3. Why is the rich getting richer?
4. Select a country or region and evaluate its performance (GDP per capita, distribution of income, etc.) before and after trade liberalization.
5. Which countries are more likely to benefit from the ASEAN agreement and why? Discuss.

Case 20: Chinese[17] Management Skills

Cultures can influence competency of management skills. Research shows that there are significant differences between countries based on the respondents' technical, human relations, and conceptual skills. In some cases, younger managers demonstrated higher technical skills than older respondents and this is probably due to the fact that older workers tend to be in professional or managerial positions as a result of promotions and their many years of experience in the workplace.

With the Chinese population, we have seen that managers who earned a doctorate degree have higher technical skill than those with a high school or an undergraduate degree. On the contrary, when compared with a master's degree, Chinese managers who earned a doctorate degree have a lower level of technical skill. In reality, managers whose educational level are high school or below may have lower ability to learn complex things compared with others. Managers with doctorate degree credentials may contribute most of their time in scientific research, so they have few opportunities to improve their practical skills. Education and management experience tend to have a significantly positive influence on human skill. If a manager has not been well educated, not trained on interpersonal skills or lacks sufficient management experience, then it may negatively affect his or her human skills. This research with Chinese managers demonstrates that those with less than six years of management experiences have relatively lower conceptual skill. This may be because they are young and lack enough opportunity to improve their cause and effect decision-making capacity. Of course, conceptual skills can be acquired from experience in solving complex departmental and interpersonal problems.

Discussion Questions:
1. Would college education in China increase a person's technical, human or

---

[17] Contributed by Han Ping, The School of Management, Xi'an Jiaotong University.

conceptual skills and why?

2. Based on your knowledge, do Chinese and Indian cultures focus more on technical skills, human relations skills or conceptual skills? Discuss.
3. Is there a relationship between gender and management skills? Discuss.
4. Based on your knowledge, do Iranian and Pakistani cultures focus more on technical skills, human relations skills or conceptual skills? Discuss.
5. Can age enhance a person's focus on management skills? Discuss.
6. Based on your knowledge, do Thai and Vietnamese cultures focus more on technical skills, human relations skills or conceptual skills? Discuss.
7. Do cultures make a difference in the management skills of college graduates? What evidence exists?
8. Based on your knowledge, do German and American cultures focus more on technical skills, human relations skills or conceptual skills? Discuss.

Case 21: Religious Values and Ethics in Pakistan[18]

Having a significant geo-strategic position on the world map, Pakistan has the potential of attracting business practices of the entire world. This country serves as a hub to have business with Asian and far Eastern countries, and is a gateway to Central Asian countries which are endowed with innumerable natural reservoirs. Immediately after gaining independence, this country started to establish administrative structures, since then, Pakistan has made tremendous efforts to get rid of its colonial past in a way of its development. In this course, Pakistan faces many upheavals of democratic, economic, and socio-cultural nature, which has further crippled the development process at times.

Business ethics has been an important issue in Pakistan as this country's leaders are trying to enhance their perception of having a fair business environment, as demonstrated by international surveys. Would religious values have the power to direct people's behaviors to do what is most ethical in each situation? Theoretically there are many schools of ethics but Islamic work ethics are the most feasible and acceptable for Pakistani work environment because of the majority of the country population (97%) is Muslim. It would not be surprising to know that the natives of the sub-continent were inspired in their business by the fair dealings of Muslim traders and therefore embraced Islam.

Moreover, Islamic values related to work and social interactions are based on honesty, integrity, truthfulness, keeping promises, fair appraisal, public responsibility and fair compensation. At the same time it negates the concept and practices of bribery, fraudulent practices, discrimination, harassment, nepotism, exploitation of subordinates, favoritism, and all other unfair business practices aimed at earning profit at the cost of affecting someone negatively. Islam teaches the following: Let there arise out of you a band of people inviting to all that is good, enjoining what is right, and forbidding what is wrong (Quran, 3:104); but let there be amongst you traffic and trade by mutual consent (Quran, 4:29). Give measure and weight with (full) justice (Quran, 6:152).

---

[18] Contributed by Razia Begum, University of Peshawar, College of Home Economics.

Researchers that have conducted research on the Pakistani telecom industry about Islamic work ethics and its effect on managerial performance concluded that religion does inspire the work practices of its followers. Therefore, the adoption of Islamic work values is of significant importance in contributing work ethics enhancement for daily decision-making of employees and managers. It has been shown that Islamic values promote strong ethical leadership and greater employee and customer satisfaction.

Discussion Questions:
1. Can religious values enhance business ethics in a society?
2. What can managers of a diverse workplace that employees with different religious beliefs do to make sure their employees behave ethically at all times?
3. What are some values that are commonly promoted among Muslims, Christians, Jews, Hindus, Buddhists, and other religions? Discuss.

Case 22: Economic Development in Cuba[19]

The challenges and opportunities which Cubans have been weathering for over fifty years now could unwittingly serve to provide a positive scheme for its reconstruction. Although its infrastructure has been drastically damaged and its human capital weakened due to sanctions and isolation from some of its developed neighbors, its deprivations should provide a population in a state of being receptive to and appreciative of even drastic changes. These changes and transitions of course, however, should not be too hard to trigger since Cuba will be starting from almost ground zero in terms of some aspects of socioeconomic development.

Before presenting our analysis and suggestions, and in order to understand the origins of the Cuban transition to socialism, it will probably be appropriate to make reference to a speech pronounced on July 26th 1968 by Fidel Castro in his official commemoration of the 15th anniversary of the attack to the Moncada Barracks that marked the beginning of his struggle against Fulgencio Batista's regime. This important ideological proposition represents the initiation of a whole era of economic behaviors that may have made Cuba highly dependent on Soviet aid and compromised any possibilities of escaping socioeconomic alienation. The conclusion of this speech, according to some Cubans, represents the definite endorsement to an idealistic and, ultimately, historically proven catastrophic economic policy, based on a distorted version of the theory of the Fair Price. Fidel Castro said at that time:

> We should not use money or wealth to create political awareness. We must use political awareness to create wealth…To give a man participation in more collective wealth because he does his duty and produces more and creates more for society is to turn political awareness into wealth…The road is not easy. The task is difficult, and many will criticize us. They will call us petty bourgeois, idealists; they will say we are dreamers; they will say we are

---

[19] Contributed by Pedro F. Pellet, Nova Southeastern University.

bound to fail. And yet, facts will speak for us, realities will speak for us, and our people will speak and act for us because we know our people have the capacity to comprehend these roads and follow these roads!

The main themes of this "utopian" speech can be summarized by the struggle or dichotomy between ideology and necessity, revolutionary ethics and economic rationality. The specific economic spheres of influence were: 1)- moral versus material incentives; 2)- role of money and markets; 3)- budgetary versus self-financed enterprises.

Discussion Questions:

1. Have the Fidel Castro regime's leadership and policies been helpful or hurtful to the economic development of Cuba? Provide evidence as compared to other countries with similar conditions and challenges.
2. What should be the main economic influences driving the decisions of politicians in Cuba (socialist) and other countries that are capitalistic?
3. Can the future of the Cuban people be substantially improved if they move away from socialism to a mixed economy and neoclassical capitalism?
4. What is the difference between socialism, neoclassical capitalism and mixed-economies?

BIBLIOGRAPHY

Adair, W., J. Okumura, and T.M. Brett. (2001). Negotiation behavior when cultures collide: The U.S. and Japan. *Journal or Applied Psychology* 86(3): 371-385.

Adler, Nancy J. (1991). *International dimensions of organizational behavior*. 2nd ed. Boston, MA: PWS-Kent Publishing Company.

Adler, N. J. & Bartholomew, S. (1992). Academic and professional communities of discourse: Generating knowledge on transnational human resource management. *Journal of International Business Studies*, 23(3), 551-569.

Adler, N. (1983). A typology of management studies involving culture. *Journal of International Business Studies*, 14: 29-47.

Allman, H.F. (1995). *Transliteration of Coca-Cola Trademark to Chinese Characters*. Retrieved January 23, 2001, from the World Wide Web: http://www.urbanlegends.com/products/coca-cola/coca-cola_chinese.html

Annan, K. A. (December 2006). *As Secretary-General prepares to step down, five lessons learnt during difficult but exhilarating decade*. By the Secretary-General Kofo A. Annan, Truman Library. December 11, 2006. Retrieved from the United Nation's website on December 14, 2006 from: http://www.un.org/News/ossg/sg/stories/statments_full.asp?statID=40.

Artley, J. B., Mujtaba, B. G., Barnes, B., and Pellet, P. F. (2009). Leadership practice influences on the Generation X employee commitment in the workplace. *Global Review of Business and Economic Research,* 5(1), 67-87.

Ayguen, A. K., and Imamoglu, E. O. (2002). Value domains of Turkish adults and university students. *Journal of Social Psychology, 142*(3), 333-351.

Awbi, A. (2006). Tesco Shifts Focus as foreign business booms. *Food & Drink Europe.com*). Retrieved August 21, 2006 from http://www.foodanddrinkeurope.com/news/ng.asp?id=68453

Ajzen, I. (1988). *Attitudes, personality and behavior*. Chicago, IL: The Dorsey Press.

Backman, M. (Revised Ed.). (2001). *Asian eclipse: Exposing the dark side of business in Asia*. Singapore: John Wiley & Sons (Asia) Pte. Ltd.

Bakhtari, H. (1995). Cultural effects on management style: A comparative study of American and Middle Eastern management styles. *International Studies of Management and Organization*, 25(3): 97-118.

Bhargava, V. (2005). *The Cancer of Corruption*. Retrieved April 2, 2006, from http://web.worldbank.org/WBSITE/EXTERNAL/EXTABOUTUS/0,,contentMDK:20666591~pagePK:51123644~piPK:329829~theSitePK:29708,00.html

Beck, C. E. (1999). *Managerial Communication/ Building Theory and Practice*. Upper Saddle River, NJ: Prentice Hall. ISBN 0-13-849886-5

Becker, K. (2000). *Culture and International Business*. Binghamton: International Business Press.

Bedeian, Arthur G. (2004). The gift of professional maturity. *Academy of Management: Learning and Education,* 3(1): 92-98.

Bernard, C. I., (1938). The executive functions. In Ott, S. J. (1996) *Classical Readings in Organizational Behavior* (2nd ed.): 181-183. Orlando, FL: Harcourt Brace & Company.

Black, J. S. & Porter, L. W. (1991). Managerial behavior and job performance: A successful manager in Los Angeles may not succeed in Hong Kong. *Journal of International Business Studies*, 22(1): 99-113.

Blackman, C. (1997). *Negotiating China: Case studies and strategies.* St. Leonards, Australia: Allen & Unwin Pty. Ltd.

Bond, M. H. (1996). Chinese values. In M. Bond (Ed.), *The handbook of Chinese psychology* (pp. 208-226). New York, NY: Oxford University Press.

Burns, J. M. (1978). *Leadership.* New York: Harper & Row.

Cascio, W. F. and Aguinis, H. (2005). *Applied psychology in human resources management* (6th ed.). New Jersey: Pearson Prentice Hall.

Cavico, Frank J., and Mujtaba, Bahaudin G. (2013). *Business Ethics: The Moral Foundation of Effective Leadership, Management, and Entrepreneurship.* Boston: Pearson Custom Publishing.

Cavico, F. J. and Mujtaba, B. G. (2008). *Legal Challenges for the Global Manager and Entrepreneur.* Kendal Hunt Publishing Company. United States.

Cellich, C., & Jain, S. (2004). *Global Business Negotiations- A Practical Guide.* South-Western. Mason, Ohio: South-Western, part of the Thomson Corporation.

Chen, M. (2004). *Common Culture, Different Styles. The Chinese Business Review,* 31, 5, 53-58.

Chopra, S., & Sodhi M., S. (2004). Managing risk to avoid supply-chain breakdown. *MIT Sloan Management Review, 46*(1), 53-61. Retrieved February 19, 2005, from EBSCOhost database.

Clem, A. H. and Mujtaba, B. G. (2010). Infusing value: application of historical management concepts at a modern organization. *Journal of Management and Marketing Research*, 4(1), 1-16.

Crum, T. F. (1987). *The Magic of Conflict: Turning a Life of Work into a Work of Art.* Touchstone; Simon and Schuster.

Covey, S. R. (1989). *Seven Habits of Highly Effective People.* United States: Free Press.

Covey, S. R. (1995). *Principle-centered leadership.* New York: Simon & Schuster.

Cuevas, P., Beda-Andourou, A., Bernal, M., Bolivar, M., and Mujtaba, B. G. (October 2011). Lessons from Fred Bailey's Expatriate Experience in Japan: Proactively Preparing Employees for International Assignments. *Journal of Business Studies Quarterly*, 2(4), 42-52.

Daft, R. L. (2004b). Theory Z: Opening the corporate door for participative management. *Academy of Management Executive, 18*(4), 117-121.

Department of Homeland Security (DHS) website. Retrieved February 16, 2005, from http://www.dhs.gov/dhspublic/

De Rugy, V. (2004, October). What does homeland security buy? *American Enterprise Institute for Public Policy Research.* Retrieved February 10, 2005, from http://www.aei.org/publication21483/

Dessler, G. (2001). *A Framework for Human Resource Management.* 2nd edition. Prentice Hall.

Dessler, G. (2003). *Human Resource Management.* Upper Saddle River, New Jersey: Prentice Hall.

Discipline without Punishment. A CRM Learning Video. 2215 Faraday Avenue. Phone: (800) 421-0833. Retrieved on 10, 06, 2005 from: http://www.crmlearning.com/product.cwa?isbn=111472V

Dolan, John P. (2006). How to Prepare for Any Negotiation Session. *Dispute Resolution Journal*, 61, 2, 64. ABI/Inform Global. Retrieved November 3, 2006 from: http://www.nova.edu/library/eleclib/databases.html.

Dowling, P.J., Welch, D.E. (2005). *International Human Resource Management: Managing People in a Multinational Context (4th ed.)* Italy: Thompson South-Western.

Drucker, Peter F. (2004). What makes an effective executive? *Harvard Business Review*, 82(6): 58-64.

Drucker, P. F. (2002). *Managing the Next Society: The CEO in the next millennium.* New York, NY: St. Martin's Press, 10010.

Drucker, P. F. (2001). *The Essential Drucker* (3rd ed.). New York: Harper Collins.

Drucker, P. F. (1974). *Management: Tasks, Responsibilities, Practices* (special edition prepared for The Presidents Association). New York: Harper & Row.

DuBrin, A. J. (2004). *Leadership: Research Findings, Practice, and Skills* (4th ed.). New York: Houghton Mifflin Company.

Dunning, J.H. (1997). *Micro and macro organizational aspects on MNE and MNE activity. International Business: an emerging vision*, Columbia, SC: University of South Columbia Press.

Elashmawi, F. & Harris, P. R. (1993). *Multicultural Management.* Houston: Gulf Publishing.

Fang, T. (2006). Negotiation: The Chinese Style. *Journal of Business & Industrial Marketing* 21[1], 50-60. 8-1-2006.

Feather, N. T. (1970). Educational choice and student attitudes in relation to terminal and instrumental values. *Australian Journal of Psychology, 22*-2, 127-143.

Feather, N. T. (1999). *Values, achievement and justice: Studies in the psychology of deservingness.* New York, NY: Kulwer Academic/Plenum Publishers.

Fiedler, F. E. (1969 March). Style or circumstance: The leadership enigma. *Psychology Today* 2(10), 38-43.

Fiedler, F. E. (1967). *A theory of leadership effectiveness.* New York: McGraw-Hill.

Follett, M. P., (1918). *The new state: group organization the solution of popular government.* London. Longmans, Green & Co.

Follett, M.P. (1933), *The essentials of leadership", lecture delivered at Department of Business Administration, London School of Economics and Political Science.* Reprinted from the book, Freedom and Coordination, Chapter IV, pp. 47-60. edited by L. Urwick (1949), The Management Publications Trust, Ltd.

Franklin, E. and Mujtaba, B. G. (March 2007). International Growth and Human Resource Management Challenges: a Review of Hewlett-Packard's Efforts to Maintain the HP Way. *Journal of Business Case Studies,* 3(1), 5-14.

Friedman, M. (1994). *The social responsibility of business is to increase its profits.* In A. W. Wines and A. Stevens (Eds.), *Reading in business ethics and social responsibility* (pp. 137-141). Iowa: Kendall and Hunt Publishing.

Gable, W. and Ellig, J. (1993). *Introduction to Market-Based Management.* Fairfax, VA: Center for Market Processes.

Gibson, Jane (1995). *The supervisory Challenge* (2nd. Ed.). Prentice-Hall: USA.

Gibson, Jane (1991). *Organizational Communications*: A Managerial Perspective, 2nd edition. Harper Collins: USA.

Gibson, Jane (1985). *Reading and Exercises in Organizational Behavior.* Academic Press: United States.

Glick, N. D. (2001).The impact of culture on sales force management. *Journal of Applied Management and Entrepreneurship,* 6(2): 116-129.

Goldsmith, Marshal (July 2004). *Personal Communication on Situational Leadership and Coaching.* Last day of the one-week workshop by Dr. Hersey at 'The Center for Leadership Studies." Escondido, CA. July 11-18.

Graham, J.L., Hodgson, J.D., & Sano, Y. (2000). *Doing business with the new Japan.* Lanman, Maryland: Rowman & Littlefield.

Griffin, T.J., and Daggatt, W. R. (1990). *The Global Negotiator.* Harper Business: Division of HarperCollins Publishers. USA

Hall, E. T. and Hall, M. R., (1987). *Understanding Cultural Differences.* Intercultural Press, Inc. USA.

Hamel, Gary (2007). *The future of management.* Boston: Harvard Business School Press.

Harris, P., Moran, R., Moran, S. (2004). *Managing cultural differences: Global Leadership strategies for the twenty-first century* (6th ed.). Elsevier Butterworth-Heinemann.

Herbig, P. A., & Miller, J. C. (1992). Culture and Technology: Does the Traffic Move in Both Directions? *Journal of International Marketing,* 6(3), 75-105.

Hersey, P. (2000). *Management of Organizational Behavior: Leading Human Resources.* (8th ed.) Boston: Prentice Hall/Pearson Education.

Hersey, P. & Campbell, R. (2004). *Leadership: A Behavioral Science Approach.* California: Leadership Studies Publishing.

Hersey, P., Blanchard, K., and Johnson, D. (2001). *Management of Organizational Behavior.* 8th ed. Prentice Hall. ISBN: 013-032518X.

Hodgetts, R. M., & Luthans, F. (2003). *International Management* (5th ed.). Boston: McGraw-Hill.

Hofstede, G. (2001). *Culture's consequences: Comparing values, behaviors, institutions and organizations across nations* (2nd ed). Thousand Oaks, CA: Sage Publications.

Hofstede, G. (1993). Cultural constraints in management theories. *The Executive, 7,* 81-94.

Hofstede, G. (1983). National cultures in four dimensions: a research-based theory of cultural differences among nations. *International Studies of Management and Organization, 13*, 46-74.

Hofstede, G. (1980). *Culture's consequences: International differences in work-related values.* Beverly Hills, CA: Sage Publications.

Hofstede, G., & Hofstede, G. J. (2005). *Cultures and Organizations: Software of the Mind* (2nd ed., Rev.). New York: McGraw-Hill.

Hofstede, G., and Bond, M. (1984). Hofstede's culture dimensions: An independent validation using Rokeach's Value Survey. *Journal of Cross-cultural Psychology, 15*(4): 417-433.

House, R.J. (1971). *A Path-Goal Theory of Leadership Effectiveness. Administrative Science Quarterly,* 16, 321-338.

Jensen, Eric (1997). *Brain compatible strategies.* Brain Store Publications: USA.

Johnson, B. & Weinstein, A. (2004). *Superior Customer Value in New Economy.* 2nd ed. CRC Press.

Jones, G. R., George, Jennifer M. (2011). *Contemporary Management,* 7th ed. New York: McGraw-Hill.

Jones, M. and Mujtaba, B. G. (2008). Becoming a management legend by making history through the Hawthorne Studies: a conversation with Alfred A. Bolton. *Journal of Applied Management and Entrepreneurship,* 13(1), 101-108.

Jones, M. B., Mujtaba, B. G., Williams, A., and Greenwood, R. A. (December 2011). Organizational Culture Types and Knowledge Management in U.S. Manufacturing Firms. *Journal of Knowledge Management Practice,* 12(4), 1-11.

Kaifi, B. A. and Mujtaba, B. G. (October 2011 - March 2012). The Emergence of a New Era of Management: The Leadership Traits and Skills of Eastern Indian and Afghan Women. *Tecnia Journal of Management Studies,* 6(2), 1-9.

Karadjova-Stoev, G. and Mujtaba, B. G. (2009). Strategic Human Resource Management and Global Expansion Lessons from the Euro Disney Challenges in France. *International Business and Economics Research Journal,* 8(1), 69-78.

Katzenbach, J. R. (1998). *Teams at the top: Unleashing the potential of both teams and individual leaders.* Boston: Harvard Business School.

Katzenbach, J., & Smith, D. (2005). The Discipline of Teams. *Harvard Business, Review, 83*(7), 162-170.

Katzenbach, Jon R. & Smith, Douglas K., (1993). *The Wisdom of Teams.* Harvard Business School Press.

Kennedy, J. W., Heinzman, J. and Mujtaba, B. G. (2007). The Early Organizational Management Theories: The Human Relations Movement & Business Ethical Practices Pioneered by Visionary Leader Mary Parker Follett. *Journal of Business and Economics Research,* 5(3), 27-36.

Kluckhohn, C. M. (1962). Values and value-orientations in the theory of action. In T. Parsons and E. A. Shils (Eds.), *Toward a general theory of action* (pp. 388-433). New York: Harper and Row.

Kluckhohn, C. (1951). The study of values. In D. N. Barrett (Ed.), *Values in transition* (pp. 17-45). Notre Dame, IN: University of Notre Dame Press.

Kluckhohn, F. R. and Strodtbeck, f. L. (1961). *Variations in value orientations.* New York: Peterson.

Koch, C. G. (2007). *The Science of Success: How Market-Based Management Built the World's Largest Private Company.* Wiley Publications; United States.

Kohlberg, L. 1981. *The philosophy of moral development.* San Francisco: Harper & Row.

Kohlberg, L. 1984. *The psychology of moral development.* San Francisco: Harper & Row.

Lamb, A. & Johnson, L. (2004). *Are You an Effective Leader?* Retrieved on September 6, 2005, from http://eduscapes.com/sms/management.html

Latz, M.E. (2004). *Gain The Edge! Negotiating to Get What You Want.* New York: St. Martin's Press.

Lundrigan, M., Tangsuvanich, V., Yu, L., Wu, S., and Mujtaba, B. G. (2012). Coaching a Diverse Workforce: The Impact of Changing Demographics for Modern Leaders. *International Journal of Humanities and Social Science,* 2(3), 40-48.

Maslow, A. H., (1970). *Motivation and Personality.* New York, NY: Harper & Row.

McFarlane, D. A., Mujtaba, B. G., and Cavico, F. J. (December 31, 2009). The Business School in the 21ˢᵗ Century and Beyond: Integrating Knowledge Management (KM) Philosophy. *Journal of Knowledge Management Practice,* 10(4).

McGregor, D. (1960). *The Human Side Of Enterprise.* New York.

McShane, S. L., & Von Glinow, M. A. (2003). *Organization Behavior: Emerging Realities for the Workplace Revolution.* McGraw-Hill/Irwin.

Mead. R. (2005). *International Management: Cross-Cultural Dimensions (4ᵗʰ Ed.).* Malden, MA: Blackwell Publishing.

Morris, T. & Pavett, C.M. (1992). Management style and productivity in two cultures. *Journal of International Business Studies,* 23(1): 169-179.

Mujtaba, B. G. (2011). Stress Perceptions and Diversity Management: a Study of Respondents in India and the United States based on Gender, Age, Education, and Nationality. *International Journal of Management and Administrative Sciences,* 1(1), 08-22.

_____ (2010). *Workplace Diversity Management: Challenges, Competencies and Strategies.* ILEAD Academy: Florida USA.

_____ (2007). *The ethics of management and leadership in Afghanistan (2ⁿᵈ edition).* ILEAD Academy: Florida USA.

_____ (2006). *Cross Cultural Change Management.* Llumina Press, Tamarac, Florida.

_____ (2008). Interpersonal Change through the "Inside-Out-Approach": Exercising the Freedom to Choose Our Responses during Conflict and Stressful Situations. *RU International Journal,* 2(1), 1-12.

_____ and Cavico, F. J. (2013). Corporate Social Responsibility and Sustainability Model for Global Firms. *Journal of Leadership, Accountability and Ethics,* 10(1), 01-11.

_____ and Isomura, K. (2012). Examining the Japanese leadership orientations and their changes. *Leadership & Organization Development Journal*, 33(4), 401 – 420.

_____ and Pohlman, R. (Autumn 2010). Value Orientation of Indian and U.S. Respondents: A Study of Gender, Education, and National Culture. *SAM Advanced Management Journal*, 75(4), 40-49.

_____ and Shuaib, S. (December 2010). An Equitable Total Rewards Approach to Pay for Performance Management. *Journal of Management Policy and Practice*, 11(4), 111-121.

_____ and Franklin, E. (2007). A retailer's steady growth strategy: should Publix stay national or go global? *Journal of Business Case Studies*, 3(4), 33-42.

_____ and McCartney, T. (2007). *Managing Workplace Stress and Conflict amid Change*. Llumina Press, Coral Springs, Florida, USA. ISBN: 1-59526-414-0. Phone: (866)229-9244 or (954)726-0902. Website: Website: http://www.llumina.com/store/managingstress.htm

_____ and Sims, R.L. (2006). Socializing Retail Employees in Ethical Values: The Effectiveness of the Formal versus Informal Methods. *Journal of Business and Psychology*, 21(2), 261-272.

_____, Cavico, F. J., and Plangmarn, A. (2012). Corporate Social Responsibility and Globalization. *Proceedings of the 17th International Conference of Asia Pacific Decision Sciences Institute* (APDSI), pp. 89-109. Chaing Mai, Thailand. July 22 - 26, 2012. ISSN: 1539-1191.

_____, Tajaddini, R. and Chen, L. Y. (2011). Business Ethics Perceptions of Public and Private Sector Iranians. *Journal of Business Ethics*, 104(3), 433-447.

_____, Afza, T., and Habib, N. (May 2011). Leadership Tendencies of Pakistanis: Exploring Similarities and Differences based on Age and Gender. *Journal of Economics and Behavioral Studies*, 2(5), 199-212.

_____, Tajaddini, R., and Chen, L. Y. (August 2011). Perceptions of Ethics by Public and Private Sector Iranians. *Asian Journal of Business and Management Sciences*, 1(2), 104-118.

_____, Lara, A., King, C., Johnson, V., and Mahanna, T. (April 2010). Stress at Work in a Slowing Economy. *Journal of Applied Management and Entrepreneurship*, 15(2), 26-42.

_____, Knapp, P., Baker, D., and Ahmed, M. (October 2009). Stress Overload Perceptions of American MBA Students in Recessionary Times. *The IUP Journal of Organizational Behaviour*, VIII (4), 73-87.

_____, Wolf, F., and Kolacek, J. (2009). Task and Relationship Orientation of American MBA Students. *International Leadership Journal*, 2(1), 27-52.

Navia, N. A. and Mujtaba, B. G., (2008). Alveolar's International Human Resources Faux Pas: Their History and One Manager's Influence! *Journal of Business Case Studies*, 4(3), 35-42.

Nguyen, L. D. and Mujtaba, B. G. (2011). Stress, Task, and Relationship Orientations of Vietnamese: An Examination of Gender, Age and Government Work Experience in the Asian Culture. *Competition Forum*, 9(2), 235-246.

Northouse, P. G. (2007). *Leadership: theory and practice*. 4th edition. SAGE Publications. Thousand Oaks, London.

Ochoa, R. M. and Mujtaba, B. G. (August 2009). The Application of Historical and Modern Management Theories in the Financial Industry: An Analysis of How Management Practices Affect Employee Turnover! *Journal of Business and Economics Research,* 7(8), 19-32.

Peak Experiences. (2005). *Power and Influence.* Retrieved on August 11, 2005, from www.peak.ca/articles/power.html

Ping, Han, Mujtaba, Bahaudin G., and Jieqiong, Cao (2012). Management Skills' Structure in Chinese Small and Medium-Sized Enterprise. *SAM: Advanced Management Journal,* 77(1), 13-21.

Pohlman, R.A. (1997). *Value Driven Management,* Faculty Working Paper 97-01, School of Business and Entrepreneurship, Nova Southeastern University.

Pohlman, R. & Gardiner, G. (2000). *Value Driven Management: How to Create and Maximize Value Over Time for Organizational Success.* New York: AMACOM.

Pritchett, P. and Pound, R. (2005). *A Survival Guide to the Stress of Organizational Change.* Reviewed in 2005.

_____, P. and Pound, R (1993). *Business as Unusual: The Handbook for Managing and Supervising Organizational Change. 3rd Ed.* Pritchett & Associates, Inc. Dallas, Tx.

_____, P. (1993) *Culture Shift. The Employee Handbook for Changing Corporate Culture.* Pritchett & Associates, Inc. Dallas, Tx.

_____, P. and Pound, R. (1993) *High-Velocity Culture Change: A handbook for managers.* Pritchett & Associates, Inc. Dallas, Tx.

_____, Price and Pound, Ron (1992). Team ReConstruction: Building a high performance work group during change. This is a hand book for managers.

Progressive Discipline, (2005). *Legal and Effective Progressive Discipline.* A 23 minute video. COASTAL Human Resources. Available through Video Training, Inc.; Phone-(800) 600-1555 or (206) 682-1555.

Ramamoorthy, N., & Flood, P. (2004). Individualism / collectivism, perceived task interdependence and teamwork attitudes among Irish blue-collar employees: A test of the main and moderating effects. *Human Relations, 57*(3), 347-367.

Robbins, S. P. (2005). *Organizational Behavior.* (10th ed.). Upper Saddle River, NJ: Prentice Hall, 2001.

Robinson, C. (1996). *Effective Negotiating.* London, England: Kogan Page Limited

Rokeach, M. (1973). *The nature of human values.* New York: Free Press.

Schein, E. (1992). *Organizational culture and leadership.* San Francisco, CA: Jossey-Bass Company.

Schermerhorn, J. R., Hunt, J. G., & Osborn, R. N. (2000). *Organizational behavior* (7th ed.). New York: Wiley.

Schwartz, S.H. (1990). Individualism-collectivism: Critique and proposed refinements. *Journal of Cross-Cultural Psychology*, 21, 139-157.

Selmer, J. (1996). What expatriate managers know about the work values of their subordinates: Swedish executives in Thailand. *Management International Review,* 36 (3): 231-242.

Senge, P. M. (1990). *The Fifth Discipline: The Art and Practice of the Learning Organization.* New York, NY: Currency/DoubleDay.

Seyoum, B. (2001). *The State of the Global Economy 2001/2002: Trends, Data, Ranking, Charts*. New York: Encyclopedia Society.

Smith, P. B. (1992). Organizational behavior and national cultures. *British Journal of Management*, 3: 39-51.

Sungkhawan, J., Mujtaba, B. G., Swaidan, Z. and Kaweevisultrakul, T. (August 2012). Intrapreneurial Workplaces and Job Satisfaction: The Case of Thai Employees. *Journal of Applied Business Research*, 28(4), 527-542.

Suvattanadilok, Montajula and Mujtaba, B. G. (January-June 2011). Decision-Making Factors in Renting an Apartment: A Study of Tenants and Small Business Owners in Lat Krabang, Bangkok. *Journal of International Business & Finance*, 3(1), 61-85.

Tajaddini, R. and Mujtaba, B. G. (2011). Stress and Leadership Tendencies of Respondents from Iran: Exploring Similarities and Differences based on Age and Gender. *Public Organization Review*, 11(3), 219-236.

Teowkul, K., Seributra, N. J., Sangkaworn, C., Jivasantikarn, C., Denvilai, S, and Mujtaba, B. G. (2009). Motivational Factors of Graduate Thai Students Pursuing Master and Doctoral Degrees in Business. *RU International Journal*, 3(1), 25-56.

Tichy, N. M. (1983). *Managing strategic change: Technical, political and cultural dynamics*. New York: John Wiley & Sons.

Trompenaars, F. (1993). *Riding the Waves of Culture: Understanding Diversity in Global Business*. New York: Irwin.

Tung, R. L. (1987). Expatriate assignments: enhancing success and minimizing failure. *Academy of Management Executive*, 1(2), pp. 117-26.

Tung, R.L. (1984). *Business Negotiations with the Japanese*. USA: Lexington Books.

Udechukwu, I. I. and Mujtaba, B. G. (2007). Determining the probability that an employee will stay or leave the organization: a mathematical and theoretical model for organizations. *Human Resource Development Review*, 6(2), 164-184.

Vogl, F. (1998). The supply side of global bribery. *Finance & Development, 35*(2), 30-32.

Vroom, V. (2003). Educating managers for decision-making and leadership. *Management Decision, 41*(10), pp. 968-978.

Walters Balfour, C. C., and Mujtaba, B. G. (2009). Are Male Employees Promoted More Often Than Females Who Are Just As Qualified? *Journal of Diversity Management, 4*(2), 7-18.

Wang, T. (2004). From general system theory to total quality management. *Journal of American Academy of Business, 4*(1/2), pp. 394-402.

Wei,S. J. (2001). *Corruption and Globalization*. Retrieved April 2, 2006, from http://www.brookings.edu/comm/policybriefs/pb79.htm

Wilhelm, P. G. (2002). International validation of the corruption perception index: Implications for business ethics and entrepreneurship education. *Journal of Business Ethics, 35*, 177-189.

Williams, B. A. and Mujtaba, B. G. (November 2010). Creating and Maintaining an Efficient "Built Ford Tough" Learning Organization: The Evolution of

Organizational Success. *Proficient: An International Journal of Management,* 2(5), 30-41.

Wolf, F. and Mujtaba, B. G. (2011). Sustainability in Service Operations. *International Journal of Information Systems in the Service Sector*, 3(1), 1-20.

World Development Report 2005: *A Better Investment Climate for Everyone.* Retrieved February 15, 2005, from http://worldbankgroup.com/.

Wren, Daniel A. (2005). *The evolution of management thought.* (5th ed.). New York: John Wiley & Sons, Inc.

Wren, D. A., and Bedeian, A. G. (2009). *The Evolution of Management Thought (6th edition).* John Wiley and Sons, United States.

Wren, D.A., & Greenwood, R. G., (1998). *Management innovators.* Oxford University Press, New York.

Yooyen, A., Pirani, M. and Mujtaba, G. B. (October 2011). Expectations versus Realities of Higher Education: Gap Analysis and University Service Examination. *Contemporary Issues in Education Research*, 4(10), 25-35.

Index Table

www.ingramcontent.com/pod-product-compliance
Lightning Source LLC
Chambersburg PA
CBHW021429180326
41458CB00001B/189